THE WORKS OF SRI CHINMOY

PRAYERS
VOLUME III

THE WORKS OF SRI CHINMOY
PRAYERS
VOLUME III

★

TWENTY-FIVE ASPIRATION-FLAMES • GRATITUDE-FLOWER-HEARTS
MY LORD'S LOTUS-FEET VERSUS MY DEVOTION-HEART
THREE HUNDRED SIXTY-FIVE FATHER'S DAY PRAYERS
O MY PILOT BELOVED • PRAYER-PLANTS
I PRAY BEFORE I LIFT, I MEDITATE WHILE I LIFT,
I OFFER MY GRATITUDE-CRIES AND GRATITUDE-SMILES
MY CHILD, YOU AND I ARE IN THE SAME BOAT
MY TWENTY-SEVEN HUNGRY PRAYER-TEARS
MY LORD SUPREME, I AM FALLING ASLEEP
VOLCANO-AGONIES OF THE SEEKERS
MY LORD, HOW CAN YOU BE SO HEARTLESSLY CRUEL TO ME?
MY LORD, MAKE ME YOUR HAPPINESS-CHILD
SOMEBODY HAS TO LISTEN • O MY HEART, WHERE ARE YOU?
O MY ASPIRATION-HEART, WHERE ARE YOU?
MY SWEET FATHER-LORD, WHERE ARE YOU?
MY LORD, I PRAY TO YOU
SADNESS-HEART-SILENCE. MADNESS-MIND-ELOQUENCE
MY ASPIRATION-HEART CYCLES • MY RACE-PRAYERS
MY BLESSINGFUL AND PRIDE-FLOODED DEDICATION TO THE INDOMITABLE
RUNNERS OF THE 3100-MILE SELF-TRANSCENDENCE RACE
MORNING PRAYERS. POEMS ON WAR

LYON · OXFORD
GANAPATI PRESS
XCIV

© 2025 THE SRI CHINMOY CENTRE

ISBN 978-1-911319-61-0

See appendix for notice regarding this edition.

FIRST EDITION WENT TO PRESS ON 24 FEBRUARY 2025

PRAYERS

VOLUME III

PART I

TWENTY-FIVE ASPIRATION-FLAMES

TWENTY-FIVE ASPIRATION-FLAMES

1

Let us pray to God to grant us the capacity,
   Out of His infinite Bounty,
To sleeplessly serve the peace-aspiring world.

Let us pray to God
To give us the most beautiful face
   Of a oneness-world-family.

Let us pray to God
To give us the most powerful heart
   Of a oneness-world-home.

2

A long twenty-three years ago my Beloved Supreme Absolute brought me to America to be of most soulful service to Him in the West. He blessed me with His infinite Hope, infinite Inspiration and infinite Aspiration to serve Him in the West.

You are my sweet children. You are my service-plants. You will one day become huge banyan trees. I am not only helping you; I will make you realise the Absolute Supreme and I will manifest Him in and through you at His choice Hour. You are my choice children. With you and in you I see the perfection of humanity's heart and life.

Love the Supreme in me infinitely more. Be devoted to the Supreme in me infinitely more. Lo, yours will be the sleepless joy and breathless satisfaction. Yours will be the complete perfection that humanity has been longing for centuries and centuries.

3

Peace in the world's oneness-home
   Is the supreme fulfilment
      Of humanity's
Birthless and deathless promise
     To God.

4

As your spiritual Father,
I am crying and I shall be crying
Inside your minds for Illumination,
Inside your lives for Liberation,
Inside your hearts for Realisation,
Inside your souls for your attainment
    Of God's ever-transcending Vision,
Inside your Inner Pilot for His sleepless,
   Birthless and deathless Satisfaction
      In you and through you.

5

At last I have pleased my Lord Supreme,
But I wish to please Him more,
   Infinitely more.

6

My Beloved Supreme powerfully loves me.
Therefore, I have His Infinity's Happiness.
My Beloved Supreme compassionately needs me.
Therefore, I am His Immortality's Peace.

7

I love my Beloved Supreme only,
Not because He has done
So many things for me unconditionally,
But because He is my life's only Hunger,
My heart's only Meal,
My soul's only Satisfaction
And my birthless and deathless Eternity's All.

8

My son, the unknowable can be known.
My son, the unknown can be known.
My son, the known can easily remain unknown.
My son, the knowable can eternally remain
   Unknowable.

9

My Lord Beloved Supreme,
It is now so clear to me that
You do not care for me.
My Lord, You do not care for me.
Is it because my mind is insincere?
Is it because my heart is impure?
Is it because I criticise You
Inwardly and outwardly every day?
Or are there some other reasons
Why You do not care for me?

"My child, if it is true that
I do not care for you,
Then it is not because of
   your mind's insincerity,
Not because of your heart's impurity,
Not because of your cruel criticism of Me,
But because you dare to live
And do succeed in living
Without My Heart's Compassion,
   Love, Blessing and Light."

10

My mind tells me that my heart
  Is not a sincere God-lover.
My heart tells me that my mind
  Can never be transformed
  And will never be transformed.
But my Lord Supreme is secretly telling me
That both my mind and my heart
  Are totally mistaken.
He is telling me that my heart
Is definitely a sincere God-lover,
And that my mind will before long
  Be transformed —
Amazingly transformed
  And unimaginably transformed.

11

My heart's spontaneous faith in my mind
  Is a divinely beautiful dream.
My mind's implicit faith in my heart
  Will be a supremely powerful reality.

12

My sisters and brothers,
You want to know from me
How I make tremendous progress every day,
   Every hour, every minute, every second.
I am telling you my supreme secret:
I keep dreaming, dreaming and dreaming
   God-Dreams sleeplessly.

13

I have lost my mind's purity.
That means I have lost much.
I have lost my heart's faith.
That means I have lost more.
I have lost my love of God.
That means I have lost all,
   I have lost everything.
I have lost God the powerful Creator.
I have lost God the beautiful creation.
My Lord, my Lord, my Lord,
Do tell me how I can regain my mind's purity,
   My heart's faith and my love for You.

"My child, go and sing inside your heart-garden.
You will regain your mind's purity.
My child, go and play with the blue-gold child
   Inside your heart.
You will regain your heart's faith.
My child, go and meditate with the breath
Of your newly-acquired blue-gold child-friend.
You will regain your love for Me."

14

Because of my outer courage
My Beloved Lord Supreme,
Out of His boundless Compassion,
Is giving me what He has:
Bliss, His Eternity's infinite Bliss.

Because of my inner courage
My Beloved Lord Supreme,
Out of His boundless Affection,
Is giving me what He is:
Fulfilment, His Infinity's immortal Fulfilment.

15

My soul is God-Eternity's God-lover.
My heart is God-Eternity's God-dreamer.
My mind is God-Eternity's God-seeker.
My vital is God-Eternity's God-warrior.
My body is God-Eternity's God-server.
My life is God-Eternity's God-enjoyer.

16

   My soul is of God
The Vision Transcendental.
   My heart is for God
The Compassion Universal.

17

Only because of my soul's
Birthless and deathless surrender unconditional
　　To God's Will,
God has forgiven me countless times,
And He may do the same
　　Forever and forever.

18

Even when I am shamelessly ungrateful
　　To my Lord Supreme,
He forgives me immediately,
And my soul forgives me ultimately.
But I want to dislike my heart,
　　My mind, my vital and my body
　　　　Vehemently and ceaselessly.
I shall not forgive them so easily.

19

During the entire day
If I do not please my Beloved Lord Supreme
　　Even once,
Then in the evening
My soul helplessly and pitifully cries
Like a child completely lost
　　In a thick forest.

20

My Pilot Supreme most powerfully loves me
    Because my soul knows
Who my Pilot Supreme is
And where my Pilot Supreme is.

My Pilot Supreme most affectionately loves me
    Because He knows
That soon my heart will start loving Him
    Unconditionally.

21

My hopeful heart
Is the most powerful blessing
From my Lord Beloved Supreme.

22

My sweet Lord Beloved Supreme,
Most compassionately You are telling me
That You are responsible
For the perfection of my life.

My Lord, I wish to tell You
That from today on
I shall be fully responsible
For the satisfaction of Your Heart.

23

What have I left undone?
I have not yet entered
Into the Heart-Garden
Of my sweet Lord Beloved Supreme.

What else have I left undone?
I have not yet claimed
My sweet Lord Beloved Supreme
As my own, very own.

24

I know, I know
That my little heart-cries
Are the harbingers
Of the world-seekers' Heaven-Life
   On earth.

25

May my heart-sorrows
Not only purify my aspiration-life
But also awaken all human beings
Who are enjoying their life-long
   Ignorance-sleep.

Notes to *Twenty-five Aspiration-Flames*

1. 3 February 1987.
2. 13 April 1987.
3. 27 April 1987.
4. 21 June 1987. Father's Day Message.
5. 18 October 1987.
6. 18 October 1987.
7. 18 October 1987.
8. 21 October 1987.
9. 24 October 1987.
10. 25 October 1987.
11. 25 October 1987.
12. 25 October 1987.
13. 15 November 1987.
14. 15 November 1987.
15. 21 November 1987.
16. 6 December 1987.
17. 6 December 1987.
18. 6 December 1987.
19. 6 December 1987.
20. 6 December 1987.
21. 14 December 1987.
22. 14 December 1987.
23. 14 December 1987.
24. 14 December 1987.
25. 14 December 1987.

PART II

GRATITUDE-FLOWER-HEARTS

GRATITUDE-FLOWER-HEARTS

1. The New Year's Message for 1985

Don't expect!
Don't expect!
Give, give and give
If you want to really survive.

2. February 1985

In this month
    I shall succeed,
I shall definitely succeed
    In my outer life.
Do you know why?
    Because
I have compelled my old enemy, ignorance,
    To return my determination-fire.

In this month
    I shall proceed,
I shall amazingly proceed
    In my inner life.
Do you know why?
    Because
My old Friend, God, my Beloved Supreme,
Is once more blessing me
    With His infinite Compassion-Suns.

3. March 1985

    A sleepless self-giver
Is another name
For God's Victory-Banner.

    A sleepless self-giver
Is God's Victory-Banner-carrier.
    A sleepless self-giver
Is God's Dream-fulfiller.
    A sleepless self-giver
Is God's creation-transformer.
    A sleepless self-giver
Is God's Heart-biographer.
    A sleepless self-giver
Is God's Life-publisher.
    A sleepless self-giver
Is God's Breath-giver.

Although there have been few,
    Very few in number,
Mother-Earth is extremely happy
To have such sleepless self-givers.
Give; you become.
    Give; you are.
Do not give; you are lost.
    Do not give; you are dead.
Give and give and give
Only to the Supreme in humanity.

4. April 1985

We must not and must not surrender
   To the bitter frustrations
      Of the past.

We must and must make friends
   With the sweet hopes
      Of the present and the future.

5. May 1985

Darkness-temptation there is.
That does not mean
I shall have to surrender
   To darkness-temptation.

Failure-frustration there is.
That does not mean
I shall have to become
   A giant failure-frustration.

God-Perfection there is.
Who dares to tell me
That I cannot become
   Another God-Perfection?

6. June 1985

My Beloved Lord Supreme,
   You have forgiven me limitless times.
      Will You not forgive me this time?

"My sweet child,
There was a time
When you used to please Me
   In My own Way.
But alas, those golden days
Are buried in oblivion.
Will you not start pleasing Me once again
   In My own Way?"

7. July 1985

I have to take seven steps in order to become a perfect instrument of my Beloved Supreme:

1. Love
2. Devotion
3. Surrender
4. Gratitude
5. Obedience
6. I belong to my Beloved Supreme.
7. Him to manifest in His own Way I came into this world.

If I take all these seven steps cheerfully, willingly and unconditionally, then my Beloved Supreme, without fail, will consider me a supremely chosen instrument, an absolutely perfect instrument of His.

8. August 1985

The Supreme and your soul are not going to please your body, vital, mind and heart with the hope that in return your body, vital, mind and heart will please your soul and the Supreme. If you have an iota of wisdom, then start threatening your idle body, aggressive vital, suspicious mind and insincere heart.

Just think for five minutes of what you were before you joined the spiritual path. Just think for ten minutes of what you have become on the spiritual path. Just think for an hour of what you will become in the future if you leave the spiritual path.

May this calamity-month be transformed into a prosperity-month for those who are doing extremely well and are trying most sincerely to please their Beloved Supreme in His own Way.

9. September 1985

If your mind has sincerity,
    Then only
The Supreme will tell you
    What to do.

If your heart has determination,
    Then only
The Supreme will teach you
    How to do everything.

If your life has unconditional surrender,
    Then only
The Supreme Himself
Will do everything and everything
    For you.

10. October 1985

My Lord Supreme,
 I am alive
Because You are
Your Eternity's Compassion.

My Beloved Supreme,
 I shall remain alive
Because You will be
Your Immortality's Forgiveness.

My Lord Supreme,
 You are alive
Because my heart
Sleeplessly needs You.

My Beloved Supreme,
 You will remain alive
Because my life
Will unconditionally love You.

11. November 1985

Let us not take a break, let us not.
    Let us continue
With our poor aspiration
And with our feeble dedication.

Let us not take a break, let us not.
For God-realisation is still a far cry,
God-manifestation is almost an impossible task
And God-satisfaction is far, far, far
    Beyond our imagination.

Let us not take a break, let us not.
For there may come a time
When our Beloved Lord Supreme,
Out of His unconditional Compassion,
    Will infinitely increase
The purity of our aspiration
And infinitely increase
The beauty of our dedication
    To realise Him,
        To manifest Him
            And to satisfy Him
                In His own Way.

12. December 1985

    My Beloved Lord Supreme,
I have failed, I have failed, I have failed.
I have failed in the world of aspiration-cry.
I have failed in the world of dedication-smile.
I have failed in the world of manifestation-dance.

    My Lord,
I implore You to give me one more chance
    To be worthy
Of Your Eternity's Compassion-Feet,
    To be worthy
Of Your Infinity's Forgiveness-Eye
    And to be worthy
Of Your Immortality's Satisfaction-Heart.

13. The New Year's Message for 1986

    The New Year will be
The year of teeming surprises —
Heaven-descending golden Dreams,
Earth-ascending silver realities —
    For the seekers
Who sleeplessly and unconditionally live
For the Compassion-Eye-Manifestation
    And
For the Satisfaction-Heart-Manifestation
Of their Beloved Supreme
Throughout the length and breadth
Of the entire world.

14. January 1986

My dear Lord Supreme,
From today on I shall please You,
Please You,
   Please You
In Your own Way,
For that is my heart's only choice.

15. February 1986

In the month of February
There will be a continuous fight
Between the hope of surrender-dream
And the frustration of ego-reality.
I am praying to my Beloved Supreme
   For the supreme victory
Of the hope of surrender-dream.

16. March 1986

    This is the month
Of visible and recognisable self-transcendence.
If I am a genuine seeker,
In this month my supreme achievements
Will surprise my own imagination.
And even if I am not a genuine seeker,
I shall feel something divine, inspiring
    And illumining
In my unlit mind.
    Whether or not
I am genuine in my aspiration,
This month I shall treasure
In the very depths of my heart.

17. April 1986

The Golden Boat of our Liberator Supreme
Is sailing unimaginably fast,
Carrying the silver heart-passengers.
May my sincerity-cry tell me
That I am a supremely choice passenger.

18. May 1986

Some seekers have failed.
That does not mean you also will fail.
　No!
You can and you must succeed
In the spiritual battlefield
　Of your divine life.
If you are simple,
If you are sincere,
If you are humble,
If you are pure,
If you are devoted,
If you are disciplined,
If you are determined
And if you are surrendered
To your Lord Beloved Supreme,
Then you are bound to succeed.
The Absolute Supreme needs your heart
　And wants your life
To manifest His transcendental Vision
　Here on earth.

19. June 1986

　In the month of June
The Inner Boat of the Absolute Supreme
Will be sailing extremely fast.
Only those who dare to claim Him
　As their own, very own,
Will be able to dive deep
Into the Supreme's
　Supreme Heart-Destination.

20. July 1986

The strength of my sound-life
Surrenders to the power of my silence-life.
The power of my silence-life
Surrenders to the Vision-Eye
   Of my Lord's Compassion-Heart.
My Lord's Compassion-Heart
   Is now telling me,
"My child, My Immortality's Dream-child,
Speed up! The Goal is within your easy reach.
   The Goal is all yours.
You and My Eternity's Liberation-Light
Will before long be transformed
   Into My Infinity's
Absolute Satisfaction-Delight."

21. August 1986

My Lord Supreme,
   My Soul-Reality's All,
Countless times I have withdrawn from You.
I have withdrawn my promise-oneness.
I have withdrawn my willingness-oneness.
I have withdrawn my soulfulness-oneness.
I have withdrawn my surrender-oneness-bliss.
Still You have not withdrawn from me.
You remain Your Eternity's Compassion-Eye.
You remain Your Infinity's Forgiveness-Heart.
You remain Your Immortality's Vision-Fulfilment-Cry.

22. September 1986

"Who is telling you that you will not be able to surrender to God's Will cheerfully and unconditionally? Do not listen to your mind. Your mind is a fool!

"Who is telling you that you will not be able to become a supremely perfect instrument of your Beloved Supreme? Do not listen to your mind. Your mind is a fool!

"Who is telling you that you will never be able to please your Beloved Supreme even for a single day in this lifetime? Do not listen to your mind. Your mind is a fool!

"My child, I am your Eternity's Friend, and you are My Immortality's friend. I am telling you only one thing: do not try to possess Me; do not try to possess Me; do not try to possess Me.

"If you want to possess Me, you will badly fail in your inner heart of aspiration, and you will miserably fail in your outer life of dedication.

"But if you pray to Me to possess you in My own Way, then your Eternity's earth-existence and your Immortality's Heaven-existence will be inundated with My Infinity's Light and my Infinity's Delight."

23. October 1986

My Supreme, my Supreme, my Supreme,
I shall never, never taste
The bitterness of frustration-night-defeats.
I shall forever and forever enjoy
The sweetness of satisfaction-light-victories,
For it is You who want to manifest
Your Immortality's Delight
   Completely and permanently
In and through
   The purity of my aspiration-heart
   And the beauty of my dedication-life.

24. November 1986

Supreme, my Supreme, my Lord Supreme,
My Absolute Supreme, my Beloved Supreme,
You are Your Immortality-Infinity's
   Unconditional Compassion,
And I am my mortal life's
   Fleeting gratitude-breath.

25. December 1986

No undivine strength,
No hostile force,
No inconscience-monster
Can slow down the fastest speed
Of our aspiration-dedication-boat
That is arriving at the Golden Shore
   Of our Beloved Supreme
     At His own choice Hour.

26. The New Year's Message for 1987

For the Mountain-Truth-climbers
And the Fountain-God-lovers,
The New Year will be the year
Of unprecedented inner aspiration-progress
And unlimited outer manifestation-success.
    The Truth-climber
Is a God-chosen God-compeer.
    The God-lover
Is a God-crowned future world-liberator.

27. February 1987

The beauty of a sweet hope
Has to be transformed into
The duty of a powerful promise,
And the promise has to be manifested
As the divinity of an infallible fulfilment.

28. March 1987

Go fast, My sweetness-child!
You are of My Immortality's Vision-Eye.

Go faster, My fondness-child!
You are inside My Eternity-Infinity's
    Heart-Nest.

Go fastest, My oneness-child!
I am for you,
I am all for you
And I am only for you.

29. April 1987

My child,
My Infinity's blue child,
I love you,
I love your Eternity's hunger-cry.

My child,
My Immortality's gold child,
I need you,
I need your Divinity's progress-promise.

30. May 1987

They came only to go,
But I came to stay —
   Forever to stay —
Inside the Golden Boat
Of my Beloved Lord Supreme.

31. June 1987

Supreme, my Supreme,
My Lord Supreme, my Beloved Supreme,
My soul came from
Your Compassion-Light-Eye,
   And at the end
Of my earth-journey's close
My soul will go back
To Your Satisfaction-Delight-Heart.

32. July 1987

My Lord Supreme, my Lord Supreme,
   My Lord Supreme,
You are utterly displeased with me
Not because my mind
Is completely ungrateful to You,
Not because my heart
Is completely ungrateful to You,
But because I have totally forgotten
My yesterday's aspiration-cry-promise,
My today's realisation-smile-promise
And my tomorrow's
   Transformation-dance-promise.
Yet, my Beloved Supreme,
Out of Your boundless Bounty,
You are giving me another chance.
This time, my Beloved Supreme,
I am praying to You to make me worthy
Of Your Forgiveness-Light,
For in Your Forgiveness-Light
Is the perfect fulfilment of Your Dream,
Eternity's Dream, Infinity's Dream,
   Immortality's Dream.
This Dream of Yours will grow into
   Your supreme Reality
      At Your choice Hour.

33. August 1987

Supreme, my Supreme, my Lord Supreme,
   My Beloved Supreme!
Do give me the sleepless willingness,
   Willingness,
     Willingness
To change my entire life.

Supreme, my Supreme, my Lord Supreme,
   My Beloved Supreme!
If my life remains unchanged,
Then how can I love You,
How can I serve You,
How can I manifest You,
How can I fulfil You
And, finally, how can I please You
   In Your own Way?
Supreme, my Supreme, my Lord Supreme,
   My Beloved Supreme!

34. September 1987

My Supreme, my Lord Supreme,
My Absolute Supreme, my Beloved Supreme,
During my soulful meditation
I have seen Your Divinity's Face
   Many, many times.
How is it that still I am unhappy?

"My child, My dear child,
My sweet child, My Eternity's child,
   You can be happy
Only when you need and have
My Immortality's Heart-Nest,
And nothing else."

35. October 1987

My dear Lord Supreme, many have failed; many more are failing; still many more may eventually fail. Please tell me my status. Where do I stand with regard to my spiritual life?

"My child, because of your disobedience you have already failed once. My child, because of your impurity in your entire being you are failing now. My child, because of your ingratitude you will eventually fail again."

My dear Supreme, that means mine is a hopeless case!

"My child, perhaps it is so.

"Now, My child, I want to tell you something most secret and most sacred. Listen to Me devotedly and soulfully once and for all. When I talk to you about your soul, you have to realise that your soul is always, always aware of My infinite Compassion, of My infinite Concern, of My infinite and unconditional Affection and Love for you. Your soul is always and always at My Protection-Feet, and from My Protection-Feet sleeplessly it receives My Illumination-Light.

"I am proud of your soul because it knows who I am, because it wants to please Me always in My own Way. Because of your soul I repeatedly forgive you. Because of your soul I grant you again and again chance after chance to please Me in My own Way.

"Your soul has not yet accepted defeat, and it will never accept the final defeat. Therefore, I shall give you innumerable chances to please Me and be a perfect instrument of Mine.

"I consider you a human being just because of your soul. I consider you an instrument of Mine just because of your soul. If your soul gives up the fight in the battlefield of your life, then yours will be a perpetual failure.

"So, My child, believe in your soul, the real reality, and not in your body, vital, mind or even your heart. If you do what I am asking you to do, then your soul and I will definitely succeed, not only in the battlefield of your life but also in manifesting My Immortality's Divinity in and through you."

36. November 1987

My Lord Supreme, my Justice-Light Supreme,
I have so many things to tell You,
And I have so many things to ask You,
My Lord Supreme, my Justice-Light Supreme.
But You are never available;
You are never approachable.
Will You ever be available,
Will You ever be approachable,
My Lord, My Eternity's Lord Supreme?

"My child, My dear child, My sweet child
    And My fond child,
My Compassion-Height is speaking to you.
I shall be available only when you give Me
    Your purity's heart-lotus.
I shall be approachable only when you give Me
    Your humility's life-grass."

My Lord, my Lord, my Lord,
Do You have anything to tell me?
Do You have anything to ask me?

"My child, I have only one thing to tell you:
    I loved you, I love you
And I shall forever love you unconditionally.

My child, I have only one thing to ask you:
    When will you claim Me
As your own, very own,
To make Me happy in My own Way?"

37. December 1987

    Since I am one
Of the supremely fortunate chosen few,
My Lord Beloved Supreme,
Out of His infinite Compassion-Light,
Is telling me that He will definitely finish
    My self-perfection-journey.
I just have to start, here and now —
Here, at this angel-blessed place;
Now, at this gratitude-blossomed moment.

38. The New Year's Message for 1988

My only Lord Beloved Supreme,
  Do bless me
With Your absolutely choice,
Secret and sacred Advice
  For the New Year.

"My child, win My Heart
And thus win My All —
  My Eternity's All,
  My Infinity's All
And My Immortality's All."

My only Lord Beloved Supreme,
How can I win Your Heart?

"My child, by loving Me only
And by needing Me only."

My only Lord Beloved Supreme,
How can I love You only?
How can I need You only?

"My child, be punctual in your heart's
  Aspiration-cry.
Be regular in your life's
  Dedication-smile."

My only Lord Beloved Supreme,
I have badly failed You this year.
I have all along failed You unquestionably.

But, my Lord, will I ever succeed?

"My child, you must and you will.
Just sleeplessly illumine your mind
   And convince your heart
That you are of My Eternity's Hunger only
And you are for My Immortality's
    Satisfaction only."

My only Lord Beloved Supreme,
I know that my living death will be
When You withdraw from me completely.
But will You ever withdraw from me?

"My child, do not think of My withdrawal,
But pray to Me to be with Me in My Boat
To reach your supreme Destination —
My complete Satisfaction in you, with you
   And for you.
I have so far not withdrawn from you.
   But,
My child, wake up!
It is already very late.
How long do you expect Me to hold
   My Golden Boat
On this side of ignorance-ocean?
You have to realise that either I am your All
Or you are all for yourself
   And all by yourself."

GRATITUDE-FLOWER-HEARTS

39. February 1988

My Lord Supreme, my Beloved Supreme,
Do tell me if I am correct in my feeling
    That when I soulfully cry,
I add something beautiful to Your Compassion,
And when I unreservedly smile,
I add something powerful to man's life.

"My child, you are correct,
    Absolutely correct."

40. March 1988

My Supreme, my dear Supreme,
My Lord Supreme and my Beloved Supreme,
Over the years, out of Your infinite Bounty,
You have shown me innumerable ways
    To please You in Your own Way.
But today do tell me
Which is at once the easiest and fastest way
    To please You in Your own Way.
"My child, My sweet child,
My Divinity's child
    And My Immortality's child,
For you, the easiest and fastest way
    To please Me
Is to sincerely feel
In the inmost recesses of your heart
That I love you sleeplessly,
Compassionately, blessingfully
    And unconditionally.

"My child,
Your soulful question has deeply pleased Me.
Therefore, I am telling you
A most secret and sacred Dream of Mine.
Every night, without fail,
I have one single Dream.
In My Dream I clearly and unmistakably see
That you have become
An absolutely perfect instrument of Mine."

41. April 1988

When I tell You, my Lord Supreme,
That I am going to leave You,
You immediately tell me
That Your Soul's Smile
    Will secretly guide me
And Your Heart's Cry
    Will openly follow me.
My sweet Lord,
That means I will never be able
To run away from You.

"My sweet child, that means
Your heart's unconscious affection for Me
And My Heart's conscious Affection,
    Love, Concern and Compassion
Will eternally remain together,
    Inseparable and immortal."

42. May 1988

O my heart's rainbow-gratitude-tears,
    Where are you?
I need you desperately
To please my Lord Beloved Supreme sleeplessly.
O my heart's rainbow-gratitude-tears,
You are my life's lightning progress-speed.
You are my life's fulfilling peace-beauty.
You are the only perfect bridge
Between my life's dreamland
And my Lord's Nectar-flooded Country-Home.

43. June 1988

My Supreme, my dear Supreme,
My sweet Supreme, my Lord Supreme,
My Absolute Supreme, my Beloved Supreme,
You have the most powerful Dream,
And I have the most soulful reality.
Your Dream is to make
My aspiration-heart and my dedication-life
   Absolutely perfect,
And my reality is to make You happy,
See You happy and keep You happy
   Sleeplessly and unconditionally.

44. Father's Day Message, June 1988

Without the leaves, flowers and fruits,
The tree is nothing, absolutely nothing.
   I am that nothing.
But with you, my children,
I am the fulness-tree.
The Supreme Father in me is telling you
That your kindness and your oneness
I appreciate far beyond your imagination.
   Because of your kindness,
I am successful here on earth.
   Because of your oneness,
I shall be fulfilled here on earth
   And there in Heaven.

45. July 1988

God the Compassion-Height requests me
To be regular in my dedication-life.
God the Justice-Light commands me
To be punctual in my aspiration-life.

46. 3 July 1988

America's Independence Day
Is God the dreaming Child's
    Very special
Rainbow-Birthday-Smile.

47. August 1988

In His inner Heart,
I am my Lord's only Choice.
In His outer Life,
I am my Lord's only Voice.

48. 27 August 1988

Supreme, Supreme, I bow to Thee.

Supreme, my Supreme, my dear Supreme,
My sweet Supreme, my Lord Supreme,
   My Beloved Supreme,
May Thy Victory be proclaimed
At every moment in and through
My aspiration-heart and my dedication-life.

Supreme, my Supreme, my dear Supreme,
My sweet Supreme, my Lord Supreme,
   My Beloved Supreme,
Those who are not consciously with You
And those who are not soulfully for You
Can never, never be my oneness-friends
Or ever, ever be in Your Infinity's
   Vision-flooded Golden Boat.

Supreme, my Supreme, my dear Supreme,
My sweet Supreme, my Lord Supreme,
   My Beloved Supreme,
Do make my heart a sleepless hunger-cry
   For You, only for You.

PART III

MY LORD'S LOTUS-FEET VERSUS MY DEVOTION-HEART

MY LORD'S LOTUS-FEET VERSUS MY DEVOTION-HEART

PART 1

MY LORD'S LOTUS-FEET VERSUS MY DEVOTION-HEART

1

My Lord,
Now that my love for You
Is strong once more,
And my faith in You
Is strong once more,
I have decided to address
All my petitions and supplications
To Your Lotus-Feet once more.

2

My Lord,
When I pray and meditate,
I most lovingly clasp
The Smiles of Your Eye.
Will You not clasp
The tears of my heart
   In return?

3

My Lord,
You do know the depth
Of my love, devotion
   And surrender.
I must say, they all come
From the depth
Of my sincerity-heart.
My Lord, do You
Agree with me?
"My child, I do, I do."

4

My Lord,
One day You inject
Elephant-confidence in me.
Next day You inject
Lion-confidence in me.
This way, alternately,
   You give me
The elephant-lion-confidence
Early in the morning.
But, alas, as the day advances,
My confidence disappears.
I become an object
Of pity-insecurity.

MY LORD'S LOTUS-FEET VERSUS MY DEVOTION-HEART

5

My Lord, fulfil me.
Fulfil me, my Lord.
Why delay any further?

6

My Lord,
Inwardly I may argue with You
In season and out of season
But, rest assured,
If You are ever in need of me,
I will immediately throw myself
   Heart and soul
     At Your Feet.

7

My Lord,
I know I argue with You
All the time inwardly,
But I know You are the only One
   To take notice of me,
You are the only One
   To take care of me,
You are the only One
   To tolerate me,
You are the only One
   Who has not lost
   Even an iota of hope
     In me.

8

My Lord,
Whether You give me permission
Or not,
I shall go here, there
And everywhere
Telling the whole world
That I am Yours,
Solely Yours.

9

My Lord,
Now it has become
An open secret.
Every day we barter:
You give me
   Your Compassion-Eye;
I give You
   My gratitude-heart.

10

My Lord,
I stand in front
Of the world-assembly
And pray and meditate,
And speak so highly of You.
Can You not secretly come to me
And whisper a sweet word to me —
Even once?

MY LORD'S LOTUS-FEET VERSUS MY DEVOTION-HEART

11

My Lord,
You have told me time and again
That when I am desperately
    In need of You,
You will come to my rescue.
My Lord,
I need You badly.
How is it that You are neglecting
Your Promise to me?

12

My Lord,
    Every day
I am sending my heart-letters
    To You
And asking You when both of us
    Will meet once again.
Perhaps You do not know
Or You do not care to know
Of my heart's excruciating pangs.

13

My Lord,
I am swimming
In the sea of ecstasy,
For You are deeply enjoying
   My heart-garden.
I am commanding my eyes
Not to lose sight of You,
Even for a fleeting second.

14

My Lord,
Everybody has special possessions.
My only priceless possession:
Your Forgiveness-Feet
Inside my heart-home.

15

My Lord,
Sorrows attend my eyes
And tears attend my heart
When I fail to be intoxicated
By Your outer Beauty
And Your inner Fragrance.

16

My Lord,
I admit that I have made
Most serious blunders
And I admit that my faults
   Are innumerable.
That does not mean
That You cannot overlook
   My faults.
That does not mean
That You cannot forgive me.
If You cannot overlook my faults,
If You cannot forgive me,
How are You going to preserve
Your reputation that You are
The Compassion-Forgiveness-Lord
   Of the fallen?

17

My Lord,
My outer life is fast asleep,
But my inner life is fully awake.
Do not abandon me because of
   My outer life's misbehaviour.
There shall come a time,
   I am sure,
When my outer life
Will follow my inner life
Happily and proudly.

18

My Lord,
We know that earthly happiness
Is of short duration.
How is it that
We do not increase every day
The speed
Of our climbing aspiration?

19

My Lord,
Every day I want to wash
Your Feet
With my heart's gratitude-tears.
Nothing else ever concerns me.

20

My Lord,
I want to adore
Your Compassion-Feet
Sleeplessly and breathlessly.
My Lord,
I want to enjoy indifference
   To all else.

MY LORD'S LOTUS-FEET VERSUS MY DEVOTION-HEART

21

My Lord,
My entire being is burning
With love, devotion
And surrender for You.
I simply cannot understand
How You can remain aloof.

22

My Lord,
Now that You have allowed me
To gain Your Compassion,
Please never allow my love
　To wane.

23

My Lord,
I am unable to steal Your Heart
　With my love
Because Your Heart is too vast.
Since my heart is so tiny,
Can You not steal my heart
With Your Love infinite?
I am sure You can do it
　Easily.

24

My Lord,
When I serve You,
   I pray to You,
Do not pay me with Your
Affection-Gratitude-Smile.
What I need from You
Is Your express Command
To please You always
   In Your own Way.

25

My Lord,
Why do both of us boast
   Unnecessarily?
Who chose whom first
Is of no consequence.
As long as we love each other
   Unreservedly,
Let us put an end
To our sweet dispute.

MY LORD'S LOTUS-FEET VERSUS MY DEVOTION-HEART

26

My Lord,
You have allowed me
To remain seated at Your Feet
    All the time.
What an extraordinary favour
I have received from You!
    Now I need
Another favour from You:
    Please destroy
My shamelessly towering pride
    Immediately.

27

My Lord,
You have given me the capacity
    To serve You
Day in and day out.
If You want to bless me in return,
Then I pray to You to grant me
Your Ocean-Delight as a reward
    And nothing else.

28

My Lord,
I want to be deeply attached
To Your Compassion-Eye
And Forgiveness-Feet
Exactly the way a desiring man
Is attached to his desire-life.

29

My Lord,
Your Love has entrapped my eyes,
    My heart, my life and my all.
May I be allowed to entrap
The hallowed dust of Your Feet?

30

My Lord,
I know what I offer You
Is always small, very small,
Yet Your Heart overflows
    With Nectar-Delight.
I am prepared
To come into the world
    Again and again
Only to fathom Your Love
    Unfathomable.

31

My Lord,
Why are You so indifferent
   To me today?

"My child,
I do not even know the meaning
   Of indifference.
Therefore, your opinion of Me
Does not apply to Me."

32

My Lord,
Today I want You to avoid me,
The impurity of my presence.
I am really ashamed
To call You my own.

"My child,
If I do not accept you
   As you are,
Then how can I claim you
To be My own, very own?"

33

My Lord,
I have been waiting
For a long time
To hear from You.
Why do You not ask for me?
Does it cost You anything?

34

My Lord,
Time and again
You are commanding me
    To come to You
Not as a beggar, but as a prince,
    Your prince.
My Lord, are You sure
You mean what You are saying?

35

My Lord,
I have forgotten
The beauty, fragrance,
Majesty and divinity
    Of Your Feet.
Do run towards me
Fast, faster, fastest.
    Your absence
Is stabbing my heart.

36

My Lord,
There is no real reason for me
To torture You
For Your outer attention.
Alas, alas, yet why...?

37

My Lord,
Since I am not pleasing You
    In Your own Way,
Please do me the greatest favour:
    Please hand me over
To the darkest oblivion-night.

38

My Lord,
I live in earth-bound time,
But I am certain that a mere glance
    From Your Compassion-Eye
Can chase away the power of time
    That has enslaved my life.

39

My Lord,
You have shown me many things,
But out of Your infinite Compassion,
Do show me Your own Path
   Through my life.

40

My Lord,
I beg of You to give me
The capacity to ceaselessly cry
   At Your Lotus-Feet
Until all my voice is lost.

41

My Lord,
It seems to me
That You have ceased
   To care for me.
If I am right,
   Do show me the way
And if I am wrong,
   Then prove it.

MY LORD'S LOTUS-FEET VERSUS MY DEVOTION-HEART

42

My Lord,
If I jump into Your Arms,
Will You hold me
   Or drop me?

"My child,
If you believe in your courage,
Then I believe in My Concern."

43

My Lord,
I have purified my mind,
I have widened my heart.
Is there anything more
You expect?
"My child,
Only one thing more:
Patience."

44

My Lord,
I have given myself
    Another name:
Earth-bound suffering.
"My child,
If you do not mind,
    I can add
One more name:
Heaven-free delight."

45

My Lord,
Every day I sing
Your Victory-Songs
For at least four hours.
May I know from You
What You do for me?

"My child,
You do your work
And I do My Work.
I energise your mind
And inspire your heart."

MY LORD'S LOTUS-FEET VERSUS MY DEVOTION-HEART

46

My Lord,
You ask me to keep
 My consciousness
One inch above my head
 When I meditate.
Is there any reason?

"My child,
Your mind is inside your head.
I want you to remain
Outside your mind-jungle,
At least when you meditate
 On Me."

47

My Lord,
My love does not please You.
My devotion does not please You.
My surrender does not please You.
Is there anything I have
 That can please You?

"My child,
Cultivate more sincerity.
Cultivate more eagerness."

48

My Lord,
My desire-life who chose,
   If not You?

"My child,
If you think that way,
Then I have something new
   For you:
Aspiration-heart."

49

My Lord,
I am proud
Of my gratitude-heart-tears.
Do You have anything
To be proud of?

"My child,
I have nothing
To be proud of.
From time immemorial
I have been performing
My self-imposed Task:
   I love you.
   I care for you."

50

My Lord,
You have sent for me
And I am now here.

"But, My child,
I have asked your whole family
    To come.
You and your body only are here.
Where is the rest of your family —
Vital, mind and heart?
    How is it
That you have come to Me
Leaving them behind?
Alas, I wanted to take
Your whole family
Together with Me
To My new Home:
    Satisfaction."

51

My Lord,
Everything is topsy-turvy
In this world.
I am supposed to run after You.
You are running after me
Instead.

52

My Lord,
Have You any idea how beautiful
Your Compassion-Eye is?
My Lord,
Have You any idea how powerful
Your Protection-Hands are?
My Lord,
Have You any idea how merciful
Your Lotus-Feet are?
My Lord,
Have You any idea how blissful
Your Satisfaction-Heart is?

"My child,
I do not know.
But if you think
That I should know,
Then let Me hear it from you."

My Lord,
On one condition,
I expect Your undivided attention.

"Of course, My child, of course."

MY LORD'S LOTUS-FEET VERSUS MY DEVOTION-HEART

PART 2

MY LORD'S LOTUS-FEET VERSUS MY DEVOTION-HEART

53

My Lord,
Did You think of me
When I was swimming
In ignorance-sea?

"My child,
Definitely My Mind
Was thinking of you
And My Heart
Was missing you."

54

My Lord,
I have come to realise
That my mind-palace
Has no peace.
Could You suggest
Another place?

"My child,
Yes, I can:
Your heart-cottage."

55

My Lord,
What is more important —
For You to tell the world
That I belong to You,
Or for me to tell the world
That You belong to me?

"My child,
Let us broadcast
Simultaneously."

56

My Lord,
Can You enjoy Your Beauty
The way we enjoy Your Beauty?

"My child,
You do your duty
And I do My Duty:
I enjoy at every moment
Your heart-beauty."

57

My Lord,
Please bless me
With that kind of love for You
That will pass the examination
Of Time.

58

My Lord,
Please tell me frankly
If I am ready for a divine life.

"My child,
Right now if I answer
The question,
I shall say without a shadow
Of doubt
That you are ready.
But if I have to answer
The question
At another time,
Then I may have
A different opinion."

Why, my Lord?

"My child,
The time that elapses
May drag you down
And you may not then be ready
For the spiritual life."

59

My Lord,
I see a criminal in me,
I really do.
Please tell me
What You see in me.

"My child,
I see in you
My highest Divinity's
Sweetest dove."

60

My Lord,
I most sincerely
Want to manifest You,
But I do not know how.
Please tell me how I can.

"My child,
Instead of wasting your time
By manifesting Me,
Pray to Me to manifest Myself
More and better
In and through you."

61

My Lord,
You do not sleep.
You meditate and meditate;
You work and work.
I am Your child.
Will I ever be
As great and as good
As You are?

"My child,
I never thought that you could be
Such a fool!
How can there be any difference
Between Father and child?
Is the child not the creation
Of the Father?
I am conscious of what I have
And what I am.
Unfortunately, you are not.
This is the difference
That forces you to swim
In the seas of inequality
And unworthiness."

62

My Lord,
Everything has a meaning.
May I know the meaning
Of Your Compassion-Breath?

"My child,
My Compassion-Breath means
Your ignorance-death!"

63

My Lord,
If I have two new eyes,
Will I not be able
To appreciate You
And admire You more?

"No, My child,
You will be able
To appreciate and admire
Me more
Only if you feed
Your God-hunger more."

MY LORD'S LOTUS-FEET VERSUS MY DEVOTION-HEART

64

My Lord,
Every year my earthly years
Advance,
And I lose something precious
From my childlike heart.
Is it because of the advancement
Of the years that I am losing
My divine qualities?

"No, My child,
It is not exactly so.
Your passing years have nothing
To do with it.
But every year, unfortunately,
You are over-feeding your mind.
Therefore, the tragedy continues."

65

My Lord,
Every word You say
Melts my aspiration-heart.

"My child,
Every promise you make
Enlarges My Cosmic Vision."

66

My Lord,
When You smile at me,
I see inside Your Smile
The Beauty of Your Divinity.

"My child,
When you smile at Me,
I see in you
A completely new world
Blossoming
In all its promises."

67

My Lord,
I want You
To saddle me.
Why do You
Cradle me?

"My child,
The hour is fast approaching
For Me to please you
In your own way."

MY LORD'S LOTUS-FEET VERSUS MY DEVOTION-HEART

68

My Lord,
I have started making
My gratitude-list.
But it never ends.

"My child,
So much the better
For both of us."

69

My Lord,
Please tell me one thing:
Do You want me to realise You,
Or do You want me to please You?

"My child,
Where is the difference?"

70

My Lord,
I want to end my earth-journey.

"My child,
I have given you freedom
In many aspects of your life,
But not here."

71

My Lord,
How I wish You would live
In the tears of my heart
Bravely.

"My child,
How I wish you would live
In the Smiles of My Eye
Happily."

72

My Lord,
I was born to be
A choice instrument of Yours.

"My child,
Unlike you, I never forget."

73

My Lord,
Is there any special reason
Why You have come to me
So late at night?

"My child,
It is the only time
I can catch your mind
And try to tame it."

MY LORD'S LOTUS-FEET VERSUS MY DEVOTION-HEART

74

My Lord,
I am giving up everything
Until I find You.

"My child,
Instead of giving up everything,
Try to find Me in everything.
That is the real way,
The only way
That will make Me happy
And will make you happy as well."

75

My Lord,
If I give You
My unconditional surrender,
I am afraid You will misuse it.

"My child,
Just give Me
Your unconditional surrender first.
If I misuse it,
You are at perfect liberty
To withdraw it."

76

My Lord,
I am begging You
To keep me with You all the time
And not to allow me to go away.

"My child,
I have the same prayer."

77

My Lord,
My heart breaks into millions
Of pieces
When I do not feel You
Inside my heart.

"My child,
You are not alone in your boat.
How is it that you do not see Me
Beside you?"

78

My Lord,
May I dare to become
One of Your favourite children?
"My child,
I think you already are one."

MY LORD'S LOTUS-FEET VERSUS MY DEVOTION-HEART

79

My Lord,
When I was young,
You told me that I was too young
To accept the spiritual life.
And now that I am old, too old,
You are telling me
That I am not meant
For the spiritual life.
Why did You not tell me this
When I was still an adult
With my whole life ahead of me?

"My child,
Allow Me to explain.
You were meant
For the spiritual life,
But you were not ready,
You are not ready
And you will never be ready
For the spiritual life
Until you feel that the spiritual life
Is the only life,
And there is no other life for you."

80

My Lord,
Will my life ever be
Your sole possession?

"My child,
The moment you hand it over
To Me."

81

My Lord,
Is there anything I can do
To make You happy?

"My child,
Claim Me immediately
As your own, very own."

82

My Lord,
Why does my body sleep so much?
And is that why I cannot meditate?

"My child,
I am also victim to the same thing,
But I force Myself to meditate.
Look how happy I am
And how proud I am!
I want you to do likewise:
Force your body."

83

My Lord,
Is there any secret way
For me to free myself
From my sufferings?

"My child,
There is one.
Just identify yourself
With My universal Suffering.
Lo, your suffering is gone,
Completely gone."

84

My Lord,
Why are You not making my life
A bit easier?

"My child,
I am asking you
The same question."

85

My Lord,
In the battlefield of life
When I am repeatedly defeated,
Do You feel sorry for me?

"My child,
My defeats are infinitely
More deplorable."

86

My Lord,
Are You not proud of me
That I have accepted You
As my Teacher
And discarded my old teacher:
Ignorance?

"My child,
Proud is an understatement!
Only I am sad
That you did not think of Me
Long ago."

MY LORD'S LOTUS-FEET VERSUS MY DEVOTION-HEART

87

My Lord,
Do You not feel sorry that
Instead of our being
At Your Mercy,
You are at our mercy?

"No, My child.
When I am at your mercy,
I try to add more Compassion
To My infinite Compassion
And more Forgiveness
To My infinite Forgiveness.
Unconsciously,
You are giving Me an opportunity
To sing the song
Of My ever-transcending Beyond."

88

My Lord,
What are You doing
Inside my mind?
Do You not know that my mind
Does not care for You?

"My child,
I know, I know.
I am just paying a visit,
In case your mind
Wants to change its mind."

89

My Lord,
Have You any idea
How much my heart is suffering
From Your absence?
"My child,
I truly have no idea.
But I am immediately sending
My Compassion-Eye
To make serious inquiries."

90

My Lord,
You do not come to me.
Is it because
My heart is too insignificant,
My mind is too impure,
My life is too imperfect?

"No, My child,
Not for that, no.
I do not come to you
Because your love for Me
Is still too shallow."

MY LORD'S LOTUS-FEET VERSUS MY DEVOTION-HEART

91

My Lord,
I am extremely tired.
Please tell me a story
So that I can immediately
Fall asleep.

"My child,
I am the wrong person.
I am infinitely more tired
Than you are.
Therefore, sleep has already
Captured My Eye."

92

My Lord,
I am fully awake.
Cheerfully and self-givingly
I am at Your Command.

"My child,
Are you sure?
I plead with you,
This time do not
Eat your promise
Like previous times."

93

My Lord,
Each time I come near You,
You just run away.
Why, why, my Lord?

"My child,
Just to increase your heart-hunger
In measureless measure."

94

My Lord,
Every day I write heart-letters
To You.
Do You get a chance to read them?
Be honest.
Do You really like them?

"My child,
My Heart hungers
For your heart-letters."

MY LORD'S LOTUS-FEET VERSUS MY DEVOTION-HEART

95

My Lord,
Will there be a day
When I will be able to come to You,
Fulfilling all Your expectations,
And show You my delight-flooded
Victory-face?
"My child,
What you need is a little more Grace.
Your red-letter day
Is fast approaching you."

96

My Lord,
I do not know how I dare
To show my face to You,
Since I displease You
In so many ways.

"My child,
How do I show My Face to you
Without fulfilling
So many desires of yours?
Even if we do not please
Each other,
Let us continue showing our faces."

97

My Lord,
I speak ill of You
In season and out of season.
How is it that You never
Speak ill of me?

"My child,
My Mind and My Heart
Are always fully occupied
With things
Infinitely more important
Than being your worthy rival."

98

My Lord,
I know world-criticism is bad.
How can self-criticism also be bad?

"My child,
Both are unmistakably
And equally bad.
Your world-criticism
Lengthens the pride
Of your stupidity-flooded mind.
Your self-criticism
Indefinitely delays
My divine manifestation
In and through you."

MY LORD'S LOTUS-FEET VERSUS MY DEVOTION-HEART

99

My Lord,
Do You really know everything
That I say and do?

"My child,
Although I have the capacity
To know
Everything that you do and say,
I prefer to do something else:
I am desperately trying
To turn you into another God
So that I can entrust you
With some of My Responsibilities."

100

My Lord,
Do You mind
When I do not please You
Every day?

"My child,
I am afraid
That I will never be able
To answer your question
Adequately."

101

My Lord,
I need to know
When I shall realise You.

"My child,
I need to know first of all
When you will give Me your all
And when you will claim Me
To be your own."

102

My Lord,
I love Your Eye so much.
Do You love anything of mine?

"My child,
I love the blooming-blossoming
Smiles of your eyes
More than you can ever love
My Eye."

MY LORD'S LOTUS-FEET VERSUS MY DEVOTION-HEART

103

My Lord,
Will my life's service-tree
Be able to inspire
One hundred seekers?

"My child,
Only one hundred?
What a shock!
What an insult to your soul
And to Me!"

104

My Lord,
Do You think I shall ever be able
To realise You in this lifetime?

"Yes, My child, yes.
No, My child, no."

What do You mean, my Lord,
'Yes and No'?
Please be explicit.

"Yes, when you are faith-nectar.
No, when you are doubt-poison."

105

My Lord,
Is it such a difficult thing
For You to make a solemn promise
To me
That You will always remain
With me,
Whether I speak highly of You
Or speak ill of You?

"My child,
I shall always remain with you,
And I have
A special piece of advice for you:
Speak ill of Me if you have to,
For this is the only way
You can empty yourself
Of your doubt-poison.
But speak highly of Me if you can,
So that I can immediately
Start singing and dancing
Inside your heart-garden."

MY LORD'S LOTUS-FEET VERSUS
MY DEVOTION-HEART

PART 3

106

My Lord,
Whenever I tell You lies,
You immediately catch me.
But how is it when You tell me lies,
I cannot catch You?

"My child,
Here is the proof
That I am infinitely smarter
   Than you are."

107

My Lord,
When I fall sick, You cure me,
And this happens quite often.
But when You fall sick,
I can never cure You.

"My child,
There are many things
That you can do,
But I cannot do."

My Lord,
Please name only one.

"My child,
You have established friendship,
　Permanent friendship,
With ignorance-night,
A thing impossible for Me
　To accomplish."

MY LORD'S LOTUS-FEET VERSUS MY DEVOTION-HEART

108

My Lord,
I am planning to write
   My autobiography.
Do You have any objection?

"My child,
I do have an objection."

Why, my Lord, why?

"I shall be terribly jealous
   Of you.
I want you to write
My Biography first."

109

My Lord,
Do You think
You will ever care
To write my biography?

"My child,
I shall write
An excellent biography
   Of your life
The day you completely stop
   Criticising Me."

110

My Lord,
You tell me to be careful
    Of my ego.
It will destroy me.

My Lord,
When I extol You to the skies,
Will You not have the same fate?

"No, My child,
Long, long before you were born,
I completely destroyed My ego."

111

My Lord,
Be frank at least once
    In Your lifetime!
It seems to me
That You are jealous
Of my mixing with ignorance.

"My child,
Why should I not be?
After all, you are My child.
I do have every claim
To have you only for Myself."

MY LORD'S LOTUS-FEET VERSUS MY DEVOTION-HEART

112

My Lord,
The more I satisfy You,
The more You demand.
Before You wanted from me
Only love, devotion and surrender.
Now You have added obedience.
If I start obeying You,
Then You will invent
   Something more!

"My child,
You failed miserably
In your love-devotion-surrender-examination.
I want you to study
The obedience-course,
Which is abundantly easier."

And, my Lord,
If I fail in Your obedience-course,
Will You have something
   Even easier?

"My child,
Yes, I will have something
   For you
Easier than the easiest —
My last resort —
A sesquipedalian cane
   And
An iron rod!"

My Lord,
Before You go that far,
I am immediately starting
My obedience-love-devotion-
   Surrender-life.
I shall obey You
   Most sincerely.
I shall start loving You
Most sincerely.
I shall devote myself
To Your service
   Most sincerely.
I shall give You
My unconditional surrender
   Most sincerely.

"Then, My child,
Come, come, come
And sit beside Me
On My Golden Throne."

MY LORD'S LOTUS-FEET VERSUS MY DEVOTION-HEART

113

My Lord,
When I do anything wrong,
You immediately scold me
Ruthlessly.
But when I do many things right —
I mean, most satisfactorily —
You do not say even one word
Of appreciation.
Is it fair?
"My child,
When you do things
To My great Satisfaction,
I am all admiration for you.
But, alas, your giant pride
Does not understand My language.
What is worse, it deafens
Your two long and beautiful ears.

"My child,
At that time you should sympathise
   With Me,
Instead of finding fault with Me.

"My child,
I do hope
I have defended My case
Most honourably
And most satisfactorily."

My Lord,
In that case,
I am terribly sorry for You.
Or, should I say,
I surrender completely
   And unconditionally
To Your inscrutable Cleverness.

114

My Lord,
I try so hard to please You,
But I can never please You.
Therefore, what is the use
Of trying again and again,
Only to fail again and again?

"My child, do not give up!
Let us not give up.
It is a joint effort.
The moment you succeed,
I shall succeed as well.
Your success has to precede Mine."

MY LORD'S LOTUS-FEET VERSUS MY DEVOTION-HEART

115

My Lord,
No matter how hard I try,
No matter how many ways
I kill myself to please You,
I can never please You.
Now it has come to a point
That I am arguing with myself
Whether I should continue trying
    To please You.
Is it really worthwhile?

"My child,
I am sharing a top secret with you.
I have been also doing
    The same thing.
You have no idea how hard
    I have been working
    To make you happy.
Alas, it is of no avail.
But something within Me
Is telling Me to continue,
So I shall continue.
And I am requesting you
    To do the same.
I am sure there will come a time
When both of us will succeed.
As you know, our philosophy
    Is never to give up.
So before long,
We are bound to succeed."

116

My Lord,
What do You think of astrology?

"My child,
In My case
I really do not want
To go backward
In order to go forward.
I want only to go forward —
Faster than the fastest
And farther than the farthest."

117

My Lord,
What do You think of palmistry?

"My child,
   My Heart
Is infinitely more beautiful
   Than My Palm.
Therefore, I want to spend
   All My Life
Appreciating, admiring, adoring
   And loving My Heart."

118

My Lord,
Am I correct when I tell You
That finally I am making progress
   In my spiritual life?

"My child,
You are absolutely right.
But do not forget
To give Me a little credit."

119

My Lord,
Five days a week we work;
Two days we get rest.
Similarly, in the spiritual life,
Can we not pray and meditate
Five days a week
And two days enjoy rest?
"My child,

I have no idea
Whether you get a salary
On the days you do not work.
But in My case I cannot afford
To give you your salary
The days you do not work for Me."

My Lord,
What is Your salary, after all?
"My child,
My salary is
My Affection, My Love,
My Gratitude and My Pride."

MY LORD'S LOTUS-FEET VERSUS MY DEVOTION-HEART

120

My Lord,
Do You know everything
That I do for You
And say about You?

"My child,
I know only one thing:
I love you, I love you,
I love you unconditionally."

121

My Lord,
Do You not think
It is high time
For You to create
A better world?

"My child,
I thought you are supposed
To do that.

"Please, My child,
Do not thrust upon
My two weak Shoulders
Your heavy responsibility.
You may not believe Me,
    My child,
But I am already overburdened."

122

My Lord,
I cry for You every day,
Every hour, every minute,
   Every second.
Do You, my Lord, ever cry
   For me?

"My child,
If I also do the same,
Then who will be able
To console whom?
Now, I am serious, My child —
I do cry for you sleeplessly."

123

My Lord,
I do not know why
You become so sad
   When You see me.
Is it because You are not satisfied
With me,
Or is it because of something else?

"My child,
I become sad when I see you,
Not because you are not good,
   But because your visits
Are quite infrequent
   And unreliable."

MY LORD'S LOTUS-FEET VERSUS MY DEVOTION-HEART

124

My Lord,
You tell me that
You always care for me.
Where were You
When I was wandering
   In my mind-forest?

"My child,
Unnoticed,
I was following you,
Lovingly and faithfully."

125

My Lord,
When I take one step,
You immediately tell me
That I am great,
　Very great.

My Lord,
When I take two steps,
You tell me
That I am good,
　Very good.

My Lord,
What will You say
When I take all the steps?

"Then, My child,
In no time,
I will tell you
That you are
Absolutely perfect."

MY LORD'S LOTUS-FEET VERSUS MY DEVOTION-HEART

126

My Lord,
When I leave You,
Do You still care for me?

"My child,
My Mind may not,
But My Heart definitely does."

My Lord,
Why does Your Mind
Not care for me?

"My child,
You will not believe
How much time I spend caring
For all your brothers and sisters!"

127

My Lord,
Will it ever be possible
For me to love You
   Unconditionally?
"My child,
This much only
I can tell you:
Many are your predecessors
    And
Many will be your successors."

128

My Lord,
If You really love me,
How is it I cannot prove it
To the world at large?

"My child,
My Love for you
Is not for your demonstration,
But for your life's illumination
    And nature's transformation."

129

My Lord,
Is there anybody on earth
Who is pure in heart?

"My child,
You use your mind-eye.
Therefore, you see everybody
    As impure.

But I use My Heart-Eye.
Therefore, I see that
All My children,
With no exception,
    Are pure."

MY LORD'S LOTUS-FEET VERSUS MY DEVOTION-HEART

130

My Lord,
I have made millions of mistakes
　In this life.
Have You ever made any mistake,
　My Lord?
Be sincere, once and for all.

"My child,
So far I have not made any mistake,
But I have decided to make one:
I want to withdraw My Concern
From the disobedient human beings.
Needless to say, you top the list!"

131

My Lord,
It is so easy for me to feel
　That You love me,
But why is it so difficult
For me to feel
　That I love You?

"My child,
Do not worry.
As long as you feel
　My Love for you,
Your road will remain
　Amazingly clear."

132

My Lord,
I promise to You
That I shall give You my heart,
 If You promise
To break my mind first.

"My child,
Amen! A million times, Amen!"

133

My Lord,
I have called You
At least a thousand times.
 But alas, no reply.

"My child,
You and I are playing
 The same game.
I have called you
At least a million times.
 But alas, no reply."

134

My Lord,
When You get angry with me,
What shall I do?

"My child,
Just give Me a cute smile."

MY LORD'S LOTUS-FEET VERSUS MY DEVOTION-HEART

135

My Lord,
When am I supposed to arrive
   At the Golden Shore?

"My child,
   Now,
At this very moment."

136

My Lord,
I need from You
The capacity to cultivate
More love, more devotion
   And more surrender.
Do You need anything from me,
   My Lord?

"Yes, My child:
More prayerful tears
   And
More soulful smiles."

137

My Lord,
Alas, I am not ready
To rise above daily trifles.

"But, My child,
I am all ready
To give you My Divinity's All.
Take it.
Just take it."

138

My Lord,
I have brought my mind
To be Your slave,
Your Eternity's slave.

"My child,
I do not need any slave.
I need only a friend,
My Eternity's friend."

PART IV

THREE HUNDRED SIXTY-FIVE FATHER'S DAY PRAYERS

THREE HUNDRED SIXTY-FIVE FATHER'S DAY PRAYERS

1. NOWHERE

Nowhere to live?
Try my heart-home.
 I think you will like it.

Nowhere to sleep?
Try my soul-room.
 I am sure you will love it.
  Just love it.

2. A BEGGAR

Yesterday
I acted like a beggar
 By asking God
To give me a smile.

Today
I am acting like a beggar
 By asking God
To give me His Power.

Tomorrow
I shall be acting like a beggar
 By asking God
To make me His only perfect instrument.

3. FATHER, DO I HAVE A MISSION?

Father, do I have a mission?
Daughter, you have not one
   But two missions,
    secret and sacred.
Your heart of life is your secret mission.
Your life of heart is your sacred mission.

4. DO YOU KNOW, DAUGHTER

Do you know, daughter,
   Why God loves you?
No, Father, I do not know.
   He loves you
     Because
You are a good player of love-game.

Do you know, daughter,
   Why God is devoted to you?
No, Father, I do not know.
God is devoted to you
   Because
You are a superb player of devotion-game.

Do you know, daughter,
   Why God has surrendered to you?
No, Father, I do not know.
God has surrendered to you
   Because
You are an excellent player of surrender-light.

THREE HUNDRED SIXTY-FIVE FATHER'S DAY PRAYERS

5. WHAT ARE THEY

What is earth,
If not the splendour of sacrifice-might?
What is Heaven,
If not the splendour of vision-light?
What is humanity,
If not the splendour of expectation-soul?
What is divinity,
If not the splendour of ecstasy-sea?

6. YOU ARE THINKING

You are thinking of yourself.
Lo, you are descending
   From
The human life to the animal life.

You are thinking of God.
Lo, you are ascending
   From
The human life to the Life divine.

You have started loving God.
Lo, you are singing and playing
   With
   God's Silence-Height
   And
   God's Oneness-Light.

7. A FULL AND COMPLETE TRUTH

    I love God.
        Indeed,
This is a stark lie.
    I think of God.
        Indeed,
This is a quarter truth.
    I do not find faults with God.
        Indeed,
This is a half truth.
    I never doubt God's existence.
        Indeed,
This is a full and complete truth.

8. BELIEVE ME

There is no difference
    And
There can be no difference
    Between
Love-touch and God-Touch.
Believe me, O aspiration-soul!

There is no difference
    And
There can be no difference
    Between
Fear-touch and death-touch.
Believe me, O desire-life!

9. YESTERDAY, TODAY AND TOMORROW

Yesterday
I cried to live
In God's Dream-Boat.
Today
I long to reach
God's Reality-Shore.
Tomorrow
I shall pine to be
God's Perfection-Smile.

10. YOU WANT TO KNOW

You want to know my past:
I was an unparalleled escapist.
You want to know my present:
I am a shameless opportunist.
You want to know my future:
I shall become
And end my life
As a false idealist.

11. A SERIES OF MYSTERIES

Earth-body
Is a mystery of loveliness.
Earth-vital
Is a mystery of strangeness.
Earth-mind
Is a mystery of loneliness.
Earth-heart
Is a mystery of holiness.
Earth-soul
Is a mystery of perfectiveness.

12. MY THREE DREAMS

My old dream
Is nothing but a faded flower.
My new dream
Is nothing but a wild animal.
My God-dream
Is nothing but a climbing life.

13. MY MIND-LIFE, MY HEART-LIFE, MY SOUL-LIFE

My mind-life
Is a useless thing to ignore.
My heart-life
Is a holy thing to see.
My soul-life
Is a perfect thing to offer.

14. I DO NOT KNOW

Where is God?
I do not know.
Who is God?
I do not know.
Shall I become
  Someday
Another God?
I do not know.
  But,
One thing I do know:
He loves me
  And
He is all for me.

15. WHEN I ESCAPED

  When I escaped
From ignorance-river
  The ocean of ignorance
Captured me, my earth-body
    And
  My Heaven-soul.
When I escaped
From the ocean of ignorance
  The Infinity of God-Love
    And
  God-Pride
Embraced me, my all.

16. GOD-POWER IS ALWAYS WITHIN ME

I have no money-power
   Yet
I am unmistakably happy.

I have no earth-power
   Yet
I am exceedingly happy.

I have no friend-power
   Yet
I am constantly happy.
   How?
Just because God-Power is always within me.

17. ARE YOU A SEEKER

Are you a seeker
   Of silence-life?
Then come in, please.
   Indeed,
This is the right place.

Are you a seeker
   Of sound-life?
Then leave this place immediately.
   Indeed,
This place can never welcome you.

18. THE BOUNDARIES

Daughter, these are
The boundaries of your unseen life:
    Your black ego-life
    Your red jealousy-life
    Your brown doubt-life
    Your gray insecurity-life.

Daughter, these are
The ever-transcending boundaries of your life unknowable:
    Your green aspiration-life
    Your blue realisation-life
    Your gold revelation-life
    Your white perfection-life.

19. NOTHING IS IMPOSSIBLE

Nothing is impossible
    When
I have an iota of love for God.
Nothing is impossible
    When
I have a fragment of sacrifice for man.
Nothing is impossible
    When
I realise I am oneness-perfection.

20. WHY, MY DAUGHTER, WHY

Father, I love Your Eyes.
   Why, My daughter, why?
Because they elevate my heart-breath.

Father, I love Your Hands.
   Why, My daughter, why?
Because they protect my earth-life.

Father, I love Your Heart.
   Why, My daughter, why?
Because it feeds my Heaven-soul.

21. THOUGHT AND DESPAIR

Thought is transitory;
   Therefore
Don't worry.
It will die soon.
Despair is stationary;
   Therefore
Don't worry.
You can leave despair alone
And triumphantly run away.

THREE HUNDRED SIXTY-FIVE FATHER'S DAY PRAYERS

22. NOISE, VOICE AND CHOICE

What do I like?
    A noiseless noise.

What do I love?
    A voiceless voice.

What do I admire?
    A faultless choice.

23. YOUR THREE ENEMIES

The enemy of your past life:
    Pride, a sky-vast pride.
The enemy of your present life:
    Jealousy, a sea-deep jealousy.
The enemy of your future life:
    Insecurity, an ant-feeble insecurity.

24. ALAS, YOU ARE DECEIVED AND DISAPPOINTED

Your vision of man
Has deceived me.
Alas, what can you do now?
You are doomed to stay with man.

Your realisation of the cosmic gods
Has disappointed you.
Alas, what can you do now?
You are compelled to stay with them.

25. DO YOU KNOW

   My heart,
Do you know what you are?
   You are my daily hope.

   My soul,
Do you know what you are?
   You are my daily promise.

   My God,
Do you know who you are?
   You are my daily Saviour.

26. HIS LIFE-CHRONICLE

His body is a village
   Of the sleepers.
His vital is a town
   Of the fighters.
His mind is a city
   Of the dreamers.
His heart is a province
   Of the lovers.
His life is a country
   Of the sufferers.

THREE HUNDRED SIXTY-FIVE FATHER'S DAY PRAYERS

27. EARTH-VOICE AND HEAVEN-VOICE

My earth-voice proclaims:
  "God may be of Heaven
    But
  He is for earth."

My Heaven-voice proclaims:
  "God may be for earth
    But
  His Breath is in Heaven."

28. A NEW DISCOVERY AND A SUBLIME INVENTION

  A new discovery;
I am using my heart
  To see the Face of God.

  A sublime invention;
God needs me.
  He really needs my life of love.

29. THOUGHT WILL SURRENDER

O face of thought,
  You are my abysmal disgrace.
O heart of will,
  You are my supernal lustre.
O soul of surrender,
  You are my sempiternal pride.

30. MIND-NIGHT AND HEART-LIGHT

O mind of night,
I am tired of seeing
   Your ugly face.

O heart of light,
Where are you?
   Do you really live?
   Or is it all my imagination?
   O soul of perfection,
   Do you really carry
The message of perfection-light?

31. THE MIRACLE POWER OF INFINITESIMAL GRAIN

An infinitesimal grain of Truth
   Can save you and your life.
An infinitesimal grain of Peace
   Can perfect you and your life.
An infinitesimal grain of Love
   Can immortalise you and your life.

32. WHEN YOU LIVE

When you live
In the room of your thought,
   Your life is a mighty, fruitless plan.

When you live
In the house of your will,
   Your life is a solid, splendid achievement.
When you live
In the palace of God-Love,
   Your life is a flood of glowing, illumining ecstasy.

33. THE STORY OF TIME

The Life of Time:
   Aspiration-flight.
The Heart of Time:
   Silence-Light.
The Soul of Time:
   Liberation-Delight.
The God of Time:
   Compassion-Height.

34. DO YOU KNOW

Daughter, do you know
    What I owe you?
I owe you My Perfection-Life on earth.
Father, do You know
    What I owe You?
I owe You my aspiration-soul of Heaven.
So Father, it is a mutual debt.
No, Daughter, it is a mutual self-satisfaction.

35. THE MIRACLES OF YOUR SURRENDER-LIFE

Look at the miracles
    Of your surrender-life.
You are remembering
    Your forgotten bliss.
You are enjoying
    Your cosmic silence-sleep.

36. DON'T HIDE

    Don't hide, don't hide.
If you hide, you can never be
A master sailor on the flow of Time.
    Seek, seek,
Yours will be the experience-sea,
Yours will be the realisation-mountain,
Yours will be the Perfection-Sun.

THREE HUNDRED SIXTY-FIVE FATHER'S DAY PRAYERS

37. THREE POWERS

Fear-power tells you:
   Death is at your door.
Courage-power tells you:
   Immortality is in your room.
Love-power tells you:
   Death never cares for you,
     And
   Immortality desperately needs you.

38. YESTERDAY, TODAY, TOMORROW

   Yesterday
I lived in the body of outer glory.
   Today
I am living in the heart of inner glory.
   Tomorrow
I shall be living in God's unhorizoned Glory.

39. IF YOU

   If you
Love man in God,
The adventure of consciousness-light
   Will embrace you without fail.
   If you
Serve God in man,
The consciousness-light of adventure
   Will claim you and treasure you.

40. WHEN I THINK OF YOU

    Heart, my heart,
When I think of you,
I see an aspiring height.
    Life, my life,
When I think of you,
I hear a thunderous voice.
    God, my God,
When I think of You,
I make my supreme choice.

41. SAD MUSIC AND GLAD MUSIC

O sad music of humanity,
Even God is tired of you.
O glad music of divinity,
Even earth-ignorance needs you
    Sincerely
    Desperately
      And
    Immediately.

42. YOU WANT TO KNOW

You want to know
   Where I was born.
My sincere heart speaks:
   I was born in the field of toil.
You want to know
   Where I now live.
My sincerity speaks:
   I live on prostrate soil.
You want to know
   Where will be my future home.
My sincerity speaks:
My future home will be
   In my earth-bound foil.

43. UNERRING, UNENDING AND UNCOMPROMISING

   Unerring,
Heaven-promise is unerring.
   Unending,
Earth-sorrow is unending.
   Uncompromising,
My challenge to ignorance-night
Is uncompromising.

44. THREE FRIENDS AND MY LORD

Three friends are with me now:
Yesterday, today and tomorrow.
Yesterday offers me a lingering world.
Today offers me a dying world.
Tomorrow offers me an aspiring world.
Ah, My Lord has just appeared.
   He offers me His ever-fulfilling World.

45. MY LIFE-STORY

   My body-life
Is a land of poverty.
   My vital-life
Is a land of audacity.
   My mind-life
Is a land of curiosity.
   My heart-life
Is a land of austerity.
   My soul-life
Is a land of absurdity.

46. SLOW PROCESS AND QUICK PROCESS

O slow process of mortality,
   Sleep not, wake up and strive.
I shall admire your new life.

O quick process of immortality,
   Run not, slow down and rest.
I shall adore your compassion-height.

THREE HUNDRED SIXTY-FIVE FATHER'S DAY PRAYERS

47. IN YOU

In you I saw
The light of the rising sun
   And spontaneously I saluted you.

In you I shall dare not see
The tears of the setting sun
   For I shall immediately die.

48. HER FEET HAVE DESCENDED

Her feet have descended;
   Therefore
Earth-life can treasure hope.

Her eyes have ascended;
   Therefore
Heaven-soul can fulfill its august promise.

Her heart has transcended;
   Therefore
God-Goal can manifest its Light supreme.

49. YOU WANT TO KNOW

You want to know
   What my mind is:
My mind is unlit ignorance.
You want to know
   What my life is:
My life is half-lit ignorance.
You want to know
   What my goal is:
My goal is ignorance-transformation.
You want to know
Who My Lord is:
   My Lord is Compassion-Perfection.

50. I NEED YOU

O hiding hands of love,
   I need you.
O smiling eyes of love,
   I need you.
O illumining heart of love,
   I need you.
O revealing soul of love,
   I need you.

51. TEACH ME HOW TO BECOME

Father, do teach me
　How to become.
Why, My daughter, why?
Father, if You teach me
　How to become,
Only then shall I be able
　To become
　　　Your egoless child,
　　　Your surrendered child,
　　　Your perfect child.

52. DON'T ASSAIL

Don't assail humanity.
After all,
Humanity is frail and weak.

Don't assail divinity.
After all,
Divinity is very audacious and callous.

53. FATHER, WHO AM I

Father, am I a sleeping fool?
No, daughter, you are a crying fool.
Father, am I a binding fool?
No, daughter, you are an unloving fool.
Father, am I an unpardonable fool?
No, daughter, you are an unparalleled fool.

54. HUNGRY LIVES

My body's hungry life
   Has an endless need.
My soul's hungry life
   Has two childlike needs:
      God-Beauty
        And
      Love-necessity.
My God's hungry Life
   Has only one need:
   My shadowless smile.

55. THE VOICE OF GOD AND THE CHOICE OF GOD

   Love the world.
You will be the Voice of God
      Unmistakably.
   Serve the world.
You will be the Choice of God
      Immediately.

56. I NEED YOU

O Heaven-born freedom,
   Where are you?
O earth-bound bondage,
   Where are you not?
O God-Promised land,
   I need you
      And
   I need you.

57. WHEN AND HOW

Father, when shall I realise You?
Daughter, you have already realised Me.
Father, when? Father, how?
When? The day you joined My Dream-Boat.
How? Through your surrender-heart.

58. NO, MY DAUGHTER, NO

Father, shall I worship You?
No, My daughter, no.
Father, shall I adore You?
No, My daughter, no.
Father, shall I admire You?
No, My daughter, no.
Father, shall I become like You?
Yes, My sweet daughter, yes.

59. ONLY ONE THING

"O Father, Father of my soul,
Only one thing I do not need."
  Daughter, daughter of My Heart,
  What is it?
"Life-consuming sound."
  Granted, My daughter, granted.

"Father, Father of my soul,
Only one thing I do need."
  Daughter, daughter of My Heart,
  What is it?
"Life-liberating silence."
  Granted, My daughter, granted.

60. FOUR UNIVERSES

What is really huge?
Material universe.
What is really powerful?
Spiritual universe.
What is always in the Goal?
Silent universe.
What is always the Goal?
Transcending universe.

THREE HUNDRED SIXTY-FIVE FATHER'S DAY PRAYERS

61. EXCESS OF BEAUTY AND EXCESS OF STUPIDITY

Father, what do You do
   With Your excess of Beauty?
Daughter, with My excess Beauty
   I perform My extra Duty.
Daughter, what do you do
   With your excess stupidity?
Father, with my excess stupidity
   I delay Your Manifestation-necessity.

62. FATHER, WHO WAS I

Father, who was I?
Daughter, you were the frankness
Of desire-life.

Father, who am I?
Daughter, you are the seriousness
Of aspiration-soul.

Father, what shall I be?
Daughter, you will be the sweetness,
Fruitfulness of Perfectiveness-Goal.

63. ENDEAVOUR

   My life knows
What mad-endeavour is.
   My heart knows
What sad-endeavour is.
   My surrender knows
What God-endeavour is.

64. TEACH ME HOW TO CRY

Father, do teach me
   How to cry.
Why, My daughter, why?
Father, if You teach me
   How to cry
Only then shall I be able
   To cry for You
     Soulfully
     Devotedly
       And
     Perfectly.

65. FATHER, TELL ME

Father, what is the thing You like most
   In my life?
Daughter, in your life I love most
   Your wisdom-cry.
Father, in the near or distant future
   What thing would You like most
   In my life?
Daughter, in the near future
   I shall love most
   Your perfection-smile.

66. FATHER, WHAT NEVER STOPS

Father, what never stops?
Daughter, horizon never stops.
Father, who never stops?
Daughter, the desiring beggar never stops.
Father, what always begins?
Daughter, the soul-life.
Father, who always begins?
Daughter, the aspiring-child.
Father, am I an aspiring child?
Daughter, you are much more than that.
You are a God-manifesting princess.

67. TEACH ME HOW TO LOVE

Father, do teach me
   How to love.
Why, My daughter, why?
Father, if You teach me
   How to love
Only then shall I be able
   To love You
     Unconditionally
     Eternally
       And
     Supremely.

68. DAWN

   O arms of dawn,
I love your power of beauty.
   O eyes of dawn,
I love your light of purity.
   O head of dawn,
I love your height of duty.

69. THEY ARE FOND OF

Body is fond of
The snoring hour.
Vital is fond of
The roaring hour.
Mind is fond of
The doubting hour.
Heart is fond of
The loving hour.
Soul is fond of
The dreaming hour.
God is fond of
The promising hour.

70. LIVE

Live in the heart-rose,
You will learn the song
  Of sinless progress.
Live in the soul-lotus,
You will learn the dance
  Of shadowless progress.
Live in the God-Fragrance,
You will learn the secret
  Of endless progress.

71. FATHER, WHAT WILL HAPPEN

Father, what will happen
If I touch Your Feet?
Daughter, if you touch My Feet
You will see a sea of peace.
Father, what will happen
If I touch Your Eyes?
Daughter, if you touch My Eyes
You will feel a mountain of power.
Father, what will happen
If I touch Your Heart?
Daughter, if you touch My Heart
You will become a sun of light.

72. WHY DO I NEED GOD

Why do I need God?
Just because He is great?
   No.
Why do I need God?
Just because He is good?
   No.
Why do I need God?
Just because He is for me?
   No.
Why do I need God?
Just because He is of me?
   Yes.

73. BEAUTIFUL, SOULFUL AND FRUITFUL

   Beautiful
Is your aspiration-heart.
     Therefore,
    You are great.

   Soulful
Is your realisation-heart.
     Therefore,
    You are good.

   Fruitful
Is your perfection-heart.
     Therefore,
    You are immortal.

74. REGULARITY AND PUNCTUALITY

Striking is the difference
  Between
Regularity-power
  And
Punctuality-light.
Regularity shows me
  God's Face
  Eventually.
Punctuality makes me
  God's Heart
  Immediately.

75. YOU WANT TO KNOW

You want to know
  What kind of mind I have.
Alas, I have a backward-walking mind.
You want to know
  What kind of heart I have.
Ah, I have a forward-marching heart.

76. YESTERDAY, TODAY, TOMORROW

 Yesterday
Yours was an industrious life.
 Only earth knew it.
 Today
Yours is the generous life.
 Only Heaven knows it.
 Tomorrow
Yours will be the precious life.
 Only God will know it.

77. I ADMIRE

I sincerely admire
 Four treasured things in me:
  A blossoming hope,
   An illumining oneness,
    A strengthening love,
     An ever-transcending God.

78. WHEN

    O earth-body,
    When
Will you be receptive?

    O earth-vital,
    When
Will you be perceptive?

    O earth-mind,
    When
Will you be concentrative?

    O earth-heart,
    When
Will you be contemplative?

79. WE ENJOY RECOGNITION

Heaven and I enjoy
    Simultaneous recognition.

Earth and I enjoy
    Spontaneous recognition.

God and I enjoy
    Constant recognition.

80. MY OLD-NEW-FUTURE FRIENDS

My old friends, fear and doubt
   Are calling me.
I tell them:
   I am sick of them.
My new friends, imagination and inspiration
   Are calling me.
I tell them:
   I am proud of them.
My future friends, perfection and satisfaction
   Are calling me.
I tell them:
   I am fond of them,
   Extremely fond of them.

81. BEAUTY

Body-beauty:
   Ephemeral splendour.
Heart-beauty:
   Supernal splendour.
Goal-beauty:
   Eternal splendour.
God-Beauty:
   An ever-transcending splendour.

82. HEAVEN AND EARTH

Heaven has fire.
    Earth has ire.
        God alone knows
Who is going to win.

Heaven owns smile.
    Earth owns cry.
        God alone knows
Who is going to win.

83. WHY

    Body, why do you love
The moonless night?
    Vital, why do you love
The sunless day?
    Mind, why do you love
The fruitless sky?
    Heart, why do you love
The goalless shore?

84. YOUR LIFE-STORY

    Your life-story
Is liked by God.
    What else do you want?

    Your soul-song
Is loved by God.
    What else do you need?

85. O UNCONFINED BIRD

O unconfined bird,
I love your beauty.

O unconfined wings,
I love your duty.

O unconfined flight,
I love your necessity.

86. GOD-LIGHT DAWNED

God-Light dawned
On your confusion night.
   But you failed to see.
     Why?
Because your love
Of earth-bound doubt
Far surpasses your God-faith
   And your own faith in your life
     Of inner cry.

87. GOOD NEWS

Father, give me some good news.
Daughter, your loud and wild days
   Are all over.
Father, give me some more good news.
Daughter, your evil and titan nights
   Are all over.

88. BECAUSE

   Because of my timid voice
I have failed
   To guide and please humanity.

   Because of my timid choice
I have failed
   To serve and please divinity.

89. THREE BELIEVERS

My heart is a good believer,
   Therefore
My soul loves my heart.

My soul is a better believer,
   Therefore
My God loves my soul.

My God is the best believer,
   Therefore
I always love God.

90. THREE BOATS

The boat of the past sailed
To reach the Golden Shore.
The boat of the present sails
To see the Face of God.
The boat of the future shall sail
To become the Heart of God.

91. WHEN I THINK OF GOD

When I think of God,
God tells me
He will give me all that He has.

When I meditate on God,
I clearly see that He has given me
All that He has been treasuring
From time immemorial
And all that He eternally is.

92. GOD IS ALWAYS READY

   In the world of form
God is always ready
To play with you
With His arms of Duty.
   Do you know that?

   In the world without form
You must remain always ready
To play with God
With your eyes of beauty.
   Do you know that?

93. YOU WILL WIN

Love the world-reality.
You will dauntlessly conquer
The countless soldiers of doubt.

Serve the world-necessity.
You will immediately win
The sun-warriors of faith.

94. TRANSCENDING REALITY

My heart of love treasures
    God the descending Dream.
My life of gratitude treasures
    God the transcending Reality.

95. LIVE

Live in the heart-garden;
Yours will be the angelic inspiration.
Live in the vital-jungle;
Yours will be the Satanic temptation.
Live in the soul-sky;
Yours will be the dynamic aspiration.

96. PYRAMIDS

A pyramid of beauty
   My heart enjoys.

A pyramid of height
   My mind enjoys.

A pyramid of fire
   My vital enjoys.

A pyramid of slumber
   My body enjoys.

A pyramid of light
   My soul enjoys.

97. SECRET AND SACRED

The secret influence of light
Has totally changed
   My earth-life.

The sacred influence of light
Shall make me
   Supremely
     And
   Proudly
Another God.

THREE HUNDRED SIXTY-FIVE FATHER'S DAY PRAYERS

98. DON'T SMILE

Don't smile.
Darkness-abyss
Will welcome you.
It may even capture you.

Swim.
Illumination-height
Will welcome you
And will without fail embrace you.

99. SOUL'S EYE, EAR AND ARM

Your soul has an ear.
With it you hear all about
    Earth-failure.

Your soul has an eye.
With it you see
    Heaven-satisfaction.

Your soul has an arm.
With it you create
    World-perfection.

100. ASPIRATION, REALISATION AND PERFECTION

Aspiration, my aspiration,
I want you to be the keeper
  Of my undisciplined vital.

Realisation, my realisation,
I want you to be the keeper
  Of my doubtful mind.

Perfection, my perfection,
I want you to be the keeper
  Of my timid heart.

101. WHEN

  When the morning stars sing,
I clearly see
  That earth-confusion
Is never meant for my heart-aspiration.

  When the evening stars sing,
I clearly realise
  That Heaven-satisfaction
Is meant for my vital-aggression.

102. WHEN HE PLAYS

When he plays on Heaven-organ
   Not only the cosmic gods
   But also the Lord Supreme
   Admires his miracle music of
     Unmeasured height
       And
     Unplumbed depth.

When he plays on earth-organ
   No human soul sincerely dares
   To appreciate the soul-breath
Of his life of
     Music-flow
       And
     Music-glow.

103. FOUR PRECIOUS GIFTS

   Gift of sight:
Universal beauty.
   Gift of night:
Universal peace.
   Gift of humanity:
Universal sorrow.
   Gift of divinity:
Universal smile.

104. THEY ADMIRE

Your body admires
Disciplinary endeavour.

Your mind admires
Visionary endeavour.

Your heart admires
Complimentary endeavour.

Your soul admires
Complementary endeavour.

105. WHERE ARE THEY

I see an empty church.
Where is the Christ?
Where has he gone?

I see an empty temple.
Where is Sri Krishna?
Where has he gone?

I see an empty heart.
Where is God?
Where has He gone?

106. HIS PRAYERS, HIS MEDITATION

His loving prayers
Have made his earth-life
   Clear of defects.

His silence-meditation
Has made his Heaven-journey
   Clear of obstructions.

107. MORTALS AND IMMORTALS

Mortals, they are helpless.
Immortals, they are careless.
Earth-Mother, she is sleepless.
Heaven-Father, He is speechless.

108. HE LIVED

He lived laborious days.
   Therefore
He can afford to live
   A relaxed
      And
   Retired life.
But not you, never.
You belonged to a different category.
Two things you really need:
   A heart of divinity
      And
   A life of immortality.

109. O SILENT DUST

O silent dust,
I do feel your bosom's pangs.
But what can I do?
    Insignificant is my voice.
    Impotent is my strength.

O silent dews,
I do feel your heart's agonies.
But what can I do?
    Helpless is my sight.
    Useless is my might.

110. FIRST FLOWER, FIRST FRUIT

My faith-tree's
First flower:
    Self-awakening.
My faith-tree's
First fruit:
    Self-giving.
What is self-giving
If not God-becoming?

111. INSTRUMENTS

You are a forced instrument.
   Therefore
You cannot go very far.
You are a loving instrument.
   Therefore
You can fly very high.
You are a perfecting instrument.
   Therefore
God wants to dance with you.

112. THE GREAT FACE

When the great Face
   Is behind me,
Forward I run
   Out of fear.
When the great Face
   Leads me,
Backward I run
   Out of sheer stupidity.

113. EARTH-LIFE

O my earth-life
Why do you cry
    Constantly?

O my Heaven-soul
Why do you hide
    Deliberately?

O my Heaven-Father
Why do you dance alone
    Incessantly?

114. HEART, SOUL AND GOD

Heart, my heart,
Will you make me your wisdom-height?

Soul, my soul,
Will you make me your perfection-height?

God, my God,
Will you make me Your Satisfaction-Sun?

115. SANCTITY AND INTENSITY

   The sanctity of Heaven
Is for my earth-heart to admire.
   The intensity of earth
Is for my Heaven-soul to admire.

THREE HUNDRED SIXTY-FIVE FATHER'S DAY PRAYERS

116. THOUGHT-SONGS

A white thought tells me;
　　God loves my pure heart.

A blue thought tells me;
　　God loves my clear mind.

A green thought tells me;
　　God loves my hero-vital.

A red thought tells me;
　　God loves my surrender-body.

A black thought tells me;
　　God never likes me
　　　　And
　　He has no need for me.

117. IRON GATES AND DIAMOND GATES

The iron gates of earth
　　Threaten me, frighten me
　　And compel me to be earth-slave.

The diamond gates of Heaven
　　Invite me, embrace me
　　And request me to be
　　The Prince of Heaven-Kingdom.

118. ON STRIKE

Now that your heart-sun
    Is in bed
Your vital life is on strike.
It demands more attention from you.

Now that your perfection-goal
    Is asleep
Your desire-body is on strike.
It demands more compassion from you.

119. WHAT DO I NEED

What do I need from God?
    An everlasting smile.

What do I need from earth?
    An everlasting oneness.

What do I need from Heaven?
    An everlasting concern.

120. TO BECOME

To become an immortal instrument,
I offered my Lord my soul-breath.
   My Lord has fulfilled
   My snow-white desire.

To become a perfect instrument,
I offered my Lord my heart-love.
   My Lord has clasped
   My aspiration-fire.

121. NO CONTROL

Earth has no control over me
      And
I have no control over Heaven.
Earth, I do not need
   Your wise guidance.
Heaven, I do not deserve
   Your blind disobedience.

122. ALL ARE TIRED

My mind is tired of living
   On earth.
My heart is tired of loving
   Human beings.
My soul is tired of promising
   To God.
My God is tired of advising
   My ignorance.

123. YOU ARE BRAVE

You are brave, very brave
   only because
You are still an unexamined hero.
You are pure, very pure
   only because
You are still an untempted seeker.

124. GOD'S LIFE-HISTORY

God's Life-History
Has inspired my life
Beyond my imagination's flight.

My life history
Has prompted God
To be more conscious
And cautious of ignorance-night.

125. DOUBT, OVER-CONFIDENCE AND INDIFFERENCE

   Doubt,
I am ashamed
Of our former attachment.

   Over-confidence,
I am ashamed
Of our present attachment.

   Indifference,
I am ashamed
Of our future attachment.

126. THE EMPLOYER'S COMPLAINTS

I gave death a job.
I asked death to sleep.
But death forgot to obey me.
What can I do?
I can only exercise
My forgiveness-power.

I gave Satan a job.
I asked Satan to meditate.
But Satan forgot to obey me.
What can I do?
I can only exercise
My forgiveness-power.

127. ARE YOU NOT TIRED

   Father, are You not tired
Of my life of never-ending weakness?
   Daughter, no.
I am only tired of My ever-increasing forgiveness.
   Father, are You not tired
Of my earth-bound life?
   Daughter, no.
I am only tired of My Heaven-free delay.

128. YOU WANT TO KNOW

You want to know
    Where I have been.
I have been with God the Dreamer
    In Heaven.
You want to know
    Where I have been.
I have been with God the Lover
    On earth.
You want to know
    Where I have been.
I have been with God the Liberator
    In death.

129. MY DISCOVERIES

My sleep-discovery:
    God is nowhere.
My dream-discovery:
    God is only in Heaven.
My reality-discovery:
    God is always busy.
He has no time to think of me.
He has no love to share with me.

130. THREE TEACHERS

My mind can teach
The world all about the heart's
Clouded weather.

My heart can teach
The world all about the mind's
Threatening weather.

My soul can teach
The world all about the soul's
Inspiring weather.

131. I CELEBRATE MYSELF

I celebrate myself.
Not because I am perfect,
But because I admire
Perfection's core.

I celebrate myself.
Not because I have satisfied God,
But because I am nearing
His Satisfaction-Door.

132. UNFAMILIAR, FAMILIAR AND ETERNAL GOD

To me,
God the Justice
Is an unfamiliar God.
To me,
God the Compassion
Is a familiar God.
To me,
God the Love
Is the eternal God.

133. GROWTH

Doubt is an unconscious growth
   In you.
Faith is a conscious growth
   In you.
Love is a precious growth
   In you.
Service is a sagacious growth
   In you.

THREE HUNDRED SIXTY-FIVE FATHER'S DAY PRAYERS

134. THE SONG OF MY LIFE

   Progressive
Is my heart-life.
   Regressive
Is my mind-life.
   Aggressive
Is my vital-life.
   Apprehensive
Is my body-life.

135. WHAT DO WE TREASURE

   Eagerness
My sound-life always treasures.
   Soulfulness
My silence-heart always treasures.
And what do I treasure?
I treasure the attentiveness
And perfectiveness of my Master Pilot
   Supreme.

136. NOBODY WANTS TO CONFESS

Light is the harbinger of God-Day.
   Everybody knows that.
Night is the harbinger of world-death.
   Nobody knows that.
     Why?
Just because nobody dares to expose himself.
Nobody wants to confess
That he is the sole cause of night.

137. LOOK AT HER

   Look at Her Feet,
It is all salvation.
   Look at Her Eyes,
It is all illumination.
   Look at Her Heart,
It is all perfection.
   Look at Her Soul,
It is all satisfaction,
   God-satisfaction.

138. IMPERIAL PALACE

   Mind, are you looking
For an imperial palace?
Lo, it is here.
   Heart, are you looking
For a celestial palace?
Lo, it is here.
   Soul, are you looking
For a transcendental palace?
Lo, it is here, and nowhere else.

139. HIS COMMENTS

   His comments
   On Heaven-vision
Are authentic, if not prophetic.
   His comments
   On earth-reality
Are pathetic, if not sympathetic.

140. YET

Lord, I have done my best.
   Yet
Earth-progress is a far cry.
Lord, I have loved my best.
   Yet
Heaven-success is a far cry.

141. ALAS, ALAS!

   Alas, alas!
No one will believe me
If I say that God has
   Employed me to represent Him
      On earth.
   Yet I perform my task most efficiently.

   Alas, alas!
No one will believe me
If I say that God has
   Employed me to advise Him
      In Heaven.
   Yet I perform my task most devotedly.

142. WHAT CAN I DO

You have two timid feet.
   Alas, what can I do?
   What can my feet do for you?
Indeed, it is a helpless case.

You have two timid eyes.
   Alas, what can I do?
   What can my eyes do for you?
Indeed, it is a hopeless case.

You have a timid heart.
   Alas, what can my heart do for you?
Indeed, it is a useless case.

143. MY REALISATIONS

   My morning realisation:
Receive from God, receive.
   My noon realisation:
Achieve perfection in your life, achieve.
   My evening realisation:
Conceive God-satisfaction, conceive.

144. I REALISED GOD

I slept in victory's room.
I dreamt in glory's room.
I worked in discipline's room.
I realised God in surrender's room.

145. NO MIND CAN ACHIEVE

No mind can achieve
   What the heart has already achieved.
No heart can attain
   What the soul has already attained.
No soul can reach
   What Silence has already reached.

146. O WORSHIPPERS!

O kneeling worshippers,
   Be sincere.
What you precisely need
   Is sincerity.
O adoring worshippers,
   Be pure.
What you unmistakably need
   Is purity.

147. YESTERDAY, TODAY AND TOMORROW

   Yesterday
I saw the sleeping triumph of my total doom.

   Today
I see the glorious triumph of my dedication-life.

   Tomorrow
I shall see the precious triumph
Of my all illumining perfection-soul.

148. LOVE GOD, SERVE GOD

You do not have to love me.
Love God. He is my Eternity's Soul.
You do not have to serve me.
Serve God. He is my Reality's Goal.

149. SEARCH

   Search God within.
You can become
   His Heart of celestial Beauty.
   Search God without.
You can become
   The pride of eternal Reality.

150. EARTH

   O aged earth,
My heart of love
Suffers for you.

   O caged earth,
My soul of freedom
Suffers within you.
   In me you can find
   Your heart-brother.

151. HE IS REALLY DIVINE

He thinks of God;
   Therefore
He is really divine.
   He meditates on God;
      Therefore
He is three times unmistakably
   More divine.
He has surrendered
   His Heaven-dream
      And
   Earth-reality to God;
      Therefore
He is seven times supremely more divine.

152. TO THE TEACHERS

To the mind-teacher
   I say:
"Don't teach
   since you do not know."
To the Light-teacher
   I say:
"Teach always
   since you want to know more."
To the soul-teacher
   I say:
"When will you start teaching?
   I am all ready."

153. THE FULL STAFF OF FAITH AND THE FULL STAFF OF DOUBT

Here is the full staff of faith:
    Determination, Aspiration,
    Realisation and Perfection.
Here is the full staff of doubt:
    Temptation, deception,
    Frustration and destruction.

154. REVIVE

    O my heart,
Revive your old devotion.
    O my life,
Revive your old determination.
    O my world,
Revive your old satisfaction.
    O my God,
Revive Your old Compassion.

155. HEAVEN-DREAM, EARTH-REALITY

From fear of death
    you suffered.
From fear of life
    you are suffering.
        Soon,
You will be suffering
From fear of your
    Heaven-dream
        And
    Earth-reality.

156. ONLY THREE WAYS

There are only three ways of serving God.
By constantly obeying God,
By soulfully smiling at God,
By unmistakably becoming
Another God.

157. I FORGET, I REMEMBER

I always remember
   To forget my ignorance-friend.
If I am not great,
   Who else is then great?
I always forget
   To remember my wisdom-sun.
If I am not stupid,
   Who else is then stupid?

158. TWO AND ONE

Two benedictive Hands
   on your
One contemplative heart.

Two compassionate Feet
   on your
One passionate life.

159. LORD, GIVE ME

Lord, do give me the inspiration to speak.
    Needless to say,
I shall speak only about You.
Lord, do give me the realisation to write.
    Needless to say,
I shall write only about You.

160. THEY ENJOY

My earth-life enjoys
    Infant slumber,
    Infant cry.

My Heaven-life enjoys
    Infant awakening,
    Infant smile.

My God-life enjoys
    Infant song,
    Infant love.

161. THE PRIDE

The pride of the noble
    Is constant self-giving.
The pride of the ignoble
    Is constant truth-denying.
The pride of God
    Is constant oneness-fulfilling.

THREE HUNDRED SIXTY-FIVE FATHER'S DAY PRAYERS

162. THOUGHT AND WILL

A life of thought
   Has a perishable face.
A life of will
   Has an imperishable smile.
Make your own choice
   And
Immortal make your own life.

163. WHO NEEDS

Who needs the animal past?
   The vital in me.
Who needs the human present?
   The mind in me.
Who needs the divine future?
   The heart in me.
Who needs the Eternal Now?
   The soul in me.

164. ASPIRATION

In the morning,
God in me is the giver
   Of aspiration.
   At noon,
God in me is the liver
   Of aspiration.
   In the evening,
God in me is both lover
   And fulfiller
Of aspiration.

165. I LOVE

I love the distant saint.
I do not want to expose
    His impurity.
I love the distant yogi.
I do not want to expose
    His insincerity.
      But
I do not love the distant God.
   I want Him right beside me.
      I want to reveal His supreme Divinity.

THREE HUNDRED SIXTY-FIVE FATHER'S DAY PRAYERS

166. AN IMPOSSIBLE TASK

Imagine you know nothing.
I know this is a difficult task.
Imagine you have nothing.
I know this is a most difficult task.
Imagine you are nothing.
I know this is an impossible task.

167. A PECULIAR POWER

You have a peculiar power
　To carry you through ignorance-night.

He has a peculiar power
　To save him from earth-ingratitude.

I have a peculiar power
　To free me from life-failure.

168. CHILDREN, I AM ALREADY OLD

　Children, I am already old.
　　Do not expect
Anything great from me.
　Children, I am no more bold.
　　Do not expect
Anything spectacular from me.
　Children, my heart is no longer gold.
　　Do not expect
Anything ambrosial from me.

169. I NEVER BETRAYED GOD

    It never happened.
I never betrayed God.
    It never happens.
I never ignore man.
    It shall never happen.
I shall never eat
    my realisation-fruit
        all alone.

170. THREE MESSAGES

The message of the West:
    "Let me be the winner."
The message of the East:
    "Let me see the loser."
The message of God:
    "Let me see the truth-lover.
    Let me see the life-builder.
    Let me see the love-fulfiller."

THREE HUNDRED SIXTY-FIVE FATHER'S DAY PRAYERS

171. YOU WANT TO KNOW

You want to know
Why I love my heart.
   I love my heart
      Because
Of its intensity.
You want to know
Why I love my soul.
   I love my soul
      Because
Of its immensity.
You want to know
Why I love my God.
   I love my God
      Because
Of His earth-liberating Duty.

172. EVERYBODY WATCHED ME

Everybody watched me
When I lost faith in God.
   But now I have regained
All my faith in God.
   But nobody comes to watch me.
They want me to be bound to ignorance-night.
   And what do I want?
I want them only to be devoted
   To the Light.

173. FORGET AND FORGIVE

What to forget?
   Nothing.
Whom to forget?
   None.
What to forgive?
   Everything.
Whom to forgive?
   Everyone.
What to illumine?
   Ignorance.
Whom to illumine?
   Your own self.

174. WHO

Who is your unknown enemy?
The hungry animal in you.

Who is your unknowable enemy?
The angry human in you.

Who is your unknown friend?
The soulful lover in you.

Who is your unknowable friend?
The ever-forgiving Mother in you.

175. GOD-COMPASSION

God-Compassion
Has crowned my prayer.
God-Perfection
Has crowned my meditation.
God-Satisfaction
Has crowned my surrender.

176. DO BETTER THINGS, SAY BETTER THINGS

Do better things.
Prove to Divinity
That your earth-life is something.
Say better things.
Prove to humanity
That your Heaven-realisation is something.

177. MY EARTH-FRIENDS AND MY HEAVEN-FRIENDS

My earth-friends warn me
   Not to mix with Heaven-lovers.
They say: Heaven-lovers are all rogues.
   I do not know what to do.
My Heaven-friends warn me
   Not to mix with Heaven-doubters.
They say: Heaven-doubters
Are all impossible fools.

178. DO NOT SUGGEST, JUST COMMAND

O my heart, do not suggest,
   Just command.
I am ready, more than ready.
O my mind, do not command,
   I allow you only to suggest.
I am not ready
     And
I shall never be ready
   To listen to your ignorance-commands.

179. THE REASON WHY

The reason why I write:
I long to correct myself.
The reason why I speak:
I long to perfect myself.
The reason why I love:
I long to fulfil myself.
The reason why I serve:
I long to transcend myself.

180. BELIEVE IT OR NOT

Believe it or not,
The song of self-discipline:
  Satisfaction-dawn.
Believe it or not,
The song of silver patience:
  Perfection-sun.
Believe it or not,
The song of golden surrender
  Is God-Smile.

181. YOU THINK, YOU LIVE, YOU LOVE

You think like a God
  Although
You do not live like a God.

You live like a God
  Although
You do not love like a God.

You love like a God
  Although
You are a false God.

182. WHO ARGUES

Who argues?
He who is a stranger
　To oneness-light.
　Who argues?
He who is a fond child
　Of bondage-night.

183. DON'T ARGUE

Don't argue with truth.
You will be compelled
To heave a sigh
Of an unreasonable mind.

Don't argue with love.
You will be compelled
To heave a sigh
Of an unthinkable heart.

184. MATCHLESS AND PRICELESS

Matchless is her mind.
　It perfectly shelters
　Earth's excruciating pangs.
Priceless is her heart.
　It perfectly houses
　Eternity's Height
　　And
　Infinity's Light.

THREE HUNDRED SIXTY-FIVE FATHER'S DAY PRAYERS

185. THREE DAYS AND THREE NIGHTS

Three good days:
    A day of true aspiration.
    A day of pure dedication.
    A day of total surrender.
Three good nights:
    A night of sound sleep.
    A night of sweet dreams.
    A night of august silence.

186. FOR YOU ALONE

Father, here is my crying heart.
    It is all for You,
        For You alone.
Daughter, here is My shining Pride.
    It is all for you,
        For you alone.
Father, here is my smiling soul.
    It is all for You,
        For You alone.
Daughter, here is My ever-transcending Height.
    It is all for you,
        For you alone.

187. THINK THE RIGHT THING, SAY THE RIGHT THING

Do what you think is right.
Only do not think
You are very great.

Say what you know is right.
Only do not say
You are either
   Another God
     Or
   A future God.

188. REVENGE-LIFE AND FORGIVENESS-HEART

  Revenge-life,
If that is wisdom-light,
  I definitely do not need it.
  Forgiveness-heart,
If that is not perfection-height,
  No harm, I shall all my life
  Stay with it.

189. FOUR THINGS

Four things of my life
I sincerely admire:
My angel-smile
My angel-infancy
My angel-flight
My angel-dependence.

THREE HUNDRED SIXTY-FIVE FATHER'S DAY PRAYERS

190. WHO WANTS, WHO NEEDS

A life of independence
Who wants, Father, who wants?
Not I, not I, not Your daughter.
I long for a life of prayerful dependence.
A life of independence
Who needs, Father, who needs?
Not I, not I, not Your daughter.
I long for a life of unconditional surrender.

191. I MUST SET YOU FREE

   Fear, I must set you free.
How long will you remain
   In a foreign country?
You should go back to your own country.
   Your brother Death,
What will he be thinking of you?

   Doubt, I must set you free.
How long will you remain
   In a foreign country?
You should go back to your own country.
   Your friend Satan,
What will he be thinking of you?

192. BECAUSE

Because
You are not sincere
   Heaven's smile
Is barren in your heart.

Because
You are not sincere
   God's Promise-Light
Fails to kindle
   Your aspiration-life.

193. PERFECT STRANGERS

Since you and sincerity
Are perfect strangers
   You have to climb
   A greased pole
Before you see the face of God.

Since you and sincerity
Are perfect strangers
   Your God-realisation
   Will entirely depend
On God's infinite Bounty
And not your incapacity's capacity.

194. FIGHTS

You had a mental fight
With God the Light.
You had a vital fight
With God the Power.
You had a psychic fight
With God the Delight.
You had a physical fight
With God the Compassion.

195. FROM NOW

From now on, Father, I shall love You
More than I love myself.

I am happy to hear that.
But do you want to make Me happier?

Certainly, Father, but how?

Just forget to love yourself.
I shall love you
   Most soulfully
     And
   Most devotedly
On your behalf.
I give you My Word of Honour.

196. A NIGHT OF SORROW

To think is to invite
A night of sorrow.

To pray is to invite
A day of hope.

To meditate is to invite
A sun of power-light.

197. FATHER AND DAUGHTER

From now on, Father, I shall think of You
More than You think of me.

Daughter, I am happy to hear that.
But do you want to make Me happier?

Certainly, Father, but how?

Just do not think of yourself.
I shall gladly and devotedly
Think of you on your behalf.

198. POWER

The power of harmony
Gives birth to peace.

The power of peace
Gives birth to God-manifestation.

The power of God-manifestation
Gives birth to satisfaction.

What is satisfaction?
Satisfaction is the stark necessity
Of both God and man.

199. I LOVE

I love the presence of Mother Earth.
    She tells me
    She will give me
    Everything she creates.

I love the presence of Father Heaven.
    He tells me
    He will give me
    His Light-Power
        to equal Him.

200. IT DOES NOT LAST

The pomp of power
   Does not last.
The throes of submission
   Do not last.
The reign of ignorance-night
   Cannot last.
The apparent defeat
  Of Knowledge-light
    Cannot last,
  Nay, can never last.

201. DISCOVERY AND INVENTION

Yesterday
My sterling faith
   Discovered God.
Therefore I was happy.

Today
My unknown fear
   Has invented God.
Therefore I am proud.

202. THREE MESSAGES

Death has a message
   For you:
"Do not try. Just cry."

Life has a message
   For you:
"Do not give up. Continue."

God has a message
   For you:
"Smile, always smile."

203. WHY

Why fear life?
Why fear death?
Life is your older brother
Who inspires you to transcend
Your puny self.
Death is your younger brother
Who warns you not to embrace
Pleasure-life.

204. DULY AND DAILY

Duly and daily
My heart loves God.

Duly and daily
My life needs God.

Duly and daily
My soul reveals God.

Duly and daily
My surrender becomes God.

205. I KNOW

A life of disgrace
Is a voiceless grave.
　I have known it.
A life of grace
Augments the pride of God's Face.
　I know it.

THREE HUNDRED SIXTY-FIVE FATHER'S DAY PRAYERS

206. DON'T BE

Don't be
In the luxury of power.
Destruction-shower will greet you
    Without fail.

Don't be
In the luxury of light.
Night-frown will torture you
    Without fail.

207. ETERNITY'S FASTEST TRAIN

You have snapped
    Your vital chain.
Lo, you are in the kingdom
    Of supreme gain.

You have snapped
    Your mental chain.
Lo, your life is in
    Eternity's fastest train.

208. YOUR

Your mind knows
What fear of darkness is.

Your heart knows
What fear of light is.

Your soul knows
What fear of ignorance is.

Your God knows
What fear of non-acceptance is.

209. POWERS

His Love-Power
Is the keeper
Of my earth-necessities.

His Light-Power
Is the keeper
Of my Heaven-necessities.

His God-Power
Is the keeper
Of my soul-necessities.

210. WHO

   Who saves my life?
My deep humility-friend.
   Who saves my heart?
My high hope-brother.
   Who saves my soul?
My shadowless confidence-sun.

211. WHERE IS HE

Where is he?
   I know not.

Where is his body?
   In the land of death.

Where is his life?
   In the land of the immortals.

Where is his soul?
   In the gratitude-breath of humanity.

212. BEAUTY

The love of beauty
   Is
World-power.

The beauty of love
   Is
God-Power.

The love of truth
   Is
Man-power.

The truth of love
   Is
God-Power.

213. MOTHER AND FATHER

Who is Heaven's mother?
   Light-sea.

Who is Heaven's father?
   Consciousness-sky.

Who is earth's mother?
   Patience-moon.

Who is earth's father?
   Knowledge-sun.

214. WHEN

When
Your outer spirit sings
You declare the pride
Of your vital glory.
　When
Your inner spirit sings
God Himself declares
Your achievement-heights.

215. YOU

You are dear to me
　Because
You love me.

You are dearer to me
　Because
You love meditation.

You are dearest to me
　Because
You love God.

216. UNRESERVED FORGIVENESS

Unreserved forgiveness,
Unmeasured bliss.

Perfect soul,
Perfect goal.

Transformed humanity,
Immortalised necessity.

217. GOD-LIGHT

He died before he saw
The face of truth.

He died before the birth
Of love in his life.

He died before he claimed
God-Light as his very own.

218. HOPE

Hope, my pilot-star, hope
I have seen your face.
I have felt your heart.
    Therefore
In ignorance-night
I shall no more grope.

Hope, my pilot-star, hope
You are humanity's peerless rope
For human souls to climb
God's Transcendental Height.

219. THREE SONGS

The song of Heaven-light
I immensely enjoy.

The song of earth-night
I boldly reject.

The song of God-Delight
My heart accepts,
My vital rejects,
And my mind,
In this case,
Wants to remain neutral.

220. WHAT DO I NEED

What do I need?
The seed of wisdom-light.
What do I need?
The flower of satisfaction-smile.
What do I need?
The fruit of God-attainment.

221. THE FIRST MORNING AND THE LAST MORNING

The first morning of creation
Heralded God's Compassion-Height.

The last morning of creation
Shall proclaim God's Justice-Might.

222. LIFE'S THIRST

To possess God
Is life's secret thirst.
To love God for God's sake
Is life's sacred thirst.

To please God
Always
Is life's supreme thirst.

THREE HUNDRED SIXTY-FIVE FATHER'S DAY PRAYERS

223. NOT ONCE BUT THRICE

Not once but thrice
I danced with death.
   When I fell in love
   With self-doubt;
   When I touched the tail
   Of jealousy-snake;
   When I swam in the anxiety-river.

224. I ADMIRE, I LOVE

O dreaming Heaven,
I admire your dream-boat,
   I admire.

O bleeding earth,
I love your reality-shore,
   I love.

225. HE PRAYS

He prays
  Because
    He loves.

He loves
  Because
    He has.

He has
  Because
    He is.
  He eternally is.

226. LEAVE SOME ROOM

O pilgrims of eternity,
Leave some room for me.
I shall join you.

O heart-smile of infinity,
Leave some room for me.
I shall join you
In your cosmic game.

227. PURE ESSENCE

Pure essence of life:
    Love-might.
Pure essence of love:
    Silence-height.
Pure essence of silence:
    Oneness-light.

228. DON'T TELL ME A LIE

Don't tell me a deliberate lie:
    God loves you.

Don't tell me a half lie:
    I clearly see
Your love of God is not totally
    sincere.

Don't tell me a complete lie:
    I tell you,
God does have the time
In measureless measure
    To think of you,
    To love you
And immortalise you.

229. O MY NOISY WORLD

O my noisy world,
Why do I love you?
"You love me because
My vital is surcharged
   With hero-energy
   With love-vision
   With life-emancipation."
Yes, you are perfectly right.

230. SERIOUS

The life of your pride,
   Serious.
The breath of your pride,
   Dangerous.
The life of your sincerity,
   Generous.
The life of your humility,
   Precious.

231. LOST AND GAINED

Earth-liberty lost,
Heaven-beauty lost.

Earth-transformation gained,
Heaven-satisfaction attained.

Earth-perfection manifested,
Heaven-promise executed.

232. FOUR LIVES

Human life
Is endless limitation.

Divine life
Is endless illumination.

Earth-life
Is endless caution.

Heaven-life
Is endless compassion.

233. WHAT DO YOU WANT

What do you want?
I want a night without darkness.

What do you want?
I want a day with the sun.
    Why? Why?
Because I want to hear
The song of independence,

I want to see
The dance of independence.

234. TRUTH, HEAVEN AND GOD

Truth, my truth,
You are still unemployed.

Heaven, my Heaven,
You are still ignored.

God, my God,
You are still unsought.

235. YESTERDAY, TODAY, TOMORROW

Yesterday
I saw your soul-flames.
You cannot imagine
How beautiful they are.

Today
I am seeing your soul-fire.
You cannot imagine
How powerful it is.

Tomorrow
I shall be seeing your soul-sun.
Both you and I
Will fail to know
How fruitful it is.

236. NOT ALONE

I play not alone.
   When I play
The sun and the moon join me.

I sing not alone.
   When I sing
Light and Delight join me.

I dance not alone.
   When I dance
The sky and the sea join me.

237. THE UTMOST FORCE OF HUMANITY

   Sacrifice:
The utmost force of earth.

   Smile:
The utmost force of Heaven.

   Sorrow:
The utmost force of humanity.

   Assurance:
The utmost force of divinity.

238. TRAVELLER-SEEKER-LOVER

The traveller in me dreams
   Of God's limitless Beauty.
The seeker in me dreams
   Of God's fathomless Light.

The lover in me dreams
   Of God's Victory-garland
Adorning His universal Necessity.

239. TELL ME THE DIFFERENCE

Tell me the difference
   Between
Desire-life and danger-death.

Tell me the difference
   Between
Aspiration-love and realisation-life.

240. HE

   His eyes are
As swift as clouds.
   His feet are
As slow as a tortoise.
   His will is
As fast as bullets.
   His thoughts are
As slow as death.

241. COME

O Lord of inseparable Oneness,
   Come to me first.
O Lord of supernal Love,
   Come to me next.
O Lord of supreme Glory,
   Come to me last,
     very last.

242. THE CAPTAINS

  O my earth-life
You want beauty
To be the captain of your body.
That is perfectly fine with me.

  You want purity
To be the captain of your vital.
That is perfectly all right with me.

  You want luminosity
To be the captain of your mind.
That is excellent with me.

  You want divinity
To be the captain of your heart.
That is more than perfect with me.

243. FATHER AND DAUGHTER

To love You, Father,
I have discarded
My arrows of desire.
   "Thank you, daughter."

To please You, Father,
I have stopped eating
With ignorance-life.
   "Thank you, daughter."

To become inseparably one with You,
I am challenging
The pride of my brooding night.
   "Thank you, daughter."

244. NOT BECAUSE I DO NOT LOVE YOU

Father, it is not because
I do not love You
That on rare occasions I wish
To stay all alone,
But because at times
I immensely enjoy the core of solitude.
But Father, if You think
What I am doing is wrong,
Unpardonably wrong,
Then I am running towards You,
I am flying towards You,
Father, for You alone are my Eternity's All.

245. NO LIFE, NO GOD

No health, no hope.
No hope, no love.
No love, no joy.
No joy, no life.
No life, no God.

246. WHY

I do not sing.
   Why?
Because my Lord Supreme
Sings so soulfully.
If I sing, I shall only embarrass Him.
I think that is not fair on my part.

I do not dance.
   Why?
Because my Lord Supreme
Dances so charmingly.
If I dance, I shall only embarrass Him.
I think that is not fair on my part.

247. BREAD

Man's bread:
Soul's smile.

Soul's bread:
Man's acceptance.

God's Bread:
Man's freedom.

Man's bread:
God's Assurance.

248. ALTHOUGH

Although you are
    A thoughtless youth,
God's Compassion-sea will forgive you.

Although you are
    A senseless youth,
God's Compassion-sky will forgive you.

Although you are
    A reckless youth,
God's Compassion-moon will forgive you.

249. CONFUSION AND ASPIRATION

To him,
Confusion worse than depression.
Confusion worse than frustration.
Confusion worse than destruction.

To him,
Aspiration better than realisation.
Aspiration better than revelation.
Aspiration better than manifestation.

250. WHEN I CALLED

When I called man
He was so upset
That I did not take his advice
In world-transformation-game.

When I invoked God
He was so upset
That I did not take a conscious part
In His Heaven-manifestation-game.

251. LIFE, LOVE AND GOD

Life is a challenging fact.
Both you and I know it.
Love is a revealing truth.
Both you and I know it.
God is an ever-transcending Reality.
Both you and I do not know it
    And
  Do not want to know it.
    Alas! Alas!

252. O FIRE OF LIGHT

O fire of light,
  Burn me, burn my desire-night.
O light of fire,
  Illumine me,
  My life of aspiration.
  Fulfil me,
  My heart of dedication.
  Immortalise me,
  My body of transformation.

253. BE SINCERE

Be sincere.
If not, yours will be
    A pathless journey.

Be sincere.
If not, yours will be
    A goalless shore.

Be sincere.
If not, yours will be
    A soulless goal.

254. SHE

To see her eyes
Is to enter into the world's
Beginningless beginning.

To feel her heart
Is to enter into the world's
Ever-transcending ending.

255. IN THE SOUL'S WORLD

In the soul's world
   He is quite healthy.
He never falls sick.
How?

Because there is no time
For him to be sick.
He keeps busy,
   Devotedly busy,
   Cheerfully busy,
   Unconditionally busy.

256. FOUR SISTERS

Four harmonious sisters:
   Purity and luminosity,
   Beauty and duty.

Great is purity's breath.
Tall is luminosity's heart.
Inspiring is beauty's soul.
Aspiring is duty's role.

257. THE DIFFERENCE

The difference
   Between
You and me is this:
You fast on earth
   And
You feast in Heaven.

I feast on earth
   And
I fast in Heaven.

I feel
Earth-food: fear, doubt, jealousy,
Are most delicious.
You feel
Heaven-food: peace, light and bliss
Are most delicious.

258. UNCONDITIONALLY

   Unconditionally
God stores up for my soul to use.
My soul lavishly stores up
   For my heart to use.
His Heart soulfully stores up
   For my life to use.

259. IMPERFECT AND PERFECT GIFTS

Three imperfect gifts
From the core of earth:
    Desire-life
    Ignorance-night
    Doubt-poison.

Three perfect gifts
From the core of earth:
    Aspiration-cry
    Realisation-smile
    Perfection-light.

260. MY HOPES

My
Desire-hope
Wants to possess.

My
Aspiration-hope
Wants to progress.

My
Perfection-hope
Eternally is.

THREE HUNDRED SIXTY-FIVE FATHER'S DAY PRAYERS

261. DO YOU WANT POWER

Do you want power?
Then go to the outer temple.

Do you want peace?
Then go to the inner temple.

Do you want love?
Then go to God-temple.
Where is it?
It is inside
The sea of your climbing eyes.

262. BEAUTY

Sincerity is an inspiring beauty.
Humility is an illumining beauty.
Purity is a feeding beauty.
Generosity is a bleeding beauty.
Divinity is an immortalising beauty.

263. HE EATS

He eats only twice a day.
His morning meal:
God's Compassion-Heart,
God's Meditation-Face.
His evening meal:
God's Perfection-Feet,
God's Satisfaction-Soul.

264. HIS PRAYERS

His morning prayer:
Lord, come near me.
I shall never breathe a word
    Against You.

His evening prayer:
Lord, I have emptied
My ignorance-sea
    Before You.
It is all to You
To leave it empty
Or fill it with Your
Compassion-Light.

265. NOT BECAUSE I LOVE YOU LESS

Father, not because
I love You less
That often I think
Of ignorance
But because
I have formed a bad habit.

Don't worry, my Lord,
I shall soon get rid
Of this bad habit.

266. ALAS

   Alas,
My native seas tell me:
I have lost my heart's depth.
   Alas,
My native skies tell me:
I have lost my mind's vastness.
   Alas,
My native sun tells me:
I have lost my life's divinity.
   Alas,
My native gods tell me:
I have lost my soul's immortality.

267. NOWHERE TO BE FOUND

An iota of happiness I want.
But where is it?
Nowhere to be found.

Frustration I do not want.
But where is it not?
Alas, it sighs
Even in my victory's crown.

268. I LOVE A HOLY TREE

I love a holy tree.
It inspires me to shelter
My earth-friends:
Impurity and insecurity.

I love a holy man.
He inspires me to invite
My Heaven-friends:
The cosmic gods.

269. DESIRE AND ASPIRATION

A life of desire-fire
Is an incomplete life.
A life of aspiration-sun
Is not only a complete life
But God's own Life.

270. MY BODY-LIFE

My body-life
   And
Earth-consciousness
Enjoy mutual recognition.
His heart-life
   And
Heaven-consciousness
Enjoy simultaneous recognition.
My soul-life
   And
God-Consciousness
Enjoy constant recognition.

271. PILGRIMS

O my body-pilgrim,
I see you are totally exhausted.
But look, your goal's fast approaching you.

O my soul-pilgrim,
Are you not sick
Of Eternity's Road
Infinity's Soul
   And
Immortality's Goal?

272. MY EARTH-YEARS

My earth-years have taught me
More than countless books.

My earth-years have taught me
More than Heaven's repeated instructions.

My earth-years have taught me
More than they actually promised.

273. YOUR BEST FRIEND

Your best friend is conviction.
Her best friend is discussion.
My best friend is hesitation.
Earth's best friend is dedication.
Heaven's best friend is illumination.
God's best friend is Compassion.

274. REMAIN NOT UNREALISED

   Remain not unrealised
In the sunlight of optimism.
   Remain always realised
In your quiet and sweet optimism.
Optimism is the only ladder
To climb up God's
Ever-transcending Height.

275. LORD, I LOVE YOUR SOVEREIGNTY

Body, I love your necessity.
Vital, I love your temerity.
Mind, I love your clarity.
Heart, I love your spontaneity.
Soul, I love your divinity.
Lord, I love Your Sovereignty.

276. OUR GOLDEN BOAT

  Our Golden Boat
Invites the passengers
Who are freed from
Ranklings of jealousy
  And who have learnt
The art of spreading purity
Lovingly and devotedly.

277. HUMANITY'S FACE

  In offering, we learn.
In learning, we become.
  In becoming, we perfect
Humanity's face
  And
Accelerate God's Grace.

278. DO YOU KNOW

Do you know why God has patience
In boundless measure?
    Just to make me His representative on earth.
    Just to make me His prototype.
    Just to make me His equal.
    Just to make of me another God.

279. WHEN

    When
It is a matter of God-realisation
Everybody belongs to the same boat.
    When
It is a matter of world-salvation
Everybody is a saviour supreme
In his own inimitable right.

280. DO NOT CARRY YOUR PASSPORT

    If you really want
To carry peace of mind
    Wherever you want to go,
Then do one thing:
    Do not carry your passport
Of self-importance.
    No, not even by mistake.

281. I AM TIRED

O body, I am tired
Of your constant lingering.

O vital, I am tired
Of your constant boasting.

O mind, I am tired
Of your constant whispering.

O heart, I am tired
Of your constant delaying.

O soul, I am tired
Of your constant dreaming.

282. EARTH-BORN AND HEAVEN-BORN SOULS

O earth-born souls,
You know how far to go
    But
You know not where to go.

O Heaven-born souls,
You know when to love
    But
You do not love adequately.

283. YOUR SILENCE-SELF

True,
Your earth-life,
A portion of fallen divinity.
But do not be doomed
To disappointment-night.

You will gain back
What you had
And what you were.
Just give one more chance
To your silence-self:
God.

284. TERRESTRIAL CHART AND CELESTIAL CHART

When her terrestrial chart
   Was unrolled
She realised how important
   Her presence on earth was.

When her celestial chart
   Was unrolled
She realised how desperately
Heaven needs her support,
   Soul-support.

285. THREE MESSAGES

Faith has three messages to offer.
First message:
    God is necessary.
Second message:
    God-realisation is indispensable.
Third message:
    God-Perfection is attainable
    At God's choice Hour,
    It is unmistakably attainable.

286. MEASUREMENT

The other day
I measured my desire's height.
My vital was shocked.

My soul was thrilled
After I took the measurement.

A pigmy's height
Was my desire's height.

287. LORD, I ENJOY

Lord, I enjoy Your juggling Eyes.
Lord, I love Your climbing Eyes.
Lord, I adore Your glowing Eyes.
Lord, I worship Your forgiving Eyes.
Lord, I need Your life-transforming Eyes.

288. DO YOU LOVE ME

Do you love Me?
If so, why then do you love
My arch enemy: fear?
That means when you say
You love Me,
You do not actually mean it.

Do you love Me?
If so, why then do you love
My hostile enemy: doubt?
That means when you say
You love Me,
You do not actually mean it.

289. LOVE IS A FLOWER

Love is a flower
That grows in every
Heart-garden.

Doubt is a flower
That grows in every
Mind-garden.

Progress is a flower
That grows in every
Life-garden.

God is a flower
That grows in every
Gratitude-heart.

THREE HUNDRED SIXTY-FIVE FATHER'S DAY PRAYERS

290. GO OUT

Go out
If you want to widen your mind.
   Stay inside
If you want to maintain
The purity of your heart.
   Go out and come back soon
If you want to conquer the world
Yet sustain your God-like beauty.

291. MY SUPREME SECRET

I tell you
   My supreme secret:
I used God's Breath
   To declare
My ignorant body's
   Ignorance-death.

   You can also try.
Your success is guaranteed
   For two million years
      At least.

292. ONLY THREE HUMAN BEINGS

God says
In His creation vast
   Only three human beings
Will never be old:
   A God-lover
   A truth-server
   A perfection-builder.

293. OUR PRESENT CENTURY

Our present century
Has discovered
Three undeniable but deplorable things:
   Indifference-ocean
   Confusion-sun
   Falsehood-perfection.

294. SILENCE-LIFE, SOUND-LIFE

   His silence-life
Is quite audible.
   His sound-life
Is quite inaudible.
   Why?
Because in his silence-life
Is God's great preparation
   And God's dynamic creation.
And in his sound-life
Is God's silent frustration,
   God's silent Compassion.

295. HE KNOWS

He knows,
He knows the virtue of silver patience.
   He practises it, too.
But he does not unnecessarily
   Sit and wait,
Scheme and dream.
   His inner light fixes
   God's choice Hour.
So, at God's Hour he runs
   And easily and unprecedentedly
Wins the race.

296. FRUITFUL IS GOD-DUTY

Hopeful is sunrise.
Thoughtful is moon-beauty.
Soulful is love-purity.
Truthful is life-necessity.
Fruitful is God-Duty
   Beyond sunrise.

297. YOU PRAY TO GOD

    You pray to God
In a time of necessity.
    You do not want to learn
The lessons offered
    By regularity and punctuality.
I tell you what regularity
    Can and will do for you:
Regularity will show you
    Your victory's crown
And punctuality will crown you,
    Your achievement's glory.

298. THREE VOICES

A thunderous voice,
    Who needs it?
I need it when I speak to Satan.
A generous voice,
    Who needs it?
I need it when I speak to poor earth.
A glorious voice,
    Who needs it?
I need it when I speak to Heaven.

THREE HUNDRED SIXTY-FIVE FATHER'S DAY PRAYERS

299. CERTITUDE AND GRATITUDE

My soul, you have for me
   Royal certitude
And I have for you
   Real gratitude.
My soul, you have for me
   The message of the sky
And I have for you
My inner beauty's cry.

300. HOPELESS AND USELESS

Father, I know I am hopeless
   And useless.
But since You have taken me
Into Your inner circle
   Will You not help me to be worthy
   Of that intimate circle?
I feel You certainly can.

   Daughter, I certainly must.

301. BE CAREFUL

Be careful!
If you do not meditate
A voracious earth-hour
Shall devour you.
Be cheerful.
Since you meditate
A precious Heaven-hour
Is bound to feed you,
Love you
    And
Immortalise you.

302. I LOVE YOU

Father, I love You.
Daughter, that is not enough.
Father, I love You only.
Daughter, that is not enough.
Father, I need You.
Daughter, that is not enough.
Father, I need You only.
Daughter, that is not enough.
Why do you love Me?
Why do you need Me?
I love You, I need You
Because You, You alone are
My Eternity's All.

THREE HUNDRED SIXTY-FIVE FATHER'S DAY PRAYERS

303. BECAUSE

Because
He went to God
With a timid heart
God did not accept him.

Because
He went to man
With two timid eyes
Man did not accept him.

Because
He went to Heaven
With two timid feet
Heaven did not accept him.

304. GOD-REALISATION

God-realisation
Is the most difficult attainment.
Who denies it?
    Nobody.
Life-perfection
Is the most difficult achievement.
Alas, nobody wants to admit it.
Nobody wants to try it.

305. CHOICE HOUR

Sacrifice-star
You have it.
You do not need any more.

Love-moon
You do not have.
You need it ever more.

Perfection-sun
God has kept aside for you.
He is just waiting
For His choice Hour.

306. IF AND WHEN

If and when
I have the power,
I shall definitely speak
To humanity.

If and when
I have the love,
I shall unerringly love divinity.

If and when I become
Another God,
I shall speak to myself
And never before.

THREE HUNDRED SIXTY-FIVE FATHER'S DAY PRAYERS

307. THREE TEMPLES

In the temple of Night
I saw who I was.
In the temple of Light
I have seen what I can
Eventually be.
In the temple of Delight
I see what I eternally am:
God's own Dream-boat.

308. LIMITED AND UNLIMITED

Limited is the power of the vital.
   I am sure by this time
   You have known it.
Equally limited is the power of the mind.
   I am sure by this time
You have realised it.
But unlimited is the power of the heart.
   You will realise it
   Before long.

309. HE JUST BARKS

   He barks
     But
He does not bite.
What I am telling is true.
But, if he ever bites,
His bite will be no match for his bark.

   He is clever
Therefore he does not bite.
I tell you,
   This is the only reason
Why he does not bite.

310. PRAYER, MEDITATION, REALISATION

   Each prayer
Heralds a new day of hope.
   Each meditation
Heralds a new day of promise.
   Each realisation
Heralds a new life of the Supreme.

311. POWER-KINGDOM AND LOVE-KINGDOM

Your power-kingdom
Is bound to be overthrown
　If you fail to feed
　　Humanity with love.

Your love-kingdom
Is bound to flourish
　If you serve the body and soul
　　Of humanity
　With your oneness-light.

312. PERFECT SATISFACTION

Your vital is a connoisseur
　Of wild confusion.
Your mind is a connoisseur
　Of mild confession.
Your heart is a connoisseur
　Of true illumination.
Your soul is a connoisseur
　Of perfect satisfaction.

313. GOD, I NEED

God, I need
Your old Kindness.
God, I need
Your new Forgiveness.
God, I need
Your old Intimacy.
God, I need
Your new Promise.

314. OUTER AND INNER TEMPLES

My outer body-temple
From time immemorial
Has been expecting God's Arrival.

My inner heart-temple
From time immemorial
Has been feeding God's Body
And treasuring God's Soul.

315. I BELIEVED THEREFORE I CONQUERED

I believed I could conquer,
Therefore I conquered.

   What did I conquer?

Heaven's indifference and earth's pleasure,
God's Crown and death's pressure.

316. ORIGINAL FOES

Humanity's
Original foes:
　Separation-night,
　Ignorance-dream.

Humanity's
Original friends:
　Self-giving,
　Truth-search.

317. CAME AND LEFT

Silver victory came,
Gold humility left.

Gold humility returned,
Diamond God followed.

318. FATHER

Father, at times why do I
Become hostile to You?

Is it because I feel
That You love others more
   Or
Because You are not
Helping me to conquer
My insecurity's life
   And
My jealousy's eyes?
Father, I know these are difficult questions.
You may take Your own time.

319. PERMANENT

Only four songs
Are permanent
In God's creation:
Man's song of procrastination
God's song of Compassion
Earth's song of dedication
Heaven's song of satisfaction.

THREE HUNDRED SIXTY-FIVE FATHER'S DAY PRAYERS

320. THE MIND-MAN AND THE HEART-MAN

Lord, the mind-man in me
   Is unwilling.
Shall I force him?
      Or
Shall I leave him?

Lord, the heart-man in me
   Is more than willing.
How shall I thank him?
      And
How shall I pilot him?

321. MY ASPIRATION-LADDER, MY DESIRE-LADDER

My aspiration-ladder
Took me up to show me
My face of golden ray.

My desire-ladder
Brought me down to show me
My feet of inconscience-clay.

322. DO YOU BELIEVE

Do you believe
In the life of reality?
If you believe
Then do not renounce life.
Do not indulge
In quitting activity
As long as you believe in reality;
God's omnipresent Reality.

323. ENEMY AND FRIEND

He who has a single desire
    Has a sure enemy.

He who has a little aspiration
    Has a true friend.

He who has an iota of love
    Has a pure mother
        And
    An eternal friend.

THREE HUNDRED SIXTY-FIVE FATHER'S DAY PRAYERS

324. IF YOU SAY

If you say
   He is old
I shall not object.
   But I shall appreciate it
If you just add a pithy line:
   His earth-face
Is lined with the roadmap
   Of Heaven-history.

325. WHO SAYS

   Who says
   You have to become
A God-believer first
If you want to be
A conscientious objector?
   It is not at all true.
You just need firm faith
In your discovery
   Of wisdom-light.
If that is done,
You do not have to bring God into the picture.
   After all, poor God,
He has many more important things to do.

326. HE IS WISE

He is wise
    Because
He knows how far he can run
In this world of limited boundaries.

327. NO MORE VICTORY

O my vital,
You cannot have a sweeping victory
    Any more.

My mind, sharp as shark's teeth,
Now vehemently challenges you.
    And
My heart, vast as the blue sky,
Condemns your age-long supreme authority.

328. HE IS WRONG

He thinks his outer years
Will offer him wisdom-light.
    Alas, he is totally wrong.

He thinks his mental capacities
Will offer him wisdom-light.
    Alas, this time, too, he is wrong.

Finally, he comes to realise
That it is God's Compassion-Flood
That offers him the wisdom-light.

THREE HUNDRED SIXTY-FIVE FATHER'S DAY PRAYERS

329. USE HIM

Use him to please you.
He will do it.

Use him to love you.
He will do it.

Use him to show you
The Face of God.
　　He will do it.
　　He will gladly do it.
　　He will devotedly do it.
　　　　Why?
Because in your joy
He achieves the peerless satisfaction
　　Of God-manifestation.

330. THERE WAS A TIME

　　There was a time
When I ventured to change
　　The face of the world.

And now I consider the case.

　　No more shall I be
　　A self-styled reformer.
I shall become only a God-lover
To please Him in His own Way.

331. TO HUMANITY

To humanity,
Your heart of light
Has brought the greatest
   Blessing-light.

To divinity,
Your mouth of abysmal darkness
Has brought the unparalleled curse.

332. WHY DOES HE NEED

Why does he need weapons
To accept the challenge
   Of world-gloom?
   His wisdom-light
Far transcends the power
   Of world-doom
     And
   Heaven-bloom.

333. WALK BY FAITH

"Walk by faith, not by night."
This is the only way
To reach God's
   Ever-transcending Heights
     And
   Ever-deepening Depth.
This method I have tried
   And I have succeeded,
     More than succeeded.

334. ALL IS UNCERTAIN

All is uncertain
Between womb and tomb.

All is uncertain
Between man's Heavenly promise
And earthly hope.

All is uncertain
Between man's aspiration-cry
And realisation-smile.

335. CONTROL AND INCREASE

Control your earth-desires.
  Don't you see
    That you are injuring
      Your Heaven-aspiration?

Increase your Heaven-aspiration.
  Don't you see
    That your human incarnation
      Is about to surrender
        To your animal incarnation?

336. GOD'S GOD-DECISION

  My
Desire-friend
What can I do?
My Lord wants me to play with you.
  He wants me to win,
  He wants you to lose.
If not, I would have easily allowed you
To win at times, at least.

As you know I have taken
  A solemn vow:
"God's God-Decision is always final."

337. DEAR DOUBT

Dear Doubt, after I have passed
Behind the curtain of eternity,
I might visit your country.
   But now, during my earth-sojourn,
     I shall stay only with my bosom friend
       Faith.
Once more, if you
Darken my mind-door,
I shall never leave
My Faith's immortal shore.
   So, be careful,
Doubt, my dear.

338. HE

He who loves nothing
   Knows nothing.
He who knows nothing
   Is nothing.
He who is nothing
   Is either God's inimitable creation
   Or man's insurmountable frustration.

339. EASY

Everything is easy to the willing.
   Father God and brother Heaven
      Are shining examples.

Nothing is easy to the unwilling.
   Your Himalayan ego
      And
   My Pacific insincerity
      Are shining examples.

340. YET GOD LOVES YOU

   Exception proves the rule;
You do not need God,
   Yet God loves you.

His hour for Heaven
   Has not yet struck;
Yet he has left for Heaven
   Out of bitter disgust for earth.
Needless to say,
   God has forgiven him
And has accepted the fact.

   I have brought God down
And placed Him before human beings
Quite unexpectedly.
   Yet God loves me.

THREE HUNDRED SIXTY-FIVE FATHER'S DAY PRAYERS

341. SEEKER-LOVER-MASTER

The seeker in me
   Never fears investigation.

The lover in me
   Never fears desertion.

The master in me
   Never fears humiliation.

342. ALL ABOUT GOD

I thought about God
Only to satisfy me.

I spoke about God
Only to glorify me.

I wrote about God
Only to justify me.

343. HE IS MY REAL FRIEND

God shook hands with me
Only to prove that He is my real Friend.

God blessed me on my head
Only to prove that He is my true Father.

God embraced me powerfully
Only to prove that He is my eternal Lover.

344. FOUR MEN

The desiring man
  In me declares:
    "Action, action."

The aspiring man
  In me declares:
    "Intention, intention."

The surrendering man
  In me declares:
    "God-satisfaction,
    God-satisfaction."

The realised man
  In me declares:
    "Eternal-perfection,
    Eternal-perfection."

THREE HUNDRED SIXTY-FIVE FATHER'S DAY PRAYERS

345. PROBLEMS

You have some mental problems.
Go to a psychiatrist.
I am absolutely the wrong person.

You have some physical problems.
Go to a doctor.
I am absolutely the wrong person.

You have some legal problems.
Go to a lawyer.
I am absolutely the wrong person.

Come to me only when
You have God-realisation problems
   And
God-manifestation problems.

346. I AM A FOOL

They say I am a fool.
I tell the world everything I know.

But what can I do?
How can I be mean?
I must share my knowledge with others.
After all I am practising
What I have been taught by the Supreme.

Did He not empty His Knowledge-Sun
Before me?
Whom shall I follow
If not my Father Supreme?

347. CONFESSION, PURIFICATION, SATISFACTION AND PERFECTION

  Confession
Is good for a Christian soul.
  Purification
Is good for a Hindu soul.
  Satisfaction
Is good for a surrendered soul.
  Perfection
Is good for a realised soul.

348. SATISFACTION GLOWS SUPREMELY

Confidence grows
   Slowly.
Realisation spreads
   Steadily.
Perfection flows
   Eternally.
Satisfaction glows
   Supremely.

349. A TRUTH AND A LIE

What is a truth?
What is a lie?
   A lie is the false protection
   Of my clever deception.

   A truth is the sure revelation
   Of my pure perfection.

350. I HAVE COMPARED

I have compared myself
   With God.
He has only two things
More than I have:
   Compassion
     And
   Forgiveness.

I have compared myself
   With man.
I have only two things
More than he has:
   Self-deception
     And
   Self-gratification.

351. CONFESS AND PROGRESS

   Confess, confess
If you have nothing else
   To do.

   Progress, progress.
   Indeed,
This is the only thing
   To do.

352. CONFIDENCE

Confidence, confidence.
God has confidence in me
   And
I have confidence in God.
God feels I shall be able
   To equal Him.
I am sure God will help me
   In this matter.
I feel I shall be able
   To manifest Him.
I am sure God will help me
   In this matter.

353. HE AND SHE

He is a cloud-born man.
   What can you really
   Expect of him?

She is a sun-born soul.
Is there anything
That both on earth and in Heaven
You cannot expect of her?

354. TEEMING SPOTS

Even the world-illumining sun
Has teeming spots.
Why do you worry
About my life's blackspots,
   Mother Earth?

Son, I want you to be
As perfect as Eternity's
   Father-sun
And not the time-born
   Planet-sun.

355. MY ADDED CONTRIBUTION

I have carefully read
God's Biography,
   Therefore
I know practically everything
   About God.
But one thing even now
I do not understand.
Is God responsible for this miserable creation
   Or
Am I responsible for my added contribution?

THREE HUNDRED SIXTY-FIVE FATHER'S DAY PRAYERS

356. SINCE

Since
Asking costs nothing
I ask God to love me more.

Since
Loving costs nothing
I love God more and more.

Since
Making costs nothing
I make God of my own sweet will.

357. GOD ALONE KNOWS

Talk to others,
You will learn.
Talk to yourself,
You will learn more.
Stop talking,
Remain silent.
God will talk and God will learn
For you.
You will learn everything
That God alone knows.

358. ONLY ONE QUESTION REMAINS UNANSWERED

All the questions
Have answers.
  Only one question
  Remains unanswered:
Does God ever think
If He has made
A serious blunder
  In creating this
  Animal universe?

359. INDEED

Indeed,
You are a real clever Master.
Just because I do not follow
Your path, you secretly
Tell your people
That I am not ready for the spiritual life.
Just because I have not taken you
As my Master, you openly say
That I am not meant to be your disciple.
Indeed,
You are a real clever Master.

THREE HUNDRED SIXTY-FIVE FATHER'S DAY PRAYERS

360. LOVE

Love your earth-adversaries
But tell them not
   What you have:
You have shadowless God-realisation.
If you breathe your realisation
They will refute your proclamation,
They will delay your manifestation.
   Love them
But tell them not
   What you have
And what you eternally are.

What you have
Is a glowing realisation.
What you are
Is an ever-ascending aspiration.

361. FAILURE

   What has failed you?
Your mind of wild confusion
   Has failed you.
   Blame not others.

   What has unnecessarily failed you?
Your life of mean seclusion
   Has failed you.
   Blame not others,
   Emphatically.

362. VICTORY-SPEED

Supreme,
We try so hard,
We cry so often,
How is it that
We never succeed?

Daughter, My daughter,
Try not to succeed
But
Try only to proceed.
Lo, your victory-speed
Is fast approaching you,
My daughter sweet.

363. IT NEVER ENDS

It never ends
My ignorance never ends.

It never begins
My aspiration never begins.

It never cries
My stupidity never cries.

It never smiles
My fear never smiles.

THREE HUNDRED SIXTY-FIVE FATHER'S DAY PRAYERS

364. THE BEST IS YET TO COME

The best is yet to come.
    Therefore
Give me another chance.

The best is yet to come.
    Therefore
I can begin to dance.

365. CLOSEST, CLOSER, CLOSE

You are closest to God
    Because
You never play with the role of God.

He is closer to God
    Because
His disciples compel him
To play the role of God.

I am close to God
    Because
On my own, I play the role of God.

PART V

O MY PILOT BELOVED

1. Prayer

What is prayer? Prayer is possession. What is prayer? Prayer is renunciation. What is prayer? Prayer is fulfilment.

With our human prayer we possess. With our divine prayer we renounce. With our supreme prayer we fulfil — we fulfil the Will of the Supreme soulfully, unreservedly and unconditionally.

The human prayer says, "Lord, give me." The divine prayer says, "Lord, take me." The supreme prayer says, "Lord, give me, if so is Your Will; take me, if so is Your Will. I have only one message for You: I am all for You, only for You."

Human prayer says, "Lord, give me what You have, and make me happy." Divine prayer says, "Lord, take me, along with all my possessions, and make me happy." The supreme prayer says, "Lord, in me and in others, please Yourself only in Your own Way, and thus make me happy."

Earth's prayer is a slowly ascending cry. Heaven's prayer is a speedily spreading smile. Earth prays for the immortal life. Heaven prays for the eternal satisfaction. Earth-prayer is God-Beauty's Perfection. Heaven-prayer is God-Duty's Satisfaction.

Prayer has a soulful brother, meditation. Prayer's God is high above. Meditation's God is deep within. Prayer's God is greatness and goodness. Meditation's God is fulness and oneness. Prayer is the strongest intensity in a seeker's life. Meditation is the steadiest immensity in a seeker's heart.

When I pray, I speak to God devotedly. When I meditate, God speaks to me affectionately. This is how we enjoy our fruitful conversation.

On the strength of my prayer, I go to God. I go to God and tell Him what He can most compassionately do for me. On the strength of my meditation, I bring God to me. God comes to me and tells me what I can cheerfully do for Him.

Prayer is humanity's momentous success. Meditation is divinity's continuous progress. Prayer's ultimate goal is God-Infinity's Sound-Glory. Meditation's ultimate goal is God-Eternity's Silence-Beauty.

I — O my Pilot Beloved

2. I do not know

O my Pilot Beloved, I do not know what I am praying for. But I do know that I am praying to You, to You, to You.

O my Pilot Beloved, I do not know what I am meditating for. But I do know that I am meditating on You, on You, on You.

"My Immortality's child, as long as you know that you are praying to Me and you are meditating on Me, you do not have to know what you are praying for and what you are meditating for. Since your heart's cry is sincere and your life's smile is sincere, I wish to tell you what you are praying for and what you are meditating for. You are praying for My Eternity's Compassion and you are meditating for My Infinity's Vision."

3. I wish to doubt

O my Pilot Beloved, I wish to doubt. I wish to doubt my suspicion of others' capacities. I wish to doubt my suspicion of others' aspiration-height and dedication-length. Each time I doubt others, I blight their pure hearts. While blighting their pure hearts, I weaken my own very limited aspiration and dedication-capacity. Therefore, O my Pilot Beloved, I wish to doubt my suspicion of others and thus cancel and illumine my previous blunder.

O my Pilot Beloved, I wish to be afraid of my ignorance-tiger, which is right in front of me and about to devour me. Before it devours me, I wish to run towards You for Your immediate Protection. If I am not afraid of my ferocious ignorance-tiger, then I shall not run towards You for Your ever-compassionate Protection. Therefore, to start with, I wish to be afraid of my all-devouring ignorance-tiger. Your Protection and Compassion, I know, will not only save me but also will give me the capacity one day to destroy entirely the very existence of my ignorance-tiger.

4. I adore You

O my Pilot Beloved, I adore You, but not because You are eternally great. I love You, but not because You are supremely good. I adore You because, if I do not adore You, my life cannot exist even for a fleeting moment. I love You because, if I do not love You, my heart will immediately fail. My adoration is my only meal; my love is my only nourishment.

5. I am happy

O my Pilot Beloved, I am happy because yesterday I covered the length of my desire-life.
  I am happy because today I have begun to climb up the height of my aspiration-life.
  I am happy because, from tomorrow on, I shall study at Your Realisation-School.

6. Greatness and goodness

O my Pilot Beloved, do tell me one thing. Is he really great just because he has achieved something significant in life? Is he really good just because he has given something precious to humanity? To me, he alone is great who adores Your transcendental Height. To me, he alone is good who loves Your universal Beauty.

"My child, you are absolutely right. Mere becoming is not greatness, mere giving is not goodness. I want you to develop your own greatness and your own goodness. You can develop your own greatness by becoming one with your heart's cry. You can develop your own goodness by becoming one with your life's smile. Greatness is oneness that grows and glows. Goodness is fulness that satisfies and immortalises the human in the divine and the divine in the human."

7. Justice-Sun, Compassion-Ocean

O my Pilot Beloved, aptitude I have; attitude I need.

With my unusual and exceptional aptitude I have seen Your Justice-Sun. Now I wish to see Your Compassion-Ocean with my soulful and surrendering attitude.

Millions of people on earth try to see your Justice-Sun. Alas, they sadly fail. In my case, I have done it; I have performed the great task. But I know that unless and until I can see Your Compassion-Ocean, my life will be devoid of salvation, my heart will be wanting in perfection, and my soul will be badly lacking in satisfaction.

Therefore, O my Pilot Beloved, what I need, now and forever, is Your Compassion-Ocean. In it lies everything — my dream-reality and my reality-dream.

8. The impossible

O my Pilot Beloved, there was a time when I felt the impossible. You are omniscient, omnipotent and omnipresent; nevertheless, I felt Your excruciating pangs inside my unaspiring heart.

There was a time when I saw the impossible. I saw with my own eyes the cosmic gods becoming jealous of me, of my spiritual heights.

There was a time when I heard the impossible. I heard directly from the denizens of the higher worlds that Your complete manifestation will always remain a far cry.

Now there shall come a time when I shall eventually become the impossible. I shall become another perfect God, like You.

9. I have been searching

O my Pilot Beloved, do look at me only once. I have been searching for You here on earth and there in Heaven. I have been searching for Your Vision-Eye and Your Compassion-Feet.

"My child, look, look! I have also been searching for you — for your ever-increasing receptivity-heart."

10. Accomplishment and happiness

O my Pilot Beloved, do tell me the difference between accomplishment and happiness.

"My child, accomplishment is constant self-giving and happiness is God-becoming once and for all."

O my Pilot Beloved, what is the difference between self-giving and God-becoming?

"My child, self-giving is a fruitful smile and a soulful cry: Eternity's cry and Infinity's smile. In God-becoming, the divine lover says to the Beloved Pilot: 'Lord, at long last I have come to You to offer myself — soul, heart, mind, vital and body. All that I have and all that I am, I offer to you devotedly, unreservedly and unconditionally, plus constantly.' In reply, the Lord Beloved says: 'My child, indeed, from now on you can claim Me as your own, very own. On every plane of My Consciousness, in every world that I am in, in My entire Universe, you have the most secret, most sacred and most significant place. Here on earth, there in Heaven, you will eternally remain My unparalleled instrument, My eternally unprecedented Choice. In you, through you I shall reveal Myself and fulfil Myself. I shall satisfy My Vision-World and My Reality-World only in and through you, you alone. From now on, you will be the source of My unparalleled joy, My unparalleled success and My unparalleled progress in My own Eternity's growing and glowing Vision-Reality. In everything that I do and in everything that I say, your living breath shall shine brilliantly and perpetually.' "

11. I need you

O my Pilot Beloved, I need You — not because of my inability, not because of my insincerity, not because of my insecurity, not because of my impurity.

O my Pilot Beloved, I need You because of the importance that You have given me in Your cosmic Vision and cosmic Manifestation.

12. My friends, my enemies

O my Pilot Beloved, my friends consciously help me realise You. My enemies unconsciously help me transform my unlit human nature. Would You please tell me if my friends are more important than my enemies, or if my enemies are more important than my friends?

"My child, no comparison! Unconscious help is not worth much. Unconscious help does not deserve any appreciation, let alone gratitude. But if help is conscious, then it deserves not only appreciation but also gratitude. Therefore, only offer your gratitude to your true friends, who consciously help you. But just because you do get help, even unconsciously, from your enemies, if you happen to see them as you walk along the path, you can offer them a soulful smile. You do not have to go out of your way to look for your friends, either, anywhere in My creation. Just offer them in silence your gratitude-heart.

"Again, there is only one real Friend, one eternal Friend, and that is I. It is from Me that everyone gets the things he needs to transcend his unlit animal nature and realise Me. It is I who help you to realise Me through your human friends. It is I who have been playing the role of friendship from time immemorial. Since you do not see Me, since you cannot comprehend Me in the physical, it is advisable to be constantly grateful to your so-called friends. It is your friends who are constantly helping you to realise Me. Realisation is oneness, eternal oneness, and in Me is your eternal oneness-life. He who helps you realise Me is your oneness-friend and My blessingful, fruitful chosen instrument."

13. Surrender is of paramount importance

O my Pilot Beloved, I know that in the desire-life determination is of paramount importance to bring about success. I know that in the inner life, in the life of aspiration, my implicit surrender to Your Will is of paramount importance. But my sweet Lord, how can I acquire this surrender? How can I make this surrender to You?

"My child, you know what you are right now; you are now ignorance incarnate. Also you know what your soul thinks of you, what it feels that eventually you will become. What you can become eventually, your soul knows. Although you are now ignorance incarnate, your soul knows that one day you can become a perfect instrument of Mine. But I wish to tell you that you will not only become a perfect instrument of Mine, but something more. You will become, like Me, another God. You know that this creation is Mine, the universal Vision is Mine, the transcendental Reality is Mine; but a day shall come when everything will be yours. Like Me, you will be the possessor of the universe, the indweller of the universe, the ruler of the universe. Since you know that you will eventually become another God, for the time being, you can make your surrender complete. For a few days, for a few months, for a few years or even for a few incarnations you can try to surrender your will to My Will.

"No, you are not dealing with possibility; you are dealing with inevitability. Your life of ignorance will disappear and a new Wisdom-Light will enter into your inner being. At that time, you will become like Me, My child, another God. Therefore, right now play your role. Make your surrender implicit, complete and continuous. What you will get in return as a reward is far, far beyond your imagination. Therefore, right now do the needful; just become a totally surrendered instrument of Mine. Yours will be My Infinity's life. Yours will be My Eternity's love. Yours will be My Immortality's success, fulfilment and perfection."

14. First-class, second-class and third-class disciples

O my Pilot Beloved, I am Your disciple. Do tell me if I am Your first-class or second-class or third-class disciple. Do tell me.

"My child, I shall not tell you directly whether you are My

first-class or second-class or third-class disciple. But I shall tell you who are the disciples in My first class, second class and third class. From My statement, you will know which category you belong to.

"My third-class disciples are those to whom I have given full freedom. They do anything they want to do. They say anything they want to say. They become what they want to become. I have given them full freedom. They live their independent lives. They just stay in My Boat and they feel that they are doing Me a big favour.

"My second-class disciples are those to whom I give an option. Always I keep two roads ready for them. I tell them: 'Either walk along this road or along that road. Do this or do that — whichever pleases you, in a sense. Either do this or do that, and please Me to some extent. It is up to you to make the choice. There is no compulsion. It is you who have to make the choice and thus please Me to some extent.' I do not expect them all the time to be inside My Consciousness. They, in return, do not expect all the time to receive My constant Concern, Love, Blessings and Gratitude.

"My first-class disciples are those to whom I have not given any earthbound or human freedom. For I know earthbound freedom — vital, mental and physical freedom — is infinitely worse than destruction itself. Therefore, I take full responsibility for their aspiration-life and dedication-life. I tell them what they must do; I do not ask them. If I say, 'Sit down!' they sit down. If I say, 'Stand up!' they stand up. I give them no choice. It is My Will. They have no option, no choice. They have to please Me and fulfil Me at every moment in My own Way. This is what my first-class disciples do.

"First-class disciples have no will of their own. They have no choice of their own. Their choice and their will have become inseparably one with My Choice and My Will. My Satisfaction, in My own Way, is their only satisfaction. They know that when they satisfy Me and please Me in My own Way, they will receive boundless joy, boundless peace, boundless love, boundless delight — everything, everything in boundless measure. Their sense of separativity, their individuality, their personality have totally disappeared. Only oneness-song, oneness-dance, oneness-march they enjoy divinely and supremely with Me here on earth, there in Heaven.

"You know, My child, indeed you are a disciple of Mine. Now you know where you stand: whether you are My first-class, second-class or third-class disciple.

"Third-class disciples I tolerate unconditionally. Second-class disciples I keep with the hope that one day they will try to become first-class disciples. One day in the near or distant future a new light will enter into them, and they will cry for total surrender to My Will. That is My expectation-world. That is My hope-world. With an iota of hope, an iota of expectation, I keep them in My Boat.

"First-class disciples are My veritable Pride. They carry Me the length and breadth of the entire world. They carry My Vision; they carry My Mission — eternally. It is in them I see My own Dream-Reality. It is for them I feel My Universal Existence. They are My instruments unparalleled. They are My happiness unparalleled. They are My Eternity's satisfaction as I am their Eternity's All.

"So, My child, if you feel that you are not My first-class disciple, try to become one and make Me feel that My Manifestation on earth is not an empty dream but fulfilling and fulfilled Reality."

15. The shortest distance

O my Pilot Beloved, today I have a volley of questions. Would You kindly answer them?

"Yes, I shall, My child."

Please tell me the shortest distance between two human beings.

"Peace."

Please tell me the shortest distance between You and me.

"A constant cry."

Please tell me the shortest distance between man and the cosmic gods.

"Understanding."

Please tell me the shortest distance between man's mind and man's heart.

"Concern."

Please tell me the shortest distance between Your transcendental Vision and the universal Reality.

"A oneness-smile."

Now, do tell me how the seeker in me can cover these distances.

"My child, for that you need concentration on the physical plane, meditation on the inner plane and contemplation in My all-illumining and all-fulfilling Plane. Without concentration, everything that you have and everything that you are will not be able to bring about success. Your life-tree will fall apart, your life-house will fall apart. Without meditation, your illumining and fulfilling hope-bridge that connects Heaven and earth will not last. It will fall apart. Without contemplation, the divine in you will never be able to manifest the Universal and Transcendental in you.

"Concentrate! You will achieve your goal. Meditate! You will be able to remain inside the very depth of your goal. Contemplate! You will become the goal itself. The all-illumining, all-fulfilling goal, it is you who will become."

II — Antigua prayer-messages

16

Surrender is God's God-Power in His own tiny human body.

17

We think of the Supreme because we need His Compassion. The Supreme meditates on us because He loves our hearts.

18

My Beloved Supreme is constant Forgiveness. Therefore, I am and I shall always remain a living reality.

19

My Beloved Supreme, here on earth, whoever scores the most is the winner. There in Heaven, who is the winner? Do tell me.
   "My child, in Heaven the winner is he who becomes cheerfully and inseparably one with the surrender-life and surrender-breath of the tennis ball. A human seeker can learn the message of surrender in its purest form from a tiny little tennis ball — not from the player, not even from the racquet, but from a mere ball. When you think of yourself as a mere ball, you will be able to

give the greatest satisfaction to Me, to your Beloved Supreme, your Eternity's Champion Tennis Player."

20

My Lord Supreme, do tell me the difference between a God-seeker and a God-lover.

"My child, the difference is very simple. A God-seeker is likely to be satisfied with God's transcendental Heaven, but a God-lover will never be satisfied with God's transcendental Heaven. He will be satisfied only when he is with God cheerfully, unreservedly, unconditionally and, also, eternally."

21

The searching mind will eventually win God's Compassion-Heart. The surrendering heart will immediately win God's Satisfaction-Breath.

22

Life is not life without love.
   Love is not love without oneness.
   Oneness is not oneness without perfection.
   Perfection is not perfection without satisfaction.
   Satisfaction is not satisfaction without God.
   God is not God without His Justice-Light and Compassion-Height, and Delight is the bridge between God's
   Justice-Light and His Compassion-Height.

23

A hero-seeker never, never surrenders to his despair-fate. He has heard the inner message that in the battlefield of life, he will eventually win.

24

The face of a human being can be read by another human being. But the heart of a seeker can be read only by God and by nobody else.

25

Excitement, enthusiasm and aspiration are three totally different things. Excitement leads the seeker to the darkest night. Enthusiasm leads the seeker to the clearest dawn. Aspiration leads the seeker to the brightest sun.

26

Nothing is more beautiful and more fruitful than a soulful seeker's tearful heart.

27

Purity's breath is the field. Divinity's assurance is the plough. Immortality's immortal Smile is the farmer.

28

Purity: what is it? It is the faithful and soulful companion of the heart's ascending cry. It is the life-transforming and God-manifesting companion of the soul's descending smile.

29

My Lord Supreme, what is the worst punishment that the Master can give to a disciple who deceives him?

"My child, the worst and most painful punishment is indifference. The Master's indifference is the worst punishment. Some are of the opinion that forgiveness is the worst punishment, but I say no. You can forgive again and again, but the deceptive seekers will make the same mistakes over and over in the same way. But if the Master is indifferent to them in the inner world and the outer world, if he takes no inner responsibility for what they do, what they say and what they grow into either in the inner or the outer world, then that is the worst possible punishment.

"It is of paramount importance to give this kind of punishment, for it permits the Master to give more opportunity to the other seekers who are still trying to realise the Absolute Supreme and who need more encouragement. Then the Master is able to pay more outer attention and offer more encouragement to them and congratulate them on their soulful inner cry."

30

Let us be faithful, and then we shall immediately know that our Beloved Supreme belongs to us.

Let us be pure, and then we shall immediately learn that we belong to our Beloved Supreme alone, forever and forever.

31

Meditation is absolutely necessary for the salvation of the animal in us. Meditation is absolutely necessary for the illumination of the human in us. Meditation is absolutely necessary for the perfection of the divine in us. Meditation is absolutely necessary for the satisfaction of the Supreme in us.

32

Darkness proudly declares: "I everywhere exist."
Light smilingly whispers: "I eternally am."

33

Aspiration admires the faithful duty of time. Time loves the soulful beauty of aspiration.

34

Life is an eternal play. This eternal play is the universal Bliss. This universal Bliss is our Beloved and Transcendental Supreme.

35

When I ask for it, suggestion is a supremely fulfilling satisfaction. When I do not ask for it, suggestion is an utterly devastating frustration.

36

Aspiration needs. Meditation gives. Aspiration is the hunger of the heart. Meditation is the meal-feast from the soul.

37

My Lord Supreme, early in the morning I surrender my very existence to You. At noon I run after You, I follow You. In the evening I tell You my supreme secret: I am eternally for You, for You alone.

38

We must meditate soulfully so that we can increase our faith in our Beloved Supreme. We must meditate soulfully so that our Beloved Supreme can have more confidence in us. Meditation is the most effective way to increase the seeker's faith in his Beloved Supreme and also to increase the confidence of his Beloved Supreme in the seeker.

39

I meditate on my Lord Supreme not because He is great. I meditate on my Lord Supreme not because He is good. I meditate on my Lord Supreme because both my inner world — the dream-world — and my outer world — the reality-world — entirely belong to Him.

40

To consciously neglect meditation is to deliberately betray the soul, the God-representative on earth.

41

When I pray to the Supreme, I pray with my sincerity-mind. When I meditate on the Supreme, I meditate with my purity-heart. When I love the Supreme, I love with my intensity's life-breath.

Three things we do: we pray, we meditate, we love. When we pray, meditate and love, everything is done.

The mind is so tricky. With this tricky mind, we can't do anything sincerely. But if we can sincerely pray, then we will get everything.

The heart is covered by weakness, garbage, rubbish. That is why the heart does not remain pure. But if we can meditate with a pure heart, we will get everything. And if we can love the Supreme with our intensity's life-breath, then the Supreme is caught forever.

42

I pray because I need something from above. I meditate because I have something to offer below. Prayer is getting something which we do not have. Meditation is giving something which we have.

II — My God and my Lord

43

My God and my Lord,
 I know, I know, there can be no zigzag road to my oneness-heart with You.

44

My God and my Lord,
 May faith and surrender play the role of my constant companions.

45

My God and my Lord,
 I promise, my love of You will never be vanquished either by animal arms or by human charms.

46

My God and my Lord,
 There was a time when my life-pendulum oscillated between my hope and my despair.
 But now my life-pendulum oscillates between my perfection and Your Satisfaction.

47

My God and my Lord,
 I am equally happy when You ask me to lead a mundane life and when You ask me to lead an ultramundane life.

48

My God and my Lord,
 My absence of constant faith is tantamount to my immediate failure-dream.

49

My God and my Lord,
 I do not desire to lead a theanthropic life — this moment divine and the next moment human. I long to lead always a life divine.

50

My God and my Lord,
 Appreciation from without titillates the human in me. Aspiration from within energises the divine in me.
 O give me my aspiration-nectar and not my appreciation-poison.

51

My God and my Lord,
In the morning I love You, at noon I serve You and in the evening I surrender to You. This is how I lead my secret and sacrosanct life.

52

My God and my Lord,
Why do I at times enter into the quagmire of stark depression and make my life most unbearably miserable? Why, my God and Lord, why?

53

My God and my Lord,
I do not wish my life to be marked by a plethora of activities. I wish only one thing: an active surrender to Your compassionate Will, constant and unconditional.

54

My God and my Lord,
In all my spiritual difficulties I have come to realise that my purity is a good palliative, my sincerity is a better palliative and my cheerfully surrendered oneness with Your Compassion-flooded Eye is by far the best palliative.

55

My God and my Lord,
   In my desire-life Your Forgiveness is paramount and supreme. In my aspiration-life Your Compassion is paramount and supreme.

56

My God and my Lord,
    Your Forgiveness obliterates my blunders.
    Your Compassion obliterates my sorrows.
    Your Satisfaction obliterates my failures.

57

My God and my Lord,
   Your Compassion is the only oasis in the desert of my all-destructive self-doubt.

58

My God and my Lord,
    You are my desire-life, believe it or not.
    You are my aspiration-heart, believe it or not.
    You are my realisation-breath, believe it or not.
    You are my perfection-source, believe it or not.
    You are my satisfaction supreme, believe it or not.

59

My God and my Lord,
  Although I do not have any occult power, I am sure that there are people who do have occult power. My question is, what shall I do with those who enjoy sneering disbelief and do not believe in occult power? Shall I forgive them or ignore them, or shall I do both?

60

My God and my Lord,
  When I make a serious blunder, do grant me not only a terrible sense of remorse but also an unforgettable sense of remorse.

61

My God and my Lord,
  I have come to realise that in the spiritual world a pure and self-giving heart is the only cynosure.

62

My God and my Lord,
  I am so happy to tell the world that my inner vacation with pay has been earned by my divine thoughts, my divine words and my divine deeds.

63

My God and my Lord,
    There is no difference between the desert in my mind and the jungle in my vital.

IV — Sovereign Lord

64. In You, in me

My Sovereign Lord, I and my life are two tiny drops. You and Your Compassion are two vast oceans.
    In me Your Heart, Your Soul and Your Heaven-Existence are struggling. In You my heart, my soul and my earth-existence are blossoming.

65. Only two things

My Lord Supreme, I feel I need many things to please You. Do You agree?
    "No, My child, I do not agree. You need only two things: a heart of obedience and a life of sincerity.
    "Your heart of obedience will perfect the human in you. Your life of sincerity will fulfil the divine in you.
    "My child, you need only two things, only two things, only two things."

66. The opportunity-bird

My Lord Sovereign, is the spiritual life an opportunity?

"Yes, My child, it is. Not only that, the spiritual life embodies infinitely more opportunity than anything else in My entire creation. You may like to know what opportunity actually is. Opportunity is a bird that flies and flies and flies."

My Lord Sovereign, if opportunity is a bird that constantly flies, then what am I supposed to do with that flying bird?

"My child, I am telling you what to do, You know that you have your heart's inner cry. This inner cry is a mounting flame. This flame also knows how to fly high, very high. Climb up on your inner flame, and then grab the flying opportunity-bird. After you catch it, bring it down and encage it. Use it to fulfil you in every aspect of your life. Once this opportunity-bird flies away, your life will become an inevitable failure. Once if I withdraw My opportunity from you, My child, yours will undoubtedly be the life of utter failure.

"Remember what you were before you accepted the spiritual life. Remember what you would have been if you had not accepted the spiritual life. Just think what you have become by accepting the spiritual life and what you can become eventually by remaining spiritual in the purest sense. It is only when you avail yourself of your opportunities that you can become close, closer, closest and inseparably and eternally one with My Light and Height, with My Consciousness and Delight. But if you do not avail yourself of the opportunity that I grant you at every moment, then yours will be the most destructive doom and your life will be a total and unprecedented failure."

67. My Lord Supreme does not want

My Lord Supreme does not want to know what I have done for Him. He just wants to know how I am. If He hears from me that I am happy, then He Himself becomes exceedingly happy. In unmistakable terms He tells me that my happiness is His real and only satisfaction.

My Lord Supreme does not want to hear from me what I see in Him. He just wants to hear if I feel something sweet, pure and divine in the inmost recesses of my heart. He tells me that my life-elevating feelings are, without fail, as good as seeing something divinely illumining and supremely fulfilling in Him.

My Lord Supreme does not want me to show Him how much I know. He just asks me to agree to become His oneness-companion. He tells me that in my oneness-life with Him I shall learn everything from Him. The past, the present and the future will be three open books.

My Lord Supreme does not want me to prove to Him how much I love Him. He just wishes me to cry inwardly and soulfully and to smile outwardly and wholeheartedly. He tells me that my inner cry and my outer smile are more than enough to inundate Him with my love.

Notes to *O my Pilot Beloved*

2-15. During the first three days of August 1978, Sri Chinmoy offered a number of prayers to his Pilot Beloved after meditations at the Centre, the United Nations, the Centre Church, the 144th Street Gym and the Jamaica High School track. These prayers are reproduced here.
2. 1 August 1978, 5:45 am Sri Chinmoy Centre, Jamaica, NY.
3. 1 August 1978, 6:00 am Sri Chinmoy Centre, Jamaica, NY.
4. 1 August 1978, 8:00 am Jamaica High School Track, Jamaica, NY.
5. 1 August 1978, 1:30 pm Church Centre for the United Nations, New York, NY.
6. 1 August 1978, 1:45 pm Church Center for the United Nations, New York, NY.
7. 1 August 1978, 5:45 pm 144th St Gym, Jamaica, NY.
8. 1 August 1978, 6:05 pm 144th St Gym, Jamaica, NY.
9. 1 August 1978, 6:30 pm 144th St Gym, Jamaica, NY.
10. 2 August 1978, 8:00 am Jamaica High School Track, Jamaica, NY.
11. 2 August 1978, 12:45 pm 144th St Gym, Jamaica, NY.
12. 2 August 1978, 5:45 pm 144th St Gym, Jamaica. NY.
13. 3 August 1978, 8:00 am Jamaica High School Track, Jamaica. NY.
14. 3 August 1978, 12:45 pm 144th St Gym, Jamaica. NY.
15. 3 August 1978, 7:40 pm Sri Chinmoy Centre Church, Bayside, NY.
16-42. During a holiday in Antigua, Sri Chinmoy conducted several short meditations a day and after each meditation delivered a special prayer-message. His Antigua prayer-messages are reproduced here.
16. 21 December 1978, 7:08 am.
17. 21 December 1978, 8:14 am.
18. 21 December 1978, 9:55 am.

19. 21 December 1978, 12:25 pm.
20. 21 December 1978, 12:50 pm.
21. 21 December 1978, 6:15 pm.
22. 22 December 1978, 9:48 am.
23. 22 December 1978, 5:10 pm.
24. 22 December 1978, 7:50 pm.
25. 23 December 1978, 9:45 am.
26. 23 December 1978, 5:40 pm.
27. 24 December 1978, 6:53 am.
28. 24 December 1978, 8:04 am.
29. 24 December 1978, 9:50 am.
30. 24 December 1978, 5:45 pm.
31. 25 December 1978, 4:20 pm.
32. 25 December 1978, 6:20 pm.
33. 25 December 1978, 7:15 pm.
34. 25 December 1978, 8:00 pm.
35. 26 December 1978, 11:27 am.
36. 26 December 1978, 12:30 pm.
37. 26 December 1978, 5:06 pm.
38. 26 December 1978, 6:10 pm.
39. 26 December 1978, 6:50 pm.
40. 26 December 1978, 8:03 pm.
41. 28 December 1978, 10:00 am.
42. 28 December 1978, 11:15 am.

64-67. In early May 1979, Sri Chinmoy and his disciples practised cycling mornings and evenings in Flushing Meadow Park, Queens, in training for the Pepsi-Cola Bicycle Marathon. After cycling, Sri Chinmoy would usually hold a short meditation and, at times, deliver short prayer-messages. These prayers were given on 10 and 11 May 1979.

64. 10 May 1979, 7:40 am.
65. 10 May 1979, 7:32 pm.
66. 11 May 1979, 7:34 am.
67. 11 May 1979, 7:40 pm.

PART VI

PRAYER-PLANTS

PRAYER-PLANTS

1

My Lord Supreme,
 You know what I wish to be. I wish to be Your Perfection-Seed in the inner world of aspiration-flames, and Your Satisfaction-Fruit in the outer world of dedication-games.

2

My Lord Supreme,
 Yesterday I obeyed You. My obedience was my meaningful preparation. Today I am obeying You. My obedience is my soulful realisation. Tomorrow I shall obey You. My obedience shall be my fruitful perfection.

3

My Lord Supreme,
 My willingness is the perfection of my communication with You.

4

My sweet Lord,
 Do give me immense patience so that I shall never give up in the battlefield of life.

5

My sweet Lord,
 Do give me intense devotedness so that I shall ever succeed in manifesting Your Light here, there and all-where.

6

My sweet Lord,
 You have fulfilled my first prayer: You have given me freedom within and freedom without. Do fulfil my second and last prayer: please, please do not give me freedom from the immediate consequences of freedom's misuse.

7

My sweet Lord,
 Do fulfil my two prayers. My first prayer is to have the capacity to wait endlessly after I have asked You a question. My second prayer is to have the capacity to offer You my gratitude-sea immediately after I have received Your blessingful and fruitful answer.

8

My sweet Lord,
 I wish to run in the outer world to get Your Compassion and Illumination. I wish to run in the inner world to get Your Perfection and Satisfaction.

9

My sweet Lord,
 I do not know what I am doing. At the same time, I do not want to know what I am doing, for I know perfectly well that my doing or not doing cannot liberate me. Only Your Compassion can make me see the face of Light — and it does.

10

My sweet Lord,
My faith-plant is helpless. It is not growing any more. The buffets of doubt are destroying it. Do give me the capacity to study once more in Your inner school where I can study my faith-life, my realisation-life and my oneness-life.

11

My Sweet Lord,
Do tell me when I am far away from You.
"My sweet child,
You are far away from Me when you are not devotedness-light in your outer existence-life and oneness-delight in your inner existence-life."

12

My sweet Lord,
I am grateful to You not because You have given me, out of Your boundless Bounty, a serving heart to proclaim You all-where at every moment; not because You have given me a discriminating mind to lead a peaceful detachment-life; not because You have given me everything I need; not because You have not given me the things that I do not need; but because I am enchanted with Your Eternity's Vision-Perfection and Your Infinity's Reality-Satisfaction.

13

My sweet Lord,
 I wish to lead and be led. I wish to lead my darkness-life and ignorance-death to You, and place them at Your Feet. I wish to be led by my heart's purity and my soul's luminosity to You, and be placed inside Your Satisfaction-Heart.

14

My sweet Lord,
 Let me do what I soulfully and bravely can: let me climb and climb.

15

My sweet Lord,
 I shall be extremely grateful to You if You do what You compassionately and easily can: keep me from fearful slipping and painful falling.

16

My Lord Supreme,
 Do make my life three-dimensional: cry, try, fly.

17

My Lord Supreme,
 Each day You are Your blessingful Invitation, and I am my soulful acceptance.

18

My Lord Supreme,
 Yesterday I gave up one thing: desire-life. Today I am giving up another thing: expectation-life.

19

My Lord Supreme,
 To love is to care. I know, my Lord, I know, You care about me unreservedly and unconditionally.

20

My Lord Supreme,
 My earthly devoted life and my heavenly surrendered life are two of the most direct means through which You speak to me constantly.

21

My Lord Supreme,
 Your transforming-capacity is amazing, and my receiving-capacity is amazing. Something more is amazing: earth's disbelieving-capacity.

22

My Lord Supreme,
 My pure heart is for You; my impure heart, too. All my possessions, smiling and crying, encouraging and discouraging, are for You, forever and forever.

23

My sweet Lord,
   Forgive me when I bring You my imaginary problems and my illusory complaints.

24

My sweet Lord,
   Do make me feel that one unfathomable Smile of Yours is infinitely more valuable than all my earthly possessions and all my heavenly achievements.

25

My sweet Lord,
   Do make my responsibility-life always dependable. Do make my gratitude-heart always inexhaustible.

26

My sweet Lord,
   What I *eternally* need is Your God-Oneness. What I *daily* need is Your Heaven-Love. What I at *every moment* need is Your Compassion-Ocean.

27

My sweet Lord,
I have but one very, very serious problem. I am terribly afraid of Your transcendental Height.

"My sweet child,
I too have one very, very serious problem. I am terribly afraid of your division-day and your separation-night."

28

My Lord Supreme,
Do grant me the capacity to be grateful for everything that I have, even my teeming weaknesses, for they help me to think of Your boundless Compassion.

29

My Lord Supreme,
When You hide from me, You are beautiful. When You appear before me, You are beautiful, blessingful and fruitful. When I try to hide from You, I think that I am going to accomplish something very great. When I do not hide from You, when I come to You with what I have and what I am, I see clearly and feel unmistakably that I have accomplished everything gloriously.

30

My Lord Supreme,
  When I look at the world from Your point of view, I see it as a perfection-plant of slow, steady and convincing growth. But when I look at the world from my point of view, I know that the perfection-plant is long dead, and it can be found only in the land of nowhere.

31

My Lord Supreme,
  You tell us that we are very good. The devil tells us that we are very bad. Now it is up to us whom to believe. You do not force us to believe You, whereas the devil does not want to leave us even when we reject him vehemently and totally.

32

My Lord Supreme,
  Do make me Your mirror so that You can see Yourself, admire Yourself and enjoy Your transcendental Beauty's Perfection and Your universal Duty's Satisfaction.

33

My Lord Supreme,
  In the aspiration-world I try to help those who need a new beginning.
  In the desire-world I try to help those who want a final end.

34

My Lord Supreme,
 I am truly proud of my heart's faithfulness because it helps me serve You everywhere.
 I am truly proud of my life's soulfulness because it helps me fulfil You all the time.

35

My Lord Supreme,
 Before I die, I shall leave only one legacy: my devoted life's gratitude-heart.

36

My Lord Supreme,
 Do grant me the vision to see Your endless Grace inside my small efforts, and to see inside Your Grace the smile-dance of my liberation.

37

My Lord Supreme,
 You are great when You do everything all by Yourself. You are greater when You do everything through me. You are greatest when You accomplish everything just by giving a chance to anybody You want to.

38

My Lord Supreme,
   My surrender to You has weakened my doubtful mind, has strengthened my faithful heart, has softened my angry vital and has fed my hungry body.

39

My Lord Supreme,
   Neither do You want nor do You expect my immediate perfection. What you need is my immediate willingness.

40

My Lord Supreme,
   Do tell my tongue to tell the world how great Your creation is and how good Your Vision is.

41

My Lord Supreme,
   My prayer-life is my begging hole.
   My meditation-life is my becoming whole.

42

My Lord Supreme,
   My heart counters my life's insecurity-cave with its confidence-palace.

43

My Lord Supreme,
  Do liberate my mind from its self-styled prison.

44

My Lord Supreme,
  I complain because I do not love You enough.
  I complain because I think of the world too much.

45

My Lord Supreme,
  You are infinitely higher than my highest thoughts of You.
  You are infinitely more compassionate than my heart feels.
  My Lord, my ever-compassionate Lord!

46

My Lord Supreme,
  May my death try to glorify You, as my life now tries to glorify You.

47

My Lord Supreme,
  Do make my vital a perfect stranger to discouragements.
  Do make my heart a perfect stranger to desolate days.

48

My Lord Supreme,
   Let me forgive my past so that my future can be proud of my present.

49

My Lord Supreme,
   The desire-world has bored me. It has done its job quite well. Now I have to do my job. I have to liberate my desire-world from ignorance-night.

50

My Lord Supreme,
   What I unmistakably need is an unconditionally surrendered life in order to become an effective member of Your ignorance-transforming and wisdom-manifesting team.

51

My Lord Supreme,
   A new world began with my aspiration-heart.
   A new world begins with my dedication-life.
   A new world shall begin with my surrender-perfection.

52

My Lord Supreme,
   I am always with You. I think so, at least.

53

My Lord Supreme,
  What am I missing? Alas, I am missing my sincere love for Your Compassion-Sea.

54

My Lord Supreme,
  Today Your Compassion has filled me totally. I shall not face each new day any more with wishful human expectation.

55

My Lord Supreme,
  Your universal Push awakens me.
  Your transcendental Pull liberates me.

56

My Lord Supreme,
  I am always for You. And I am certain.

57

My Lord Supreme,
  It seems that my life's awareness and Your Heart's Goodness always like to live together.

58

My Lord Supreme,
  Your Justice succeeds. Your Compassion, too, succeeds, plus proceeds.

59

My Lord Supreme,
  You are inviting me to journey with You, and I am all ready.

60

My Lord Supreme,
  I am an unparalleled fool. I am trying to make my life valuable, forgetting that You have all along been working very hard to make my life invaluable.

61

My Lord Supreme,
  Am I not Yours? Am I not eternally Yours? Am I not only Yours?

62

My Lord Supreme,
  I trusted You. Therefore You have shown me the heart of earth's cry. I trust You. Therefore You will show me the soul of Heaven's smile.

63

My Lord Supreme,
   Yesterday my name was hope. Today my name is frustration. Tomorrow my name will be either illumination or destruction.

64

My Lord Supreme,
   This world of Yours has everything else except peaceful happiness.

65

My Lord Supreme,
   A day of understanding and harmony is indeed Your Infinity's Boon.

66

My Lord Supreme,
   I love myself because You love me. Otherwise I do not see anything in me that deserves love either from me or from anybody else.

67

My Lord Supreme.
   I do not need Your Compassion-Height. I do not need Your Justice-Light. I need only Your Existence-Delight.

68

My Lord Supreme,
  Do take away only three things from me: yesterday's failure-night, today's doubt-cloud and tomorrow's death-surrender.

69

My Lord Supreme,
  Since Your Compassion-Sun I cannot claim, I do not deserve and I cannot even earn, will You not give me the capacity at least to receive Your Compassion-Sun devotedly and unreservedly?

70

My Lord Supreme,
  Do give me the capacity to feel that my self-effort can succeed only when Your God-Grace precedes.

71

My Lord Supreme,
  May Your inner Voice awaken me and inspire me and Your outer Choice perfect me and fulfil You in Your own Way.

72

My Lord Supreme,
  May Your inner Silence-Beauty bless me and Your outer Sound-Duty love me.

73

My Lord Supreme,
There was a time when I gave You everything as a duty. But now I give You everything out of love. I place my progress-smile at Your Feet.

74

My Lord Supreme,
Yesterday I failed. But today I shall not. Why? Because today I am not only with You, but also for You, only for You.

75

My Lord Supreme,
You are Your Compassion. May I become Your expression? Do give me a chance.

76

My Lord Supreme,
Each day is another step closer either to frustration-gate or to satisfaction-home.

77

My Lord Supreme,
Your encouragement I love. Your punishment I treasure.

78

My Lord Supreme,
   Your Compassion awakens the human in me. Your Justice inspires the divine in me.

79

My Lord Supreme,
   There is no difference between my flowering smile and Your Compassion-Touch.

80

My Lord Supreme,
   I am giving You my sorrow's strength. Do give me Your Joy's length.

81

My Lord Supreme,
   Physically I died to see Your Face. Spiritually I am crying to sit at Your Feet.

82

My Lord Supreme,
   Alas! My face of pride I see everywhere. Alas! Alas! My heart of humility I see nowhere.

83

My Lord Supreme,
May my life become a life of willingness. May my heart be always a heart of selflessness.

84

My Lord Supreme,
My aspiration-dedication-life knows all about You. My surrender-gratitude-life knows only You.

85

My Lord Supreme,
The outer world is a doubter's mind. The inner world is a lover's heart. Am I not correct?

86

My Lord Supreme,
Success-day I like. Progress-sun I love.

87

My Lord Supreme,
I am helping my poor mind to make a new beginning. Will You not grant me Your inspiration-encouragement?

88

My Lord Supreme,
  Do give me the vision to meet You soulfully at any time, and do give me the mission to love You unconditionally all the time.

89

My Lord Supreme,
  My life's continuous sense of incompleteness makes my heart cry for oneness.

90

My Lord Supreme,
  The human in me wants to be understood. The divine in me longs to understand.

91

My Lord Supreme,
  The unfulfilled reality loves the human in me strongly.
  The fulfilled reality loves the Divine in You even more desperately.

92

My Lord Supreme,
  Let me admire You because You are so far.
  Let me love You because You are so near.
  Let me touch Your Heart because that is what You precisely and eternally are.

93

My Lord Supreme,
How is it that Your Satisfaction does not satisfy me, whereas my satisfaction always satisfies You?

94

My Lord Supreme,
My dedication-life is fulfilling because my aspiration-life's reliance upon You is unswerving.

95

My Lord Supreme,
An unaspiring life — how can it be my goal? Do give me a different goal, I pray.

96

My Lord Supreme,
What I have is a broken heart. What I am is a smashed life. At long last they have discovered their right place — Your Compassion-Heart.

97

My Lord Supreme,
Do give my heart the beauty of a rainbow and my life the duty of a God-manifestation-hero.

98

My Lord Supreme,
 My faith in myself may die; my hope, too. But not my surrender to You, my Lord. Never!

99

My Lord Supreme,
 I have only one desire, only one aspiration — Your Compassion-Sea.

100

My Lord Supreme,
 I have only one role, only one goal — a perfection-life.

101

My Lord Supreme,
 Even You have a substitute: Love. But Your Compassion has no substitute. It is without a second.

102

My Lord Supreme,
 What I call my spontaneous faith, You call that very thing Your supreme Victory.

103

My Lord Supreme,
 My prayer needs You as the Giver. My meditation needs You as the Receiver.

104

My Lord Supreme,
 I wish to hear only one thing from You: "Follow Me." Would You kindly hear only one thing from me: "Lead me."

105

My Lord Supreme,
 I have one desire: I need only You. May I soulfully fulfil my desire?

106

My Lord Supreme,
 To love You only is to be on the right road. To need You only is to be in the right lane.

107

My Lord Supreme,
 To strengthen my faith-muscle I need a second of gratitude-exercise daily.

108

My Lord Supreme,
  My insecurity starves the human in me and hurts the divine in You. What can I do? I am so helpless and useless.

109

My Lord Supreme,
  In the inner world a cry is a two-way conversation between You and me. In the outer world a smile is a two-way conversation between You and me.

110

My Lord Supreme,
  Morning is the time for my heart's gladness in You. Evening is the time for my life's nearness to You.

111

My Lord Supreme,
  I am exceedingly happy that my worry-power has surrendered to my poise-power.

112

My Lord Supreme,
  Today Your Compassion is my name. Tomorrow Your Satisfaction will be my name.

113

My Lord Supreme,
Today I have learned that there are no small acts of self-giving and that there are no great acts of self-withdrawing.

114

My Lord Supreme,
You want me to grow day by day in wisdom, glow hour by hour with light, flow minute by minute with energy, row second by second with my soul. You want me to do all these and I shall.

115

My Lord Supreme,
Yesterday I decided to be with You. Today I am choosing to sit at Your Feet. Tomorrow I shall please You in Your own Way.

116

My Lord Supreme,
Do give me the capacity to translate my mind's great intentions into my heart's good actions.

117

My Lord Supreme,
Your Compassion deserves all my human treasures — endless tears — and all my divine treasures — gratitude and cheerfully surrendered oneness.

118

My Lord Supreme,
  Just because I did not look back yesterday, today I have been able to step forward. Just because I have stepped forward today, tomorrow I shall reach my Goal of goals: the Golden Shore.

119

My Lord Supreme,
  Just because I smile at You, my life is replete with sincerity. Just because I cry for You, my heart is complete in perfection and satisfaction.

120

My Lord Supreme,
  Every day is the right day for me to need Your Compassion and to love Your Satisfaction.

121

My Lord Supreme,
  My inner revolution and my outer resolution have the self-same source: Your Compassion-Heart.

122

My Lord Supreme,
  My heart's soulfulness is Your Grace. My life's fruitfulness is Your Face. Your Grace is Your Eternity's Assurance. Your Face is Your Immortality's Beauty.

123

My Lord Supreme,
 When You are in my prayers, I know what to do. When I am in Your Satisfaction-Thoughts, I know I have already become what You wanted me to become.

124

My Lord Supreme,
 My gratitude-heart is the cornerstone for building my satisfaction-world.

125

My Lord Supreme,
 Do accept my gratitude-life's gratitude-heart.

126

My Lord Supreme,
 You have told me a supreme secret: a day of ingratitude gives birth to teeming clouds of loneliness.

127

My Lord Supreme,
 I am grateful to You because You have given me a mind that thinks of You spontaneously. I am grateful to You because You have given me a heart that thanks You constantly.

128

My Lord Supreme,
   My prayer-heart is pure; my meditation-life is sure. Needless to say, these two love each other deeply and are unfailing friends.

129

My Lord Supreme,
   Will You let me stay with You alone, only for a day? My Lord Supreme, will You?

130

My Lord Supreme,
   When I pray, I speak to Divinity on behalf of humanity. When I meditate, I speak to humanity on behalf of Divinity.

131

My Lord Supreme,
   My heart of faith and Your Eye of Compassion have developed a tremendous friendship since I have accepted the life of aspiration-dedication.

132

My Lord Supreme,
   Do make me realise my Himalayan blunder — my self-imposed responsibility.

133

My Lord Supreme,
   Do make me realise Your Compassion-ordained duty for me.

134

My Lord Supreme,
   My soul pleases You every day. So can my body. From now on it shall just do it.

135

My Lord Supreme,
   Let me start counting Your Smiles. Then I will have no complaints. No, not even one.

136

My Lord Supreme,
   Your outer world loves the lover in me most. Your inner world loves the forgiver in me most.

137

My Lord Supreme,
   Your greatness-world fascinates my eyes. Your goodness-world liberates my eyes.

138

My Lord Supreme,
 Do give me a non-stop gratitude-growth to increase Your Compassion-Sea for me and Your Satisfaction-Sky in me.

139

My Lord Supreme,
 Alas, what am I missing? My oneness with You. Alas, alas, what am I losing? My confidence in myself.

140

My Lord Supreme,
 To reach You, we start with unknown fear and we end with known strength.

141

My Lord Supreme,
 Today I am following You soulfully. Tomorrow I shall live for You unconditionally.

142

My Lord Supreme,
 My gratitude-heart is truly fond of Your Compassion-Eye.

143

My Lord Supreme,
Every day You are changing the human in me and fulfilling the divine in me.

144

My Lord Supreme,
My life is a gift. I have accepted it gratefully. Now do give me the capacity to cherish it soulfully.

145

My Lord Supreme,
Because of Your Compassion my life is not a failure. Because of Your Satisfaction my life is perfect Perfection.

146

My Lord Supreme,
My mind says that I have to reach up to find You. My heart says that You have been knocking and knocking at its door.

147

My Lord Supreme,
Today I am really happy because Your Assurance is complete and my surrender is unmistakable.

148

My Lord Supreme,
  Do give me the heart that longs to feel You, and not the mind that tries to understand You.

149

My Lord Supreme,
  If You want to give me a mind, then give me the mind that can understand the world and not the mind that wants to be understood by the world.

150

My Lord Supreme,
  Now is the time for me to give You my outer life's all: ignorance. Now is the time for me to give You my inner life's all: gratitude.

PART VII

I PRAY BEFORE I LIFT, I MEDITATE WHILE I LIFT, I OFFER MY GRATITUDE-CRIES AND GRATITUDE-SMILES

I PRAY BEFORE I LIFT, I MEDITATE WHILE I LIFT,
I OFFER MY GRATITUDE-CRIES AND GRATITUDE-SMILES

1. May 23

My Beloved Supreme,
You are my inspiration,
You are my aspiration,
You are my realisation.
If ever I can lift up 300 pounds,
It will be 100 per cent
Your unconditional Compassion,
Unconditional Blessings,
Unconditional Fulfilment.

2. May 24

My Lord Supreme,
May Your Compassion-Light
Be the ruling king
Of my body's lethargy-flooded ignorance-night.

3. May 25

My Lord Supreme,
Do turn my life into
Your Eternity's Patience-Tree.

4. May 26

My Lord Supreme,
I know my prayer-life
Is weaker than weakness itself.
But I also know
That Your Compassion-Heart
Is Your Infinity's Power-Manifestation.

5. May 28 am

My sweet Lord Beloved Supreme,
My life is an attempt;
My heart is an experience.
My life-attempt-tree and
My heart-experience-flower
I place at Your Feet cheerfully.

6. May 28 pm

My Lord Supreme,
For immediate success
The human in me cries.
For continuous progress
The divine in me cries.
For the absolute perfection of my life
You, my Lord Supreme, sleeplessly in me cry.

7. May 29

My Lord Beloved Supreme,
Hope keeps humanity's life alive
In Your Eternity's
Compassion-Satisfaction-Heart.

8. May 30

My Lord Supreme,
This creation of Yours
Has perhaps seen
The face of happiness,
But it has not yet felt
The heart of happiness.

9. May 31

My sweet Lord,
There is no joy in giving.
There is no joy in receiving.
There is no joy even in becoming.
There is joy
Only in obeying Your Commands,
Inner and outer.

10. June 2 am

My Sovereign Lord Supreme,
Since You created only delight
And not suffering
In this world,
Will You not put an end
To all human suffering?

11. June 2 pm

My Beloved Supreme,
My happiness is my strength,
And I know, I know,
That Your Compassion-Eye
Is the only fount
Of my happiness-strength.

12. June 3

My sweet Beloved Supreme,
May Your Compassion-Eye
Conquer once and for all
Humanity's ingratitude-heart.

13. June 4

My Lord Supreme,
Although You are unknown to my heart,
My heart loves You only.
Although You are unknowable to my mind,
My mind is searching for You only.

14. June 14

My Lord Supreme,
My Beloved Supreme,
Once again I am diving deep
Into Your Heart-Eternity's Compassion-Sea.

I shall be attempting 300 pounds. After a week of rest while I was in Europe, now I am back. There also, I totally banked upon Your Compassion. You have granted me and my disciples three Peace Miles — in Berlin, Zurich and Geneva. I do not deserve Peace Miles, my students do not deserve them, but Your eternal and unconditional Compassion is with us in these illumining and fulfilling achievements for earth and for mankind.

15. June 15

My sweet Lord Beloved Supreme,
It is Father's Day.
You are our Father,
Our only Father Supreme.
On this Father's Day
We, Your children, would like to have
A supreme boon from You:
Do grant us the capacity
To be sleepless servitors
Of Your Eternity's Will.

16. June 16

My Lord, my Lord Supreme,
Father's Day is over.
But from You, O our Eternity's Father,
Your infinite Compassion-Light
And Your immortal Forgiveness-Delight
Will never, never be over.

17. June 17

My sweet Lord Beloved Supreme,
What is my success-life,
If not my mind's constant remembrance
Of Your Compassion-Sea?
What is my progress-life,
If not my heart's constant feeling
Of Your Forgiveness-Sky?

18. June 18

My Lord Supreme, my Lord Supreme,
Do make the outer world soulful
So that it needs You.
My Lord Supreme, my Lord Supreme,
Do make the inner world perfect
So that at every moment
It can sing Your Victory-Manifestation-Song.

19. June 19

My sweet Lord Beloved Supreme,
Do give me the capacity
Not to criticise the world any more.
Do give me the capacity
To better myself every day
And thus inwardly, secretly and sacredly
Try to serve the world
For its improvement.

20. June 21

My Absolute Lord Supreme,
I must concentrate soulfully
On what I am doing
And not on how or why
I am afraid to do it.
No fear!
Only Your Compassion, Your Compassion, Your Compassion
Is what I need
And what I am
And what I shall forever be.

21. June 23

My Lord Supreme,
My Beloved Supreme,
As my life is a daily examination,
Even so, You are my constant inspiration,
Constant encouragement and constant assurance.
Therefore, I shall without fail
Pass all my examinations.
My Lord,
You are my inner assurance
And You are my outer performance.

22. June 24

My Lord Supreme, tomorrow a few world champions of the highest order in the sports world, especially in bodybuilding, will join us in our celebration of my first bodybuilding-weightlifting anniversary.

My Lord, do give me the capacity to give these champions of the highest magnitude joy, abundant joy, from the very depths of my aspiration-heart.

23. June 25

My Lord Supreme, my Beloved Supreme, world champions are coming today, and I am coming to ask You to bless me with an extra supply of Your Kindness, Concern, Affection and Love. I shall soulfully offer these deep, divine treasure-qualities to these champions, who are inspirers in the world of souls and in the physical world, which is the world You have chosen for humanity for Your divine Manifestation.

24. June 26

My Lord Supreme, my Beloved Supreme, my Eternity's All, today marks the first anniversary of my weightlifting career. There was a time when You made me a runner, a sprinter, an athlete. Now You have turned me into a bodybuilder, a weightlifter. My Lord, soulfully, devotedly and unconditionally I shall become what You want me to become.

Bodybuilders of the highest magnitude, weightlifters of the highest magnitude, Olympic heroes, are here to celebrate my weightlifting anniversary. I know, I know, my Lord Supreme, what they are actually doing. They are sharing their sincere love for Your infinite Compassion in me. They are all seekers. Some are conscious seekers, while others are going to be conscious seekers before long. What do I learn from them? I learn something most significant. This lesson I have been learning from You since I was four, when I started praying and meditating with Your infinite Grace.

My Lord, You are the Infinite. You become the finite, yet You do not lose Your Eternity, Infinity and Immortality. The finite is also You. Inside the heart of the finite, You play the role of the Infinite. Here on earth, when the supreme authorities on bodybuilding and weightlifting come to see me and be part of our oneness-family, I feel that the Infinite and the finite, the big and the small, together can sing the song of oneness-peace-family and thus make You happy, offering You satisfaction in Your own Way.

My Lord, my Lord, my Lord, may my outer name and my inner name be gratitude, gratitude, gratitude — sleepless gratitude, breathless gratitude and deathless gratitude — my Lord, my Eternity's Lord, my Absolute Beloved Supreme.

25. June 28

My Lord Supreme,
Happiness does exist in this world.
My friends, my guests on earth, and I
All got boundless joy from the celebration.
It is You who granted us this joy.
May our joy be transformed into a gratitude-flower
To place at Your Feet.

26. June 29

My Lord Supreme,
I know You are unknowable.
If You want to remain unknowable,
Then do remain so.
But do give me the satisfaction
Of loving You, knowing perfectly well
That You are the Unknowable.

27. June 30

My Lord Supreme,
Do help my life grow into
A patience-tree
So that I can serve You
Devotedly and soulfully,
Much more than I am doing now.

28. July 2

My Lord Supreme,
My Beloved Supreme Lord,
You are at once God the Power
And God the Compassion.
I need You, my Lord, as God the Power
To destroy the devouring tiger-hunger in me.
I need You, my Lord, as God the Compassion
To liberate the encaged soul-bird in me.

29. July 3

My Lord Supreme,
My Beloved Supreme,
I have come to realise
That my inner aspiration
Must every day feed
My outer determination.
If not, my outer determination
Will not be able to accomplish anything
For You, in Your own Way.

30. July 5

My sweet Lord Supreme,
You are teaching me
How to forgive the world.
You are also telling me
That an act of forgiveness
Is more beautiful than the Garden of Eden
And sweeter than honey itself.

31. July 6

My Lord Supreme,
May each defeat, each failure, remind me
Of what I have already accomplished
With Your infinite Grace and Compassion,
And not of what I have not accomplished
And will never accomplish.
I know, I know, my Lord,
This "never" accomplishment is an absurdity.
For You are my inner aspiration
And outer inspiration.
Therefore, I can have no permanent failure.
I shall have success after success
And progress, continuous progress,
For that is what You want from me.

32. July 7

My Lord Supreme,
My mind is divinely prosperous
Only when it works for You;
My heart is supremely enriched
Only when it works for You, for You,
Only for You.

33. July 8

My sweet Lord Supreme,
I shall never give up hope, never!
This weak body of mine
Will have to become strong one day
So that I can serve You
In the physical world
More devotedly and more soulfully
Than I am doing now.

34. July 9

My Lord Supreme,
Your Heart's infinite Compassion is telling me
That You love me because I am lovable
And not because I am Your creation.
My Lord Supreme, I wish to tell You that I love You
Not because You are Your infinite Power.
I love You because You are Your constant
Forgiveness, Forgiveness, Forgiveness.

35. July 10

My Lord Supreme,
Do give me inner peace
To harmonise my outer life.
Do give me inner joy
To perfect my outer life.
Do give me inner gratitude
To claim You as my own, very own,
In my outer life
The way I have always claimed You
As my own, very own,
In my inner life.

36. July 11

My sweet Lord Supreme,
My heart is grateful to You because
My life is Your Infinity's Blessings;
My life is grateful to You because
My heart is Your Eternity's Choice.

37. July 12

My Lord Supreme,
Let me not proudly criticise
The division-weakness of the outer world.
Let me soulfully utilise
The oneness-strength of the inner world.

38. July 14

My sweet Lord Supreme,
I do know there is a life
That is known as the life of failure.
But I also know, I also feel,
That by Your Grace infinite
Someday, somehow, I shall overcome it.

39. July 15

My Lord Supreme,
This world is a colossal disappointment.
Do grant me an appointment with You
And teach me how to love this world
Infinitely more.
Also, do teach me how to love this world
Unconditionally
So that I can be really happy.

40. July 16

My Lord Supreme, my Lord Supreme,
I do not want to see the flower-face
Of my own victory;
But I wish to be the heart-fragrance
Of Your supreme Victory,
With Your Grace infinite, eternal
   and immortal.

41. July 21

My Lord Supreme,
I love You only
Because everything in You
Is so lovable.
My Lord Supreme,
I need You only
Because You are the only One
Who has everything that I need
And, also, who is always, always ready
To grant me everything that I need.

42. July 22

My Lord, my Beloved Supreme,
I am totally and unmistakably lost
Between the beauty
Of Your divine Manifestation
And the ugliness
Of my human frustration.

43. July 24

My Lord Supreme,
If my mind does not believe constantly
That it belongs to You,
Then why should You care for
Its illumination and perfection?

44. July 25

My Lord Supreme,
My sweet Supreme,
My Beloved Supreme,
May my body's outer success
Soulfully depend on
My heart's inner progress —
Always and always.

45. July 26 am

My Lord, my Lord, my Lord,
May Thy supreme Victory be proclaimed
Not only in the beauty
Of my heart-garden
But also in the ugliness
Of my mind-jungle.

46. July 26 pm

My Lord Beloved Supreme,
Today I am completing one year and one month
In my bodybuilding and weightlifting-life.
It is a most significant day.
Therefore, my heart of sleepless gratitude
To You I offer.

47. July 28

My Lord Supreme,
For me, there is only one way
And that way is Your Way.
For me, there is only one Goal
And that Goal is Your Compassion-flooded
Oneness-Heart.

48. July 29

My Lord Supreme,
I know, an ingratitude-heart
Is a dissatisfaction-mind.

49. July 30

My Lord Supreme,
"Give me, give me, give me":
This is a very old song.
Long, long ago, I taught that song
To myself,
And I have been singing that song
Tirelessly.
But now I want to learn a new song:
"Accept me, accept me, accept me."
This song is Yours.
Do teach me, most perfectly, my new song:
"Accept me, my Lord, accept me!"

50. July 31

My Lord Supreme,
From my success I come to realise
That You give satisfaction to my mind.
Through my progress I come to realise
That You need my life's perfection.

51. August 2

My Lord Supreme,
My Beloved Supreme,
I tell You and also I tell myself
That I need Your supreme Guidance
At every moment of my life.
But do I really mean it?
Do I really, soulfully, always welcome
Your Guidance?
Alas, no, no, no!

52. August 4

My Lord Supreme,
My Beloved Supreme,
Every day, at every moment,
I live inside Your perpetual Compassion-Eye,
And every day You believe in my life's
Eventual transformation-perfection.

53. August 5

My Lord Supreme,
My Beloved Supreme,
Do tell me why I take the side
Of my mind's doubt-night
And fight and fight
Against my heart's confidence-light.

54. August 6

My Absolute Lord Supreme,
I am praying to You
To stop forgiving and protecting
My mind's huge ego-balloon.
I am praying to You
To fully illumine and completely perfect
My purified heart's confidence-sky.

55. August 8

My Lord Supreme,
My Beloved Supreme,
My gratitude-life is now helping me
Reclaim my aspiration of the hoary past
When at every moment
I lived only for You, only for You —
Only to love You and serve You
In the heart of mankind.

56. August 9

My Lord Supreme,
My Absolute Supreme,
From now on let me not stick
To my mind's opinions.
Let me not adhere
To my heart's decisions.
Let me only faithfully follow
Your blessingful Guidance.

57. August 11

My Lord Supreme,
My Beloved Supreme,
My body's strength
Comes from my mind's happiness.
My mind's happiness
Comes from my heart's gratitude.
My heart's gratitude
Comes from my life's surrender.

PART VIII

MY CHILD, YOU AND I
ARE IN THE SAME BOAT

MY CHILD, YOU AND I ARE IN THE SAME BOAT

1

My Lord,
I am utterly lost.

My child,
You and I are in the same boat.

2

It took my Lord Compassionate Supreme
A whole day to teach me how to laugh,
A full month to teach me how to giggle,
And an unending 365 days to teach me how to chuckle.

Then God said to me,
"My child, you may be a very slow learner,
But now you have become a perfect professor."

3

My Lord,
Is there any way
I can make You laugh?

Just ask Me to trust you.

4

My Lord,
How is it possible for You
To remain always happy?

My child,
Unlike you, I talk to Myself,
And I listen to Myself.

5

My Lord,
Are You aware
Of the bad things
That I do?

My child,
No, I am not aware,
And I don't want to be.

My Lord, why?

Just because
You don't care to know
How many good things I do.

MY CHILD, YOU AND I ARE IN THE SAME BOAT

6

My Lord,
Do tell me
When You are really
Pleased with me.

My child,
I am really pleased with you
Only when you hate Me.

My Lord,
How?
How can it be true?

How, my child?
That is the only time
That you think of Me.

7

My Lord,
How can I become perfect?

My child,
You can become perfect
Just by teaching Me
For 99 years and 365 days
All that you have learnt.
From your ignorance-teacher.

8

My Lord,
Have You ever
Told me a lie?

Many, many times.

Why, my Lord, why?

Just to be even with you,
My child.
As you know,
I never accept defeat
From anybody.

9

My Lord,
Will You help me
To be as great as You are?

No.
I can't allow you
To be as great as I am.

Why?
My ego-head will be crippled.

MY CHILD, YOU AND I ARE IN THE SAME BOAT

10

My Lord,
Will You allow me
To be as good as You are?

Certainly.
Do you know why,
My child?

Why, my Lord?

Because,
If you become as good as I am,
Then I will be able
To enjoy My retirement,
Which I so desperately need.

11

My Lord,
Do you enjoy it
When I quarrel with You
Unnecessarily and foolishly?

My child,
Let Me add —
And unpardonably as well.
Am I correct,
My son?

My Lord,
Perhaps You are.
My Lord, tell me,
Why do You allow me
To indulge
In quarrelling with You?

My child,
If I do not allow you
To empty
Your overflowing poison-ocean into Me,
Then who will and who can?

12

My Lord,
People say that I am
Extremely beautiful.
Do You agree with them?

No, never!

My Lord,
Why are You so cruel to me?

Because you do not
Give any credit
To the Source.

Who is the Source
And what has the Source
Done for me?
I am the Source
And I tell you once and for all,
The beauty that you have
Is a loan from Me.
At any moment
I can compel you
To return it.
My child,
I can never understand
How a beggar-borrower
Can ever be happy and proud.

13

My Lord,
I wonder how You answer
All my questions
So easily and perfectly.

My child,
Don't forget that I am
A little bit older than you.

My Lord,
That means when I equal
You in age,
I shall be able
To answer all Your questions.

No.
I shall always remain
Older than you.

14

My Lord,
What shall I do
With my mind?
Do give me some advice.

I do not want you
To live without a mind.
Again, with a mind either.

MY CHILD, YOU AND I ARE IN THE SAME BOAT

15

My Lord,
I am always afraid of You.
Are You ever afraid of me?

Of course, of course.
I am always afraid
Of your tearful eyes.

16

My Lord,
What are You doing now?

I am arguing with Myself.

My Lord,
What are You arguing about?

My child,
I want to know for sure
Whether I am a failure
Or you are a failure.
Also, I want to know
If both of us are failures.

My Lord,
You may be a failure,
But I am not, never.

17

My Lord,
They tell me that
When everything else fails,
Try prayers.
My Lord,
Is it true?

No, it is not.
When everything else fails,
Start blaming Me.

My Lord, why?

Why?
Because My world-happiness-machine
Is always out of order.

18

My Lord,
If I give You
My mind's precious hallucinations,
What will You
Give me in return?

My child,
I shall immediately give you
My Heart's spacious Reality.

19

My Lord,
Do You want to know from me
Why I am so fond
Of my ego?
I am so fond of my ego
Because my ego is the only thing
That I can always depend on.
It always claims me.
Vice versa.

20

My Lord,
Now that my mind
Is in abysmal abyss,
What shall I do?

Tell your mind
That there is only one direction left —
Up.

21

My Lord,
Please tell me if I am alive.

My child,
Resurrect Me first.

22

My Lord,
Even when I do not
Have the right questions,
How do You
Have the right answers?

My child,
At least one of us
Has to be right.

23

My Lord,
When I do not allow You
To be inside my heart,
Where do You go?

My child,
No particular place.
I become a homeless vagabond,
Plus a sonless Father.

24

My Lord,
I forget so many things so often.
Do You ever forget anything?

My child,
You are very rich,
Especially in your mental world.
I am not as rich as you are.
Therefore, you can afford to forget.
Poor as I am,
I cannot afford to forget.

25

My Lord,
I am so grateful to You,
For You have given me so much.

My child,
I want to remain satisfied
With your gratitude-heart.
Don't ask Me for anything more.
Who knows?
This time I may disappoint you.

26

My Lord,
How can I shut up my mouth?

My child,
Just open up your heart.
Your mouth will automatically
Be sealed.

27

My Lord,
I have discovered happiness
By deceiving myself.
How have You discovered
Your happiness?

My child,
I have not yet discovered happiness.
Perhaps you can teach Me.
Who knows, your way may be
The only way for Me to be happy.

PART IX

MY TWENTY-SEVEN
HUNGRY PRAYER-TEARS

MY TWENTY-SEVEN HUNGRY PRAYER-TEARS

1

God, I need
   Your Eye.
It is so beautiful.

2

Lord, I need
   Your Heart.
It is so blissful.

3

My Lord, I need
   Your Feet.
They are so powerful.

4

My dear God, I need
   Your Hands.
They are so bountiful.

5

My sweet Lord, I need
   Your Life.
It is so peaceful.

6

My Sovereign Lord, I need
   Your Breath.
It is so merciful.

7

Supreme, I am praying
For a willingness-heart.
   I am praying.

8

My dear Supreme, I am praying
For a readiness-mind.
   I am praying.

9

My sweet Supreme, I am praying
For a fulness-life.
   I am praying.

10

   My Lord Supreme,
Do bless my mind to unlearn.
   Do bless.

11

    My Beloved Supreme,
Do bless my heart to learn.
       Do bless.

12

    My only Beloved Supreme,
Do bless my breath
     To be Your permanent heart-student.
        Do bless.

13

    My only, only Beloved Supreme,
Do make me Your sleeplessly unconditional
   Seeker-lover-server.
      Do make me.

14

God, save my mind
From self-doubt, self-criticism
   And self-torture.

15

Lord, save my heart
From insecurity, impurity
   And disloyalty-attacks.

16

My Lord, save me
From superiority, inferiority
   And partiality-absurdities.

17

My dear God, I do not want
   To judge any human being.
Please fulfil
   My heart's desire-cry.

18

My sweet Lord, I do not want
   To interrogate any human being.
Please, please fulfil
   My heart's desire-cry.

19

My Sovereign Lord, I do not want
   To defeat any human being
      In anything.
Please, please, please fulfil
   My heart's desire-cry.

MY TWENTY-SEVEN HUNGRY PRAYER-TEARS

20

Supreme,
Do make my mind see
How good You are.

21

My dear Supreme,
Do make my heart feel
How unconditional You are.

22

My sweet Supreme,
Do make me realise
How absolutely perfect You are.

23

My Lord Supreme,
May the purity of my dynamic vital
   Satisfy You.

24

My Beloved Supreme,
May the duty of my serving body
   Satisfy You.

25

My only Beloved Supreme,
May I stop drinking greatness-poison
 For good.
May I drink only
 Goodness-nectar.

26

My God the Lord,
May I grow into a prayerful heart
To quench Your Vision-Eye-Thirst.

27

My Lord the God,
May I grow into a peaceful life
To feed Your Oneness-Heart-Hunger.

PART X

MY LORD SUPREME, I AM FALLING ASLEEP

MY LORD SUPREME, I AM FALLING ASLEEP

1

My Lord Supreme,
What is the difference between
Greatness and goodness?

"My child, Greatness means
　'I am.'
Goodness means
　'Thou art'."

2

My Lord Supreme,
What do I need?
Excellence or transcendence?

"My child,
You need both.
The human in you needs excellence,
The divine in you needs transcendence."

3

My Lord Supreme,
How can my mind, my heart
And my life be truly happy?

"My child,
Your mind can be truly happy
Only by renouncing
   Its possession-greed,
Your heart, by multiplying
   Its God-hunger
And your life, by enjoying
   Its God-surrender-feast."

4

My Lord Supreme,
In Your kind opinion,
Who am I today
And what shall I be tomorrow?

"My child,
In My opinion,
You are today
   Your fantasy-dream
And tomorrow you will be
   Your ecstasy-reality."

5

My Lord Supreme,
I beg of You,
Do tell me
   What is within me
And what is without me.

"My child,
Within you are
Your heart's soft whispers,
And without you are
Your mind's loud murmurs."

6

My Lord Supreme,
May I know what You are going to do
With my desire-mind
And my aspiration-heart?

"My child,
With your desire-mind,
I have decided to dig
   My own grave
And with your
   Aspiration-heart
I have decided to create
   A new paradise."

7

My Lord Supreme,
What are You going to do
　With my desire-face
And with my aspiration-eyes?

"My child,
I have decided to reluctantly touch
Your desire-face
And I have decided to affectionately
Treasure your aspiration-eyes."

8

My Lord Supreme,
What are You going to do
With my desire-mind and
My satisfaction-heart?

"My child,
I have decided to carry
　Your desire-mind
And sink both of us
　Together
In ignorance-sea.
I have decided to carry
　Your satisfaction-heart
Inside My Golden Boat
　And sail together
To the Shores
Of the ever-transcending Beyond."

9

My Lord Supreme,
What do You do
When I demand something from You
And expect something from You
And really need something from You?

"My child,
When you demand, I immediately fall asleep
   And start snoring.

"When you expect, I quickly wake up
   And start singing.

"When you need, I sprint towards you
Like your Sudhahota Carl Lewis,
The world's fastest sprinter,
   And smilingly reach you
And affectionately give you
   What you need."

10

My Lord Supreme,
What are You going to do
With my complicated mind?

"My child, I shall very carefully
Take your complicated mind
To My new school
That will teach your mind how to unlearn."

11

My Lord Supreme,
What are You going to do
With my simplicity-heart?

"My child, I shall very proudly
Take your simplicity-heart
   To My fullness-school
That will teach your heart
How to acquire wisdom-light
More, infinitely more."

12

My Lord Supreme,
When I isolate my mind from others,
Does it affect You?

"My child,
   It does.
It definitely does.
Something within Me
Compels Me to cry most pitifully."

13

My Lord Supreme,
When I isolate my heart from others,
Does it affect You?

"My child,
   It does.
It definitely does.
Something within Me
Compels Me to die immediately."

14

My Lord Supreme,
Do I have anything to make you happy?

"My child, you do.
Your heart's faith-founded existence-life
Makes Me happy, boundlessly happy,
Far beyond your imagination."

15

My Lord Supreme,
I feel so sorry for You.
I really do.

"My child,
Why do you feel sorry for Me?"

I am so clever that I can easily convince You
That I love You, but You find it so difficult
To convince me that You love me,
Therefore, I feel sorry for You.

"My child,
I am so grateful to you that you have such
Genuine sympathy for Me.
Where can I find
Another sympathetic heart like yours?"

16

My Lord Supreme,
When I devotedly pray and soulfully meditate,
I can clearly see that my life
Is an open book to You.

But alas, no matter how hard I try to know about
Your earthly life and Heavenly life, I sadly fail.
Therefore I am begging You
To be kind to me
And share some of Your secrets.

MY LORD SUPREME, I AM FALLING ASLEEP

"My child,
I shall comply with your request
But I do not know whether My secrets
Will make you happy or unhappy.
Anyway, I leave it up to you.

"My secret number one:
Each time your desiring mind
Defeats your aspiring heart,
I cry and cry.

"My secret number two:
When you dine with your mind-doubts
And starve your heart-faith,
I cry and cry.

"My secret number three:
Each time you do not allow your heart
To fulfil its Heaven-climbing promises,
I cry and cry.

"My secret number four:
Each time you do not allow your soul to fulfil
Its Heaven-manifesting promises on earth,
I cry and cry.

"My secret number five:
When your life-boat plies
Between your depression-vital-shore
And your frustration-mind-shore,
I cry and cry.

"My secret number six:
When you become the most intimate friend
Of your body's idleness and your mind's unwillingness,
I cry and cry."

My Lord Supreme,
I don't know why I suddenly feel so tired and sleepy.
It seems that You have literally endless secrets.
"Yes, my child. I do."

Then, my Lord,
Some other day
I shall definitely hear more of Your secrets.

"My child, My child, wait, wait.
Only one more secret I wish to share with you
Before you fall asleep.

"This time, I am blessing you with My topmost secret:
You are My Today's Self-Transcendence-Dream
And My Tomorrow's Self-Perfection-Satisfaction-Reality.

My Lord Supreme,
I am fast asleep.
I cannot hear You any more.

"My child, I am still fully awake.
I shall do everything for you.
You enjoy your sweet sleep."

PART XI

VOLCANO-AGONIES OF THE SEEKERS

VOLCANO-AGONIES OF THE SEEKERS

1

My Lord,
I have so many complaints against You!
Are You kind enough,
Are You brave enough
To listen to my complaints?

"My child,
I am neither kind nor brave,
But I am wise."

My Lord,
What do You mean?

"I shall tell you what I mean later on.
   In the meantime,
Let me hear all your complaints
   Against Me."

2

My Lord,
Why have You given me
A mind thick with darkness-nights?

3

My Lord Beloved,
Why do You allow
The unfortunate memories
   Of my past
To invade and torture me
   So ruthlessly?

4

My Lord Beloved Supreme,
Can You not see
That my days and nights
Are made of insufferable afflictions?

5

My Lord,
This world of Yours does not want me.
It does not even need me.
Yet not a single day passes by
When You do not ask me
   To love and serve this world.
My Lord, tell me,
Why do You do this to me?

6

My Lord Beloved,
Over the years I have been telling You
That this world is a bed of thorns.
But You go on telling me
That this world is a bed of roses.
I am the sufferer!
To me, You are nothing but a Lecturer!

7

My Lord Beloved Supreme,
Do You think that Your Ears
Are too precious to listen
To the prayers of my innocent heart?

8

My Lord,
What can I expect from You,
Since You literally do not want to feel
The agonies of my heart?

9

My Lord Beloved,
Why do I have to convince my mind
Unnecessarily and foolishly
That without You,
My life will be compelled
To flicker feebly?

10

My Lord Beloved Supreme,
Because I pray to You the whole night
   To please You,
Sleep is displeased with me
   And it is jealous of You.
Sleep has deserted me for good.
   You have also deserted me.
Alas, where do I stand?
   Alone, helpless, worthless and useless!

11

My Lord,
Alas, my mind has taught me
Only two mantras:
   "What shall I do?
   Where shall I go?"
I am sure You have taught
These two mantras
To my mind!

12

My Lord Beloved,
You have nothing better to do
Than subject me to the pain
　　Of Your Absence.

13

My Lord Beloved Supreme,
Are You blind
That I have to give You sight to see
That I am standing in front of You
In streaming tears?

14

My Lord,
I sing Your Victory-Songs
　　At the top of my voice.
I can clearly see
　　That You have kept
Your Ears completely sealed.

15

My Lord Beloved,
There was a time
When I thought
You belonged to me
   And I belonged to You.
Now I am fully convinced
That You and I
Are two perfect strangers,
And we belong to two totally
   Different worlds.

16

My Lord Beloved Supreme,
Every day early in the morning
You send someone to lecture me.
How is it that that person
Does not tell You
That my aspiring limbs
   Are all shattered
And that I do not have even an iota
   Of love for You?

17

My Lord,
Can You not see
That my life is doomed
To watching and waiting?

18

My Lord Beloved,
It seems that Your inner plane
    And outer car
Will never start functioning.

19

My Lord Beloved Supreme,
Sometimes I burst into roaring laughter
    When I call You
"My Lord of unconditional Compassion."

20

My Lord,
You have made me mad
With the desire to see You.
I am doing my duty extremely well.
But do You believe in fulfilling Your Duty?
How is it that, even for a fleeting second,
You do not come and stand before me?
How long will You enjoy
    Your Compassion-famine-Life?

21

My Lord Beloved,
I have seen the world.
I have also seen its ways —
Deception from the beginning
　To the end.

22

My Lord Beloved Supreme,
Why do You have to hide
　Your illumination
From this world?

23

My Lord,
I cry for Your Compassion.
You enjoy watching
Your Compassion snoring.

24

My Lord Beloved,
I cry for Your Protection.
You prove to me
　That Your Heart-Dictionary
Does not house the word
　"Protection".

25

My Lord Beloved Supreme,
I cry to You
　To save my reputation.
You, as usual,
Turn Your deaf Ear
　To me.

26

My Lord Beloved,
My prayers and meditations
Are so disappointed in You
That they tell me
They are at a perfect loss.

27

My Lord,
Every day I send my pure heart
In search of You.
　With such eagerness
My heart runs here and there
To catch a glimpse of You
And prostrate before You
With such humble petition.
　Alas,
Every day it comes back to me
With utterly fruitless failure-pangs.

28

My Lord Beloved Supreme,
I wanted to be the slave
   Of Your Heart.
Perhaps it was presumptuous
   On my part.
I changed my mind.

I wanted to be the slave
   Of Your Eye.
Perhaps that too was presumptuous
   On my part.

I wanted to be the slave
   Of Your Feet.
Alas, Your lack of response
Clearly showed me
That it was nothing but audacity
   On my part.

Now I want to be the slave
   Of the dust of Your Feet.
Even the dust of Your Feet
Does not care for the pangs
   Of my heart!

My life is dancing inside
My humiliation-pride-room.

29

My Lord,
If it is too difficult to save my life
    In my own way,
At least save me and my life
    In Your own Way,
Instead of not saving me at all!

30

My Lord Beloved,
Just because I call You my own,
    Nobody wants me to be their own.
No! Not even my mind is willing
    To accept me as its own.
They have all forsaken me.

31

My Lord Beloved Supreme,
The fire of my ceaseless longing for You
Has done only one thing:
Instead of illumining my heart,
It has burned my heart to ashes!
    Alas,
Who can ever be a greater fool
    Than I am?

32

My Lord,
My mind is permanently in a rage
That I spend all my time
   Foolishly on You.
I could have spent my time,
According to my mind,
   More wisely and fruitfully.

33

My Lord Beloved,
I thought You gave me the path
Of sweet, illumining
   And fulfilling devotion.
But now I see
That the path You have given me
Is the path of birthless
   And deathless frustration.

34

"My child,
Are you not tired
Of your marathon-complaints?"

My Lord, why?
Why should I be?
If You can enjoy
Your infinite Peace and Bliss
All by Yourself
While torturing me,
   My heart,
     And even my breath,
Why should I remain silent?

But, my Lord, if You are tired,
Then I can show You
My unsolicited compassion.
And to-morrow,
At our mutual leisure time,
I can drive my complaint-train
   And give You
A longer than the longest ride!

PART XII

MY LORD, HOW CAN YOU BE SO HEARTLESSLY CRUEL TO ME?

MY LORD, HOW CAN YOU BE SO HEARTLESSLY CRUEL TO ME?

1

My Lord,
How can you be
So heartlessly cruel to me?

Why have You
So maliciously departed
From the orbit of my sight?

2

My Lord,
How can you be
So heartlessly cruel to me?

Why are You so afraid
Of accepting me
As Your own, very own?

3

My Lord,
How can you be
So heartlessly cruel to me?

Can You not see
That thickest clouds
Have completely covered
My heart-sky?
Why is Your Compassion sleeping,
Why?

4

My Lord,
How can you be
So heartlessly cruel to me?

Frustration-thunders
Are roaring.
My poor mind is totally unsuccessful
In finding its own grave.
Can You not come to rescue
My hopelessly helpless mind?

5

My Lord,
How can you be
So heartlessly cruel to me?

I have been begging You
For such a long time
To come to me
So that I can enthrone You
In my brow-waves.

MY LORD, HOW CAN YOU BE SO HEARTLESSLY CRUEL TO ME?

6

My Lord,
How can you be
So heartlessly cruel to me?

Why are You not giving me
The capacity to feel
That You are
The Be-All and End-All
Of my earth-Heaven-heart-homes?

7

My Lord,
How can you be
So heartlessly cruel to me?

Your total indifference
To my desire-life
Has devastatingly pierced me through.

8

My Lord,
How can you be
So heartlessly cruel to me?

Why are You not opening Your Eye
Even for a fleeting moment
To see the fire of longing
Sleeplessly burning
Inside my heart?

9

My Lord,
How can you be
So heartlessly cruel to me?

How long do You want me to weep
Copious tears
For Your deliberately delayed
Arrival?

10

My Lord,
How can you be
So heartlessly cruel to me?

Save me!
Save me in any way
You want to!

11

My Lord,
How can you be
So heartlessly cruel to me?

Can You not see that at long last
My mind has stopped doubting
Your Existence?
Can it not expect from You
A sky-burst Smile?
My Lord,
Your Silence is torturing me
Far beyond Your Imagination.

12

My Lord,
How can you be
So heartlessly cruel to me?

I have none to call my own.
Alas, I never thought
That my sad experience
Would be forced to include You!

13

My Lord,
How can you be
So heartlessly cruel to me?

Why are You unnecessarily delaying
In releasing me even from one
World-temptation-snare?

14

My Lord,
How can you be
So heartlessly cruel to me?

Your partiality is killing me entirely.
You have saved and lifted up
Many creatures
That were undoubtedly lower than me.
Alas, in my case,
You have given Yourself
A terribly shocking new name:
Indifference.

MY LORD, HOW CAN YOU BE SO HEARTLESSLY CRUEL TO ME?

15

My Lord,
How can you be
So heartlessly cruel to me?

Alas, how can You be one of those
Who are telling me
That all my divine qualities
Have left me for good?

16

My Lord,
How can you be
So heartlessly cruel to me?

I am crying
Because You have deliberately kept
Your listening Ears
Out of order.

17

My Lord,
How can you be
So heartlessly cruel to me?

If You really care for me,
Will You not take the trouble
Of humbling and humiliating
My impossible pride
For my life's
Perfect perfection?

18

My Lord,
How can you be
So heartlessly cruel to me?

For You I have swept my path
Readily, willingly and eagerly.
How can it be possible
For Your Compassion-flooded Eye
Not to see
What I have done for You?

MY LORD, HOW CAN YOU BE SO HEARTLESSLY CRUEL TO ME?

19

My Lord,
How can you be
So heartlessly cruel to me?

When will You give me the capacity
To claim You as my own, very own
Here, there and everywhere?

20

My Lord,
How can you be
So heartlessly cruel to me?

How is it
That it is not possible for You
To think of me at this very moment
When I am dying for You?

21

My Lord,
How can you be
So heartlessly cruel to me?

Why are You not allowing me
To be a sleepless slave
Of Your Feet?

22

My Lord,
How can you be
So heartlessly cruel to me?

When are You going to come
To extinguish the fire
Of my separation
From Your Heart?

23

My Lord,
How can you be
So heartlessly cruel to me?

Can You not feel even once
The excruciating pangs
Of Your absence
That are eating
My heart?

24

My Lord,
How can you be
So heartlessly cruel to me?

Streams of tears are falling
From my devotion-eyes
To please You in Your own Way.
But Your unwillingness to accept them
Is unearthing the roots
Of my life-tree.

25

My Lord,
How can you be
So heartlessly cruel to me?

Can You not see
The snake of our separation
Has bitten me powerfully
And shockingly,
And my life-breath is sinking
Without having a sweet glimpse
Of Your Compassion-Eye
And Your Satisfaction-Heart?

26

My Lord,
How can you be
So heartlessly cruel to me?

When will You give me
A sleepless and unquenchable thirst
For You?

27

My Lord,
How can you be
So heartlessly cruel to me?

You fool me by saying
That I am all Yours
And You are all mine.
I think and I feel
That this is the worst possible lie
That I have ever heard
From anybody!

28

My Lord,
How can you be
So heartlessly cruel to me?

Why do You allow me
To dream of anything else?
Do You not know
That I want to dream
Only of You?

29

My Lord,
How can you be
So heartlessly cruel to me?

When will Your Heart tell You
That I am always dying
To see You
And to be in Your Presence?

30

My Lord,
How can you be
So heartlessly cruel to me?

I do not want to continue
With this human life.
Give me back my animal life.
I want to be Your faithful dog
To follow You
Everywhere You go.

31

My Lord,
How can you be
So heartlessly cruel to me?

How many times have I told You
That my life is no life without You?
Yet I clearly see
That You do not care for me at all,
Either in my inner life
Or in my outer life.
Why, why?

32

My Lord,
How can you be
So heartlessly cruel to me?

How many more times
Do I have to tell You
To capture my heart
So that my heart
Becomes all sweetness
And all fondness for You?

33

My Lord,
How can you be
So heartlessly cruel to me?

If You really love me,
Will You not transform
Everything in my life
To fulfil You?

34

My Lord,
How can you be
So heartlessly cruel to me?

Why do You not come
And eat with me at my table
When I beg You again and again?
Am I an untouchable creature?
I thought You were my Creator.
It seems that I have to change
My opinion.

35

My Lord,
How can you be
So heartlessly cruel to me?

How I wish You to miss me breathlessly
Only once
The way I miss You.
Then You will realise
What my heart and I go through
In Your absence.

36

My Lord,
How can you be
So heartlessly cruel to me?

I ask You to increase my aspiration
And decrease my desire.
I cannot understand why
My desire has to increase
And
My aspiration has to decrease!
How can You not feel the sincerity
Of my intensity-prayer?

37

My Lord,
How can you be
So heartlessly cruel to me?

I pray to You for Your Closeness.
You give me success after success
So that my success-life can prevent me
From being close to You.
I assure You that one day
You will have to surrender
To my eagerness
To be in Your extreme Closeness.

38

My Lord,
How can you be
So heartlessly cruel to me?

Are You really afraid
Of my growing attachment
To You?
Do tell me frankly.

39

My Lord,
How can you be
So heartlessly cruel to me?

Please be kind to me once and for all
And tell me when I can be
A glowing detachment
From my desire-bound earth-life.

40

My Lord,
How can you be
So heartlessly cruel to me?

I try to give You my fear.
You do not accept it.
I try to give You my love.
You do not accept it.
Then tell me what I can give You
To make You happy in Your own Way.

41

My Lord,
How can you be
So heartlessly cruel to me?

For centuries I have looked for You.
Now may I not be allowed
At least for a few years
To look after You?

42

My Lord,
How can you be
So heartlessly cruel to me?

How can I believe
That I was made only of Your Joy
When I do not see You happy
At any time?

43

My Lord,
How can you be
So heartlessly cruel to me?

Have You forgotten
That You made a solemn promise
That when I fail,
You would immediately sail
To my rescue?

44

My Lord,
How can you be
So heartlessly cruel to me?

When will I be able to breathe in
Your Compassion-Smile?
And when will I be able to breathe out
My surrender-joy?

45

My Lord,
How can you be
So heartlessly cruel to me?

Why have You given me
Such feeble devotion
That can never reach
Your Feet?

46

My Lord,
How can you be
So heartlessly cruel to me?

You have never asked me
To sing for You
A rainbow-song
Of my self-giving.

47

My Lord,
How can you be
So heartlessly cruel to me?

Can You not allow my soul-flames
To illumine my entire being
Even one single time?

48

My Lord,
How can you be
So heartlessly cruel to me?

How can it be possible
That right in front of You
My aspiration-heart has not become
An ever-rising life-tree-climber?

49

My Lord,
How can you be
So heartlessly cruel to me?

Can You not give me
A special kind of morning meditation
To multiply my heart's
Aspiration-flames rapidly?

50

My Lord,
How can you be
So heartlessly cruel to me?

Can You not see
My heart's streaming tears
Running again and again
To my life's progress-start?
Can You not be of any help to me?

51

My Lord,
How can you be
So heartlessly cruel to me?

When are You going
To pass by this way?

52

My Lord,
How can you be
So heartlessly cruel to me?

Do You not think
That Your Promises are all hollow?
You have promised to me
So many times
That You will steal into my heart
And rob me of everything
That I have and I am.

53

My Lord,
How can you be
So heartlessly cruel to me?

How long are You going to remain
Unmoved and unperturbed
By my orphan-tears?

54

My Lord,
How can you be
So heartlessly cruel to me?

Will there be a day in my life,
Early in the morning
During my prayers and meditations,
When we shall consume each other
With our mutual love and affection?

55

My Lord,
How can you be
So heartlessly cruel to me?

Was Your Promise not sincere
When You told me
That You would come back
And take me with You
To visit Your transcendental Heights?

56

My Lord,
How can you be
So heartlessly cruel to me?

Is it such a difficult task
For You to break my ego
Before it breaks me?

MY LORD, HOW CAN YOU BE SO HEARTLESSLY CRUEL TO ME?

57

My Lord,
How can you be
So heartlessly cruel to me?

Can You not see
That my outer life
Is totally shattered
And my inner life
Is completely devoid of hope?

58

My Lord,
How can you be
So heartlessly cruel to me?

Please tell me
Why You have stopped answering
My heart-letters,
Why?

59

My Lord,
How can you be
So heartlessly cruel to me?

My Lord, do You not know
That when You do not smile at me,
I immediately lose
The compass and the anchor
Of my life-boat?

60

My Lord,
How can you be
So heartlessly cruel to me?

I want to realise You
As soon as possible,
But if You continuously
Break my heart,
Then I assure You
Your Heart will be next!

61

My Lord,
How can you be
So heartlessly cruel to me?

I strongly feel
That Your very Touch
Can easily transform
My mind-woods
Into
My heart-blossoms.

62

My Lord,
How can you be
So heartlessly cruel to me?

Why do You not tell me
The secret way to Your Heart,
Why?

63

My Lord,
How can you be
So heartlessly cruel to me?

Do I have to tell You
Again and again
That You heal my heart
With Your fleeting Smile?

64

My Lord,
How can you be
So heartlessly cruel to me?

Do You not realise
That in Your absence
I drown in my heart's
Loneliness-tears?

65

My Lord,
How can you be
So heartlessly cruel to me?

Do You not realise
That each act
Of Your loving Concern
Deepens my heart's love
For You?

66

My Lord,
How can you be
So heartlessly cruel to me?

My heart is simply devastated.
For me, my oneness with You
Means here and now,
At this very moment,
And not in the remote future.

67

My Lord,
How can you be
So heartlessly cruel to me?

Unspeakable selfishness
Is killing my entire being,
Yet You are completely silent.

68

My Lord,
How can you be
So heartlessly cruel to me?

My Lord, is it not high time
For You to destroy
My unwillingness-tyrant-mind?

69

My Lord,
How can you be
So heartlessly cruel to me?

I have only one prayer,
And that prayer
Is for You to make me worthy
Of Your scoldings.
But even that one prayer
You never sanction!

70

My Lord,
How can you be
So heartlessly cruel to me?

Why do You not give me any chance
To smile at You,
To make my heart
Infinitely sweeter
And my life
Infinitely richer?

PART XIII

MY LORD, MAKE ME YOUR
HAPPINESS-CHILD

MY LORD, MAKE ME YOUR HAPPINESS-CHILD

1

My Lord Supreme,
   Yesterday I was
Your Compassion-birth.
   Today I am
Your Perfection-flower.
   Tomorrow I shall be
Your Satisfaction-flute.

2

My Beloved Supreme,
   What is the thing
That I need most from You
At every hour
   Of the night and day?

"My child,
My blessingful Hand's
Blessingful Touch."

3

My sweet Lord,
I wish to make
   A most sincere confession.
I have heard the words
Eternity and Immortality
   Countless times.
To my extreme sorrow,
I do not know
   What they precisely mean.

"My child,
Eternity is
   My Heart's universal Hope.
Immortality is
   My Eye's transcendental Promise."

MY LORD, MAKE ME YOUR HAPPINESS-CHILD

4

My dear Lord,
We are Your children.
How is it
That You have not made us
   As happy as You are?

"My child,
Your way of happiness
   And My Way of happiness
Are two totally different things."

My dear Lord,
When I say happiness,
   What I mean is
My supremacy-declaration.

"My child,
When I say happiness,
   What I mean is
My Oneness-Satisfaction.

"You cannot and do not claim Me
As your own, very own.
   Therefore you are unhappy.
But I can and do claim you
As My own, very own.
   Therefore I am happy."

5

My Lord Supreme,
Every day my life-boat
   Plies between
Your two Compassion-Shores:
   Time and speed.
I pray to You to grant me
   The lightning-speed
While I am plying my boat
   To the speed-destination.
And while I am plying my boat
   To the time-destination,
Do bless me with
   Eternity's patience.

6

My Beloved Supreme,
   Out of 100,
What do You give me
   When I give You
My mind's love, my heart's devotion
   And my life's surrender?

"My child, I give you 9¼
When you give Me your mind's love.

"I give you 79½
When you give Me your heart's devotion.

"I give you 99¾
When you give Me your life's surrender."

My Beloved Supreme,
When can You give me
   100 out of 100?

"My child,
Not until you are empty
   Of your curiosity-stupidity."

7

My sweet Lord,
Can I ever be forgiven?

"My child,
Not until I am absolutely sure
That you will not
   Deliberately repeat
The same blunder."

8

My sweet Lord,
Please be sincere.
Do You really care for me?

"My child,
I care for you
Only when you want Me
   To guide you
And not when you want
   To lead Me."

9

My Beloved Supreme,
Which church can and will
    Save me?

"My child,
Not the man-built church,
But your own heart's inner
    Devotion-built church."

10

My dear Lord,
I am a staunch Catholic.
Therefore, am I wrong if I say
That I alone am entitled to Heaven?

"My child,
I am afraid if I tell you
    That you alone
Are entitled to Heaven,
Then your Protestant cousins
    Will sue Me."

My dear Lord,
Then who is entitled to Heaven?

"My child,
The human being whose heart-cry
    Can fly up to Heaven,
And whose soul-smile
    Can fly down to earth."

11

My Supreme Lord,
If I die,
Will I be able to go
   To Heaven?

"My child,
If you live
In your mind-confusion,
   No.

"But if you live
In your heart-devotion,
   Then definitely yes."

12

My Beloved Supreme,
Is there any right time for me
To do the right thing?

"My child,
Not tomorrow,
   Not even today!

"The right time for you
To do the right thing
   Is now,
At this very moment,
   Plus
Here and nowhere else."

MY LORD, MAKE ME YOUR HAPPINESS-CHILD

13

My Lord Supreme,
Are You displeased with me
   Because I have not
Cheerfully surrendered myself
   To Your Will?

"My child,
I am not displeased with you,
But the real reality in you
   Is your soul.

"Each day when it sees
That you are not making
   Your cheerful surrender
To My Omniscience,
   Omnipresence
   And Omnipotence,
Your soul carries unnecessarily
An elephant-weight,
   A volcano-frustration
   And a tornado-destruction.

"My child,
Each second
Either you surrender to My Will
Or I surrender to your stupidity.

"I can go on surrendering to you,
But if you do not surrender
To My Infinity's Compassion-Heart,
   Then each day
Is a failure-cry of your soul,
And I shed endless tears
   With your poor soul."

14

My Lord Supreme,
Why are You so unkind to me?
You have given me no capacity.
   Whereas,
You have given my soul the capacity,
   Out of Your infinite Bounty,
To be in a self-absorbing trance,
To enjoy Your Immortality's
   Infinite Compassion.

"My child,
In comparison to your soul,
You are too young.
When you become as mature
   As your soul,
I shall give you
The same kind of capacity
To do My Work on earth."

15

My dear Lord,
   I have forgotten.
Do tell me
If You have given me
   Anything to bring down
From Heaven to earth.
"My child,
I gave you My Vision-Eye
   To bring down
From Heaven to earth."

My dear Lord,
What will You be giving me
To carry from earth to Heaven?

"My child,
I shall give you
   My Manifestation-Feet
To carry from earth to Heaven."

16

My sweet Lord,
How many steps are there
   To reach God?

"My child,
There is only one step."

Only one step!
Please tell me
   The name of the step.

"It is called
Your life's union-surrender-step."

17

My dear Lord,
Please tell me
What is ahead of me.

"My child,
The beauty of My Compassion-Eye."

And what is behind me?

"The certainty of My Forgiveness-Heart."

18

My sweet Lord
Absolute Beloved Supreme,
Do give me the capacity
To worship You sleeplessly
While admiring
   Your universal Mind,
Adoring
   Your universal Life,
And loving
   Your universal Heart-Breath,
To fulfil You and please You
In Your absolutely new
And unprecedented creation.

19

My Lord Supreme,
What is the difference
Between faith and love?

"My child,
There is no difference
Between faith and love.

"Faith and love
Are two complementary souls.

"Faith is the heart of love
And love is the breath of faith."

20

My Lord Supreme,
I do not want greatness.
I do not want even goodness.
   I want only to be
A speck of humility-dust
   To remind me
Of my sleepless service-life.

PART XIV

SOMEBODY HAS TO LISTEN

SOMEBODY HAS TO LISTEN

1

Somebody has to listen.
Why not let me try
To be that fortunate one?

2

God the inner man
Gives me the capacity.
God the outer man
Gives me the responsibility.

3

O my faith-fountain-existence-light,
Only because of you
God is so close to me.

4

Be careful!
Your body's lethargy
And mind's frustrations
Are your
Most dangerous enemies.

5

God tells me that
It is infinitely easier
For Him to respond
To my aspiring heart
Than to answer
My questioning mind.

6

The beginning
May be a long road
But the satisfaction-end
Is always round.

7

Give your peace quickly
Before disquiet
Enters into you secretly.

8

I may not need God
To give good advice,
But I do need God
And God's Compassion
To set good examples.

9

There is no such thing
As
A little temptation.

10

God accepts
My heart's tears
To make
My mind peaceful.

11

How can you sincerely
Pray to God
If you do not value
Your own heart-life?

12

Aspiration may
Be kept secret
But dedication must not
Be kept secret.

13

I do not believe
In a secret dedication.
I believe only
In a sacred dedication.

14

I walk with God
To take me
Where I am supposed to go,
And not
Where He Himself has to go.

15

Alas, my Lord
Has so many times told me
That He is really tired
Of my possession-greed.

16

My renunciation-smile
Is the strength
Of my soul's joy.

17

Anger says:
"I can destroy
The whole world."
Peace says:
"Not when I work
Inside you."

18

God does not expect
Anything sublime
From our
Falsehood-infested world.

19

My heart's gratitude
Is
My life's plenitude.

20

I may not always
Please God,
But I can and must
Always try.

21

O my mind,
I may not exactly know
What you have,
But I do know
What you truly are:
You are utterly stupid.

22

There is only one task:
To bask
In the Compassion-Sunshine
Of
My Lord Beloved Supreme.

23

Not only to make
My Lord Supreme happy,
But also to make myself
Infinitely happier,
I must forgive
My so-called enemies.

24

The heart loves
Because to love
Is to become
The heart of goodness.
The mind loves
Because to love
Is to own
The thunder-sound
Of greatness.

25

When the mind
Wants to divide,
It realises that
It is an impossible task.
When the heart
Wants to unite the world,
It feels that
God has already done it.

26

Progress is
The only unmistakable
And laudable evidence
Of the spiritual life.

27

The aspiring heart
Continued to struggle.
The doubting mind did not.
Naturally, the heart
Has won the victory
Which it so rightly
And richly deserves.

28

Alas,
The man who thinks
That he is faultless
Has kept poor God
Unemployed.

29

The right attitude
Is the winner and owner
Of divine plenitude.

30

Success
Makes my vital cheerful.
Progress
Makes my heart peaceful.

31

Walk with a saint.
You are bound to inherit
His peace-saintliness.

32

The good man
Loves self-enlightenment.
The great man
Loves self-enlargement.

33

Peace is not
The absence of power.
Peace is
The presence of love.

34

If the heart
Is your choice,
Then the proud mouth
Cannot be your voice.

35

A misunderstood man
Is
A bullet-killed man.

36

Comparison
Is
Progress-prison.

37

In my inner life,
What I need
Is the strength of peace.
In my outer life,
What I need
Is the flower of prayer.

38

An eagerness-breath
And a willingness-mind
Must always
Be found together
To bring about perfection.

39

The heart-illumination-temple
Has no
Mind-confusion-room.

40

Frustration
Has been the mind's
Very old occupation.

41

The mind
Must desire only
What the heart requires.

42

A new age
Without a new Saviour
Is so strange.

PART XV

O MY HEART, WHERE ARE YOU?

O MY HEART, WHERE ARE YOU?

1

O my aspiration-angel-heart,
Where are you?

2

O my gratitude-fragrance-heart,
Where are you?

3

O my surrender-song-heart,
Where are you?

4

O my God-Satisfaction-hunger-heart,
Where are you?

5

O my God-Fulfilment-dream-heart,
Where are you?

6

O my world-service-joy-heart,
Where are you?

7

O my earth-suffering-heart,
Where are you?

8

O my silence-meditation-heart,
Where are you?

9

O my mind-transformation-promise-heart,
Where are you?

10

O my God-Dream-invocation-heart,
Where are you?

11

O my hope-sea-heart,
Where are you?

12

O my purity-blossom-heart,
Where are you?

13

O my faith-garden-heart,
Where are you?

14

O my willingness-runner-heart,
Where are you?

15

O my enthusiasm-jumper-heart,
Where are you?

16

O my determination-diver-heart,
Where are you?

17

O my doubt-cloud-illumination-heart,
Where are you?

18

O my God-Peace-Family-member-heart,
Where are you?

19

O my consciousness-existence-bliss-partner-heart,
Where are you?

20

O my God-Invitation-acceptance-heart,
Where are you?

21

O my insecurity-conqueror-heart,
Where are you?

22

O my God-Dreams-collector-heart,
Where are you?

23

O my rainbow-beauty-magnet-heart,
Where are you?

24

O my Mother-Nature-worshipper-heart
Where are you?

O MY HEART, WHERE ARE YOU?

25

O my golden boat-journey-heart,
Where are you?

26

O my oneness-world-searching heart,
Where are you?

27

O my tomorrow's vision-inner-heart,
Where are you?

28

O my temple-sacredness-heart,
Where are you?

29

O my God-Glory-revelation-heart,
Where are you?

30

O my deeper than deep dream-world-heart,
Where are you?

31

O my soul-teacher's perfection-progress-student-heart,
Where are you?

32

O my soul's Immortality-singer-heart,
Where are you?

33

O my tomorrow's God-revelation-heart,
Where are you?

34

O my intuitive God-Plans-awareness-heart,
Where are you?

35

O my Heaven-bringer-promise-heart,
Where are you?

36

O my resistance and resentment-empty heart,
Where are you?

O MY HEART, WHERE ARE YOU?

37

O my God-throb-heart,
Where are you?

38

O my soul-trust-representative-heart,
Where are you?

39

O my blue-green hope-heart,
Where are you?

40

O my life's light-speed-heart,
Where are you?

41

O my life's devotion-breath-heart,
Where are you?

42

O my complaint-disdain-renouncer-heart,
Where are you?

43

O my jealousy-stranger-heart,
Where are you?

44

O my God-love-fountain-heart,
Where are you?

45

O my God-devotion-ecstasy-heart,
Where are you?

46

O my God-surrender-perfection-heart,
Where are you?

47

O my Golden Shore-arrival-heart,
Where are you?
Where are you?

44

O my God-love-fountain-heart,
Where are you?

45

O my God-devotion-ecstasy-heart,
Where are you?

46

O my God-surrender-perfection-heart,
Where are you?

47

O my Golden Shore-arrival-heart,
Where are you?

PART XVI

O MY ASPIRATION-HEART,
WHERE ARE YOU?

O MY ASPIRATION-HEART, WHERE ARE YOU?

I

1

O my aspiration-heart,
   Where are you?
Since you left me,
I have never seen
God smiling at me.

2

O my aspiration-heart,
   Where are you?
You are my God-faith-confidence-foundation.

3

O my aspiration-heart,
   Where are you?
It is you who have given me
   The indomitable courage
Not only to brave the unknown,
But also to satisfy the Unknowable.

4

O my aspiration-heart,
   Where are you?
You are the only one
To end my earth-sufferings
And awaken my Heaven-ecstasy
   Here on earth.

5

O my aspiration-heart,
   Where are you?
Can you not see that both
My dream-world
     And
My reality-world
Are pitifully and helplessly
   Crying for you?

6

O my aspiration-heart,
   Where are you?
Without your cheerful assistance,
My ignorance-sleep of millennia
   Will not come to an end.

O MY ASPIRATION-HEART, WHERE ARE YOU?

7

O my aspiration-heart,
    Where are you?
All I need from you
Is my soul's silence-sea-poise.

8

O my aspiration-heart,
    Where are you?
Without you,
No matter which direction I take,
    It leads me
To useless nothingness.

9

O my aspiration-heart,
    Where are you?
Please come back.
I promise you that I shall give up
Leading the mind-life
    For good.
Do trust me.

10

O my aspiration-heart,
    Where are you?
Do come back.
From now on I shall give you
My cheerful and sleepless willingness.
I shall obey you and please you
    In every way.

11

O my aspiration-heart,
    Where are you?
Each time I think of you,
    I hear a new
God-throbbing melody.

12

O my aspiration-heart,
    Where are you?
I am blinded and stabbed
    By the doubt-hooligan.
Come immediately to my rescue!

13

O my aspiration-heart,
   Where are you?
Let us try once more
Carefully, soulfully and self-givingly
To walk along the path
   Of God-discovery.

14

O my aspiration-heart,
   Where are you?
Do not forget
That you are the only golden bridge
Between my hope-life
And God's Promise-Eye.

15

O my aspiration-heart,
   Where are you?
There is no retirement
   For you and me.
We must daily sing together
Our self-transcendence-song
   At the Feet
Of our Lord Beloved Supreme.

16

O my aspiration-heart,
    Where are you?
Every day you present me
With a newly-blossomed dream.
I desperately need you
    And your dream.

17

O my aspiration-heart,
    Where are you?
Have you forgotten
God's own transcendental Motto:
    "Never give up"?
Therefore, never give up on me,
Never give up on yourself,
    And specially
Never give up on my stupid mind,
For it needs God-illumination
With your and my help.

18

O my aspiration-heart,
   Where are you?
God has telephoned me
   For news about you.
I simply do not know what to say.
Please come back immediately
   And answer the phone.
Every five minutes God is phoning here
With a very significant
And private message for you,
   Only for you.
I do not know what it is all about.
Therefore, do come back immediately
   And speak to God,
And I shall be so grateful
If you can share with me
Just a little of your conversation
   With God.

19

O my aspiration-heart,
   Where are you?
God is starving
For your aspiration-food-flames.

20

O my aspiration-heart,
   Where are you?
Without you I cannot build
My hope-fulfilment-empire.

21

O my aspiration-heart,
   Where are you?
Do come back
With your silence-peace-fountain.
This time I shall not allow
My restless mind
   To disturb you.

22

O my aspiration-heart,
   Where are you?
Only with you and in you
Am I able to go far beyond
   My own competence.

23

O my aspiration-heart,
    Where are you?
Every day, without fail,
    I need from you
The capacity to maintain
My God-faith-oneness-friendship.

24

O my aspiration-heart,
    Where are you?
I cannot love God without you,
I cannot obey God without you.
Without you I cannot do anything
Prayerfully, soulfully
    And unconditionally
To see God smiling at me.

25

O my aspiration-heart,
    Where are you?
I beg your pardon.
No more shall I allow
My questioning and confusing mind
    To enter into
Your God-treasured silence-life.

26

O my aspiration-heart,
    Where are you?
My gratitude-breath I am offering
    To you
Because it was you who showed me
    How to belong only to God.

27

O my aspiration-heart,
    Where are you?
I need you desperately,
    For you embody
My fastest God-invocation-speed.

28

O my aspiration-heart,
    Where are you?
At every moment when I think of you,
Your unparalleled rose-beauty
    I see.

29

O my aspiration-heart,
    Where are you?
My God-love-bird flies
Higher than the highest
    On strongest wings
Only when you are with me
    And for me.

30

O my aspiration-heart,
    Where are you?
Without you,
My faith in God
    And
My love of God
    Disappear
Before they appear.

31

O my aspiration-heart,
    Where are you?
Without you,
My life-boat is sinking fast,
    Very fast.
I see no pilot, no destination.
What I see is the destruction-dance
    Of my earth-existence.

32

O my aspiration-heart,
   Where are you?
I cannot take
Even one single step farther
   Towards God
Without your inspiration, enthusiasm,
   Eagerness and support.

33

O my aspiration-heart,
   Where are you?
Every day I am becoming
   Increasingly aware
Of your supreme importance
In my God-manifestation
   And God-satisfaction-life.

34

O my aspiration-heart,
　　Where are you?
I am giving you what I have:
　　Promise.
I am giving you what I am:
　　Gratitude.
I shall never, never
Disappoint you again.
　　Do come back.
Let us rock together once again
On the waves of Eternity's Bliss.

II — Incredible news

35

Incredible news:
    My mind,
Instead of getting older every year,
Will now become younger every year —
    Plus, it will become wiser.

36

Incredible news:
    Every day
My mind sits beside my heart,
And with utmost sincerity
It meditates with my heart.

37

Incredible news:
Before, my mind used to mock
    At my heart's
Credulous behaviour.
Now my mind wants to be
As close as my heart is
    To my soul.

38

Incredible news:
My mind has become
A very devoted student
   Of my soul.

39

Incredible news:
The mind that used to doubt
   The soul
Once upon a time
Now has all faith in the soul.

40

Incredible news:
My mind now admits
That God knows
   More than it knows —
And this is a most sincere admission
   On the part of my mind.

41

Incredible news:
My mind's most recent discovery —
It cannot live without God,
Even for a fleeting second.

42

Incredible news:
My mind has finally surrendered
　To my heart.

43

Incredible news:
My mind has started believing
　In emptiness.

44

Incredible news:
　From now on
My mind will quite often
Take a vow of complete silence.

45

Incredible news:
My mind's best friend,
　Doubt,
Has now become
My mind's worst foe.

46

Incredible news:
My mind has said to criticism,
"I have had enough of you!
I do not need you any more,
Even for a fleeting second!
What I badly need
Is oneness-satisfaction."

47

Incredible news:
My mind is devouring
Something completely new —
    Purity.

48

Incredible news:
My new mind is in full control
    Of my old vital.

49

Incredible news:
My mind has started going
To my heart-temple
   Every day devotedly
And faithfully listening
To the most illumining lectures
Of my eternally wise soul.

50

Incredible news:
My mind is getting tremendous joy
In unlearning its old lessons
   And
Unburdening its old problems.

51

Incredible news:
My mind is sincerely ashamed
Of its past complexity-life.

52

Incredible news:
My mind is commanding
Its giant intellect
To touch the feet
Of my intuition-child
And to stay at its feet forever.

53

Incredible news:
My mind does not want
To possess God
By hook or by crook
Any more.
My mind now needs God
Soulfully and unreservedly.

54

Incredible news:
My mind has totally demolished
The fearful fear-house.

55

Incredible news:
My mind is asking God,
"Father, am I now ready?"
God is telling my mind,
"You are, My child.
You are more than ready.
Look, you have safely
And unmistakably arrived
At your final Destination:
My blue-gold Satisfaction-Shore."

O MY HEART, WHERE ARE YOU?

Notes to *O my aspiration-heart, where are you?*

1-34. These thirty-four poems were written on 23 and 24 August 1993 in New York.
35-55. These twenty-one poems were written in July and August 1982 in Florida and New York.

PART XVII

MY SWEET FATHER-LORD, WHERE ARE YOU?

MY SWEET FATHER-LORD, WHERE ARE YOU?

1

My Lord Supreme,
May I see Your Beauty's Eye
    And
Feel Your Duty's Heart
   Everywhere —
Wherever I go.

2

My Lord Supreme,
I know, I know
That my present difficulties
Will soon be removed
By Your infinite Compassion-Light
    And
Your Illumination-Salvation.

3

My Lord Beloved Supreme,
May I keep my heart-door open,
   Wide open,
Every hour, every minute
   And every second
For You to enter
With Your Compassion infinite
And play all the time
   Inside my heart-garden.

4

My Lord Supreme,
May my curiosity about spirituality
   Come to an end.
May my heart's sleepless hunger for You
   Come to the fore
And make You feel that I am all ready
   For You, only for You.

5

My Lord Beloved Supreme,
In my previous incarnations
I pleased You
With my life's strict discipline-light.
In this incarnation
I would like to please You
With my heart's sleepless surrender-delight
To Your Vision transcendental
    And
Your manifestation universal.

6

My Lord Beloved Supreme,
My heart's mounting cries
    And
My life's spreading smiles
Are my sacred gifts
Which I am placing
At Your Compassion-Feet
So that at every moment
I can please You
And fulfil You
In Your own Way.

7

My Lord Supreme,
I have given You this time
    Bravely
What I have long cherished:
My mind of confusion-night.
In return, You have given me
What You eternally are:
Your Heart's Compassion-Illumination,
Compassion-Perfection
    And
Compassion-Satisfaction.

8

My Lord Supreme,
In my previous incarnations,
My hungry heart used to cry and cry
For Your Compassion-Nectar.
In this incarnation,
My life is smiling sleeplessly
At Your Compassion-Heart,
At Your Perfection-Feet
    And
At Your Oneness-fulfilled Heart-Home.

9

My Lord Supreme,
In my previous life You wanted me
To be materially successful
And earthly great.
Therefore, You placed me into
    A royal family.
But in this incarnation
You are telling me
That to be spiritually rich
Is the most important thing.
If I can be spiritually rich,
Only then will I be able to please You
    Most satisfactorily.
My Lord, may Thy Will be fulfilled
As soon as possible in and through me.

10

My Lord Supreme,
You have removed my mind's doubts,
My mind's confusion-darkness
    And
My mind's anxiety-clouds.
You have replaced them
With climbing aspiration-cries,
With glowing dedication-smiles
    And
With Your ever-fulfilling Love and Joy.

11

My Lord Supreme,
The time has come for me
To please You in Your own Way —
To make my surrender and oneness
    Complete
In my own secret and sacred heart-room
    And
To become a choice instrument of Yours.

12

My Lord Supreme,
My unconscious fear of You
Takes me away from You,
But my conscious faith in You
    And
My conscious love for You
Not only bring me back to You
But also make me feel
That Your Compassion-Light
Is closer than the closest.
Soon You will make me feel
That throughout Eternity
Your Compassion and my surrender
Will be inseparable friends
For Your complete Satisfaction
And my complete fulfilment.

13

My Lord Supreme,
You have given me
A mind that longs for Truth,
  Your Truth,
For You as the Truth Supreme.
My Lord Supreme,
You have given me
A heart that cries for Your Heart,
  Only Your Heart.
You have made me feel
That my tiny drop-heart
Will eventually become one,
Inseparably one,
With Your larger than the largest
Compassion-flooded Ocean of Delight.
My Lord Supreme,
With Your infinite Compassion
You are making me feel
This Truth sublime, illumining
And all-fulfilling.

14

My sweet Father-Lord,
    Where are You?
How is it that I cannot see You
    All the time,
Or at least when I want to see You?

"My sweet child,
Your soul and I play hide-and-seek.
We enjoy this game immensely.
Now is the time for you to seek Me
And for Me to hide.
But soon you will try to hide from Me
And I will seek you out.
Then we shall end
Our hide-and-seek game.
I shall transform your little,
Earthly life-plant
Into a Heavenly-blossomed life-tree."

15

My Lord Supreme,
You have given me a heart
   That cries for You.
You have given me a life
   That wants to serve You.
But, my Lord, is there any way
That I can run fast, faster, fastest
In my heart of aspiration
And in my life of dedication?

"Yes, My child, there is a way,
And this way is very, very simple
And very direct.
This way is the way
Of your gratitude-offering to Me.
The more you can offer
Your gratitude-heart and gratitude-life
   To Me,
The sooner you will be able to run
Faster than the fastest
In your heart of aspiration
And in your life of dedication."

16

My Lord Supreme,
When I pray to You,
I see the sky lifting me up
High, higher, highest.
When I meditate on You,
I see the same sky descending
Slowly, steadily and unerringly
And touching my earth-existence
    Most compassionately.
My Lord Supreme, You are telling me
Not to be afraid of the Unknown,
But to love the Unknown
And become one with the Unknown,
For this unknown Reality
Will not remain forever unknown,
And my life's perfection
And my heart's satisfaction
    Will grow in it.
My Lord, make me ready
And make me worthy
Of Your blessingful Promise to me.

17

My Lord Supreme,
You are telling me that
My heart's inner cry
    And
My life's hunger for You
Must have a slow, steady
    And unerring pace.
The crown of spirituality
Cannot be achieved overnight,
In the twinkling of an eye.
Slowly, steadily and unerringly,
I shall abide by Your
Compassion-Decision about my life,
For I must be fully ready
Before the God-Hour strikes for me.
Once the God-Hour strikes,
My life has to respond immediately.
My Lord Supreme, from today on
I shall wait for Your Arrival
With the utmost confidence
    In Your choice Hour.
May Your Compassion and Satisfaction
    Climb up and down
Inside my life's patience-tree.

18

My Lord Supreme,
   I do not know
What You have in mind for me.
   I do not know
And I do not want to know.
I have only one prayer to You:
That I not be afraid
In my own spiritual life,
So that, like a divine warrior,
I can conquer my mind's giant doubts
And my life's anxiety-mountains.
I want to be what You want me to be:
A self-giving and perfect instrument
Of Your highest Vision for earth.

19

My Lord Supreme,
My Beloved Supreme,
In my previous incarnation
You showered on me
Your most powerful Blessing-Light.
I cried and cried and cried
While receiving from You
Your immortal Treasures.
In the evening of my life,
In that incarnation,
I claimed You as my own, very own.

In this incarnation,
At my journey's dawn,
I see myself seated inside
Your infinite Compassion-Heart-Garden,
And I see that You are giving me
The capacity to enjoy
The celestial Beauty
And the celestial Fragrance
   Of Your Heart-Garden.

20

My Lord Beloved Supreme,
You have given me a childlike heart.
In my previous incarnations also
You gave me a childlike heart,
And I know that You will always give me
   A childlike heart.
My Lord Beloved Supreme,
Do tell me why You gave me,
Have given me and will forever give me
   A childlike heart.

"My child, your childlike heart
Is My Divinity's most special Boon.
It is in and through this most illumining
And fulfilling Boon
That I see, I grow into and I become one with
My own universe.
Only a childlike heart can please Me.
Only a childlike heart can fulfil Me.
Only a childlike heart will reach
   My Immortality's highest Height."

21

My Lord Supreme,
My mind wants outer education.
My heart wants inner education.
My mind wants to see the Truth
    In its own way.
My heart wants to feel the Truth
The way the Truth wants to be known
    And felt.
My Lord Supreme,
You want my inner education
To come first and foremost in my life.
Make me strong, make me confident
So that I can please You at every moment
By having You as my only Teacher
    In my life's inner school.
I know that when I study
    In my heart's school,
You will not only teach me,
But also make me feel
That I will be able to claim
Your infinite Wisdom-Light-Ocean
    As my own, very own.

22

My Lord Supreme,
You have given me a simplicity-mind
And a purity-heart unconditionally.
What shall I give You in return soulfully?

"My sweet child,
You do not have to give Me anything
    In return.
Just feel that I shall do everything
In you and for you in My own Way
In accordance with My Vision's
    Choice Hour.
From this moment on may your life
    And your heart
Become only a garland
    Of gratitude-satisfaction."

23

My Lord Supreme,
You have taken me out of
 Ignorance-forest.
You have taken me out of
 Ignorance-clay.
You have taken me out of
 Ignorance-destruction.
Now You have placed me
 At Your Lotus-Feet.
Therefore, I am safe,
 Permanently safe.
May my own heart-lotus
Petal by petal blossom
And offer its gratitude-fragrance
 To You,
To Your entire creation.
May my heart of love,
May my life of gratitude,
May my entire earthly reality
Become an unconditional surrender-river
 To flow into
Your Infinity's Compassion-Ocean,
Your Immortality's Satisfaction-Ocean.
My Lord Supreme, how happy I am
To claim You, only You, only You,
 As my own, very own.

24

My Lord Supreme,
Who am I?
Do tell me.

"My child,
You are My Eternity's Dream-boat.
You are My Eternity's Dream-passenger
    And
You are My Eternity's Vision-partner.
You have the body,
But you are the soul-consciousness.
Your earthly mind-possession
You have not claimed and should not claim.
Only claim your heart as your own.
If you remain in the heart,
You will remain My friend,
   My Eternity's friend,
And your soul will remain forever
My most satisfied and most satisfying wealth.
If you can bring to the fore
Your soul-consciousness,
You will please Me infinitely more
Than even your own heart
   Can ever imagine.
Remain in the soul, remain in the soul,
   Forever and forever."

25

My Lord, my Lord, my Lord, my Lord,
My soul's Lord, my heart's Lord,
My mind's Lord, my vital's Lord,
    My body's Lord,
No matter how many times
I have failed You,
I shall never give up.
I shall please You,
I shall please You
In Your own Way,
In Your own Way.
This is my life's only promise
To You, to You, my Lord,
My Beloved Lord Supreme.

26

My dear Supreme, my sweet Supreme,
My Lord Supreme, my Beloved Supreme,
My Absolute Master Supreme,
May my mind thank You most sincerely
For all the things that it has received from You.
May my heart thank You most soulfully
For all the things that You have not given
   To my heart.

My Supremely Beloved Supreme,
My Absolute Master Supreme,
Am I correct in saying and in feeling
That my mind's world-possession-hunger
Has made me enormously happy?

My Absolute Master Supreme,
My Supremely Beloved Supreme,
Am I perfect in saying and in feeling
That my heart's bondage-renunciation-flight
Has made You proudly happy?

"My child, My Eternity's Dream-child,
My Infinity's Reality-being,
In the world of your mind
You are definitely correct,
And in the world of your heart
You are absolutely perfect.
With your mind's possession-world,
You may make yourself powerful.
With your heart's renunciation-life,

You can and will
Make My transcendental Dream beautiful
And My universal Reality fruitful."

27

My ever-increasingly
Compassionate Lord Supreme,
I am praying to You
With my heart's silence-tears.
Do accept the cheerful surrender
Of my mind's freedom.

28

My Lord,
Please, please, give me Your Peace.
"My child,
Please, please, give Me your willingness-heart."

My Lord,
Please, please, give me Your Peace.
"My child,
Please, please, give Me your surrender-life."

My Lord,
Please, please, give me Your Peace.
"My child,
Please, please, give Me your gratitude-breath."

My Lord,
Please, please, give me Your Peace.
"My child,
Please, please, give Me a new promise
That you belong to Me only,
You need Me only,
You love Me only,
You came into the world to please Me
In My own Way.

"My child,
You are My Eternity's all,
My Infinity's all,
My Immortality's all."

29

My Lord Supreme,
Your Head was aching
Because I was not pleasing You
    In Your own Way.
My Lord Supreme,
Your Heart is bleeding
Because I am not pleasing You
    In Your own Way.
My Lord Supreme,
Your Life will be dying
Because I shall not be pleasing You
    In Your own Way.
My Lord Supreme,
What can I do?
What shall I do?
I am so helpless and useless.

"My child, do not worry.
I have already forgiven you.
I am now preparing Myself
To help you embark on a new journey
And watch your heart's blossoming,
Singing and dancing rainbow-sunrise."

30

My Lord Beloved Supreme,
Greatness You have given to my mind,
Goodness You have given to my heart
    And
Oneness You have given to my life.
Now, my Supreme, my Supreme, my Supreme,
Out of Your infinite Bounty,
Do give me something else:
One heart of gratitude-tears,
Two eyes of gratitude-smiles.

31

This morning my Lord Beloved Supreme
   Is telling me
That before I dare to claim
His immortal Love,
   Immortal Joy
      And
   Immortal Pride
As my own, very own,
My own faith-heart-garden-blossoms
Must infinitely increase
Their beauty and fragrance
Inside His own Compassion-flooded Heart.

32

My Lord, my Lord, my Lord,
I am swimming in the sea of tears
Because I do not love You
    In Your own Way.
My Lord, my Lord, my Lord,
I am drowning in the ocean of death
Because I do not need You
    In Your own Way.

33

My Lord, my Lord, my Lord,
I do not love You,
    Yet You love me.
I do not need You,
    Yet You need me.
        Why, why?

"My child, let us try
To be kind to each other
    Once and for all.
You give Me what you have:
Your ignorance-forest-mind.
Let Me give you what I am:
My Oneness-Fragrance-Heart."

34

My Lord, my Lord, my Lord!
Look, I have come back to You
With my heart's mounting
   Aspiration-flames.

"My child, My child!
Look, look what I have for you:
My Heart's Happiness-Ocean."

35

My Lord, my Lord, my Lord,
How can I be a perfect instrument of Yours?

"My child, do not think of your future,
Do not think of your past,
Do not think of your present.
Just think of this very moment.
Try to see Me second by second,
And not minute by minute,
Not to speak of hour by hour.
Try to see yourself
Inside My own Heart-Garden,
And never desire to see yourself
Inside your own mind-forest.
   Behold, My child!
I am declaring to the world at large
That you are My supremely
   And eternally chosen instrument
And My proudest perfection-child."

36

My Lord, my Lord, my Lord,
Every morning when You ask
Your beloved son — sun to wake up,
Do ask me also to wake up,
And please bless my heart
With prayer-gratitude-tears
   And my life
With surrender-perfection-smiles.

37

My Lord, my Lord, my Lord,
I shall not blame You any more.
I shall not blame myself any more.
I shall only pray to You
To make me a self-giving
Instrument-child of Yours.

My Lord, my Lord, my Lord,
I came into the world
To see Your Eyes smiling
And feel Your Heart happy.
Do fulfil my hope,
Do fulfil my promise.

38

My Lord, my Lord, my Lord,
Do give me the capacity
To place at Your Feet
   Every morning
My heart's readiness,
My heart's willingness,
My heart's eagerness
     And
My heart's happiness.

My Lord, my Lord, my Lord,
Do tell me how
I can claim You as my own,
   Very own.
Do tell me how
You can claim me as Your own,
   Very own.

"My child,
Give Me what your mind has:
   Unwillingness.
If you can give Me
Your mind's unwillingness,
Then you will be able to claim Me
   As your own, very own.

"My child,
Give Me what your heart is:
   Love.
If you can give Me

MY SWEET FATHER-LORD, WHERE ARE YOU?

Your heart's love,
Then I shall claim you
As My own, very own."

39

My Lord, my Lord, my Lord,
This morning, to my mind's extreme surprise
And to my heart's extreme sorrow,
I saw the distance
From Your Heart to my mind.
The distance is unimaginably long!
This frightened me to death.
My Lord, my Lord, my Lord,
Do tell me how I can shorten the distance,
How I can nullify the distance,
How I can make Your Heart and my mind one.

"My child, My child, My child,
From today on do not remain
A student of your desire-mind.
Become a companion of your aspiration-heart.
You and your aspiration-heart
Will be able to compel your mind
   To sit at My Feet.
Once your mind is at My Feet,
My Heart and your mind will become one,
   Inseparably one.
Your mind will be illumined,
You will be fulfilled
And I shall be satisfied."

40

My Lord, my dear Lord, my sweet Lord,
My Lord Divine, my Lord Supreme,
How can I, even for a single day,
Love You in Your own Way,
Offer You my devotion in Your own Way
    And
Surrender my entire earth-existence to You
  In Your own Way?

"My sleeplessly and breathlessly
Dream-blossoming child,
It is not an impossible task.
It is not even a difficult task.
It is an unbelievably easy task.
My child, from today on,
Do not try to hide from Me
And live in your darkness-mind-cave —
  Absurd, My child, absurd!
The entire creation, the entire universe,
  Is created by Me.
I am the Body
    And
I am the Spirit of the universe.
My child, I am most affectionately,
Most blessingfully inviting you
To come and live with Me
  In My Heart-Nest.
Come, My child, come!
Come play with Me and sing with Me.
  Lo, My child,

Perfect is your love for Me,
Perfect is your devotion to Me,
Perfect is your surrender to Me.
Your name is now perfect perfection-sky,
    And
My Name is perfect Satisfaction-Sun.
My child, to make the Real in you happy,
Today, tomorrow and forever and forever
I must love you in My divine Way,
   The only Way.
My child, My child, My child!"

41

When I see my Master's sorrowful eyes,
   I cry, I cry and I cry.
When I touch my Master's sorrowful heart,
   I sigh, I sigh and I sigh.
When I feel my Master's sorrowful life,
   I die, I die and I die.
When I see my Master's God-smiling eyes,
   My God-realisation-hope blooms.
When I touch my Master's God-smiling heart,
   My God-realisation-promise blossoms.
When I feel my Master's God-smiling life,
   My God-realisation-dream-manifested reality
Feeds the God-hungry seekers of God's Universe.

42

My Lord, My Lord, My Lord,
This morning do You have
Any special Blessing-Message for me?

"My child, I do.
My child, every day,
In the small hours of the morning,
You must wake up.
   Then immediately
You must wake up your child, aspiration.
   Then immediately
You and your child, aspiration,
Must open your heart-door to My Hope.
   Then immediately
I shall open My Heart-Door
   To your promise.
   Then immediately
Give Me the beauty
Of your heart's tears
And the fragrance
Of your soul's smiles.
   I shall then immediately
Give you the Beauty
Of My Heart's Universal Dream
And the Fragrance
Of My Soul's Transcendental Reality."

43

My Lord, my Lord, my Lord,
Do bless me with
Your last-minute Advice.

"My child, My child, My child,
The higher you think of Me,
The longer you think of Me
    And
The deeper you think of Me,
The sweeter will be your heart,
The purer will be your mind
    And
The easier will be your self-giving to Me.
My child, there shall come a time
In the very near future
When you will come to realise
Who you truly are:
You are the Beauty of My Dream,
You are the Fragrance of My Reality."

44

My Lord, do prove to me
That You love me.

"My child, how?"

My Lord, if You can make me
And keep me happy
Only for an hour every day,
Then I shall feel
That You really love me.

"My child, do prove to Me
That you love Me."

My Lord, how?

"My child, if you can make Me
   And keep Me happy
Only for five minutes every day,
   Then I shall feel
That you really love Me.
My child, if you can please Me,
I shall make you and keep you happy,
Not only for an hour every day
But for the entire day."

My Lord, I want to make You happy,
But please show me the way.

MY SWEET FATHER-LORD, WHERE ARE YOU?

"My child, just give Me
Your unconditional surrender
For five minutes every day.
My child, I want to keep you happy
Throughout the entire day.
Just show Me the way."

My Lord, just give me
Your Infinity's Affection
    And
Your Immortality's Love.

45

May the beauty of the New Year
    Beautify my heart.
May the purity of the New Year
    Purify my mind.
May the simplicity of the New Year
    Simplify my vital.
May the intensity of the New Year
    Intensify my body.
May the responsibility of the New Year
    Glorify my life.
May only the divinity of the New Year
    Fully satisfy me.

46

My Lord, my Lord, my Lord Supreme,
I love You with all my heart.

"My child, from now on you will tell Me
That you love Me with all *My Heart*.
My child, your heart is too small
   To love My big Heart.
My child, if you can love Me
   With My big Heart,
Then, only then, you will feel complete
   And I shall feel satisfied."

47

My Lord, my Lord, my Lord Supreme,
Do bless me fully and compassionately.
Do give me the soul to sing,
Do give me the heart to smile,
Do give me the eyes to cry,
Do give me the life to hope,
Do give me the breath
To be Your dreamer,
   To be Your server
      And to be Your lover
         Unconditional.

48

My Lord, my Lord, my Lord Supreme,
In the small hours of this morning
    I came to You.
I saw You were extremely, extremely
    And extremely busy.
Even then You said to me,
"My child, take Affection infinite from Me."
    I refused.
"My child, take Love infinite from Me."
    I refused.
"My child, take Joy infinite from Me."
    I refused.
"My child, take Peace infinite from Me."
    I refused.
"My child, what do you want?"
    I said,
"My Lord, my Lord, my Lord Supreme,
I just want to be with You."
My Lord, You became
Your Infinity's Smile-Blossoms.

49

My Lord, my Lord, my Supreme Lord,
Please tell me
What my express need should be.

"My child, My Eternity's child,
Your express need should be
Your devotion, your sleepless devotion
    To Me."

My Lord, my Lord, my Lord Supreme,
Please tell me
What my daily need should be.

"My child, My Infinity's child,
Your daily need should be
Your love, your sleepless love
    For My Will-manifestation."

My Lord, my Lord, my Lord Supreme,
Please tell me
What my ultimate need should be.

"My child, My Immortality's child,
Your ultimate need should be
My Satisfaction, only My Satisfaction,
    In My own Way."

50

My Lord, my Lord, my Lord Supreme,
I think of You.
You do not think of me.
    Alas, why?
My Lord, I look at You.
You do not look at me.
    Alas, why?
My Lord, I come to You.
You do not come to me.
    Alas, why?

"My child, I, too, think of you.
    I, too, look at you.
    I, too, come to you.
My child, when I think of you,
You are not inside your mind.
    When I look at you,
You are not inside your eyes.
    When I come to you,
You are not inside your heart-home.

My child, if you want to know
    When I think of you,
Then keep your mind empty of thoughts.
If you want to see Me
    While I am looking at you,
Then keep your eyes pure, absolutely pure.
If you want to see Me
    While I am coming to your heart-home,
Then keep your heart-home-door wide open
    Only for Me.

51

My Lord Supreme, my Beloved Supreme,
   My Absolute Lord Supreme,
Please teach me how to sweeten my heart
   With my soulfulness-tears.
Please teach my heart how to climb up
Into the skies of readiness, willingness,
   Eagerness and selflessness.
Please teach me how to escape
   From my doubting mind,
   From my ungrateful heart
   And from my fearful life.
Please teach me how to forgive my enemies
   So that I can have newness in my life.
Please teach me how to forgive myself
   So that I can have fulness in my life.
Finally, please teach me how to love myself
   The way You love me,
For my real perfection
And for my real satisfaction.

MY SWEET FATHER-LORD, WHERE ARE YOU?

52

My dear God, my dearer God, my dearest God,
My sweet Lord, my sweeter Lord,
   My sweetest Lord,
At my journey's start You blessed me
Most compassionately and most affectionately
With quite a few divine qualities.

My life's God, my heart's Lord,
In the future if once more I displease You,
Then You may take away
All the divine qualities
   Save and except one:
Please, please, please keep with me
   My obedience-heart
To breathe prayerfully, happily
   And gloriously
In my mind, in my vital and in my body.

My life's God, my heart's Lord,
This morning my soul, that represents You
Divinely, supremely and eternally,
In soundless sound has told me
That if I continue displeasing You,
Either consciously or even unconsciously,
Then mine will be the life
Of utter failure-tears
At the end of my journey's close.

My life's God, my heart's Lord,
May my outer life of dedication
Become Your absolute Commander-Will-
    Obedience-perfection.
May my inner heart of aspiration
Become Your absolute Commander-Will-
    Obedience-satisfaction.

53

My Lord, my Lord, my Lord,
    My Lord!
If I love You just because
    You love me,
Then I am eternally and infinitely
    Worse than the worst.
But, my Lord, if I love You
Because I cannot breathe
    Without loving You,
Then do allow me to enjoy
Prayerfully, sleeplessly
    And breathlessly
The dust-beauty, the dust-fragrance
    And the dust-delight
Of Your Nectar-Feet.

54

My Lord,
My Lord Supreme,
My Absolute Supreme,
You have not allowed me to do many things.
And I shall also not allow You
To do one thing, only one thing:
I shall not allow You to surrender
To humanity's absurd
And self-aggrandising demands.

55

My Lord Beloved Supreme,
With every breath of my heart
I enter into Your Heart
To love You only in Your own Way.

My Lord Beloved Supreme,
With every breath of my heart
I sit at Your Feet
To need You only in Your own Way.

My Lord Beloved Supreme,
With every breath of my heart
I look at Your Eye
To fulfil You only in Your own Way.

Notes to *My sweet Father-Lord, where are You?*

1-24. Sri Chinmoy offered the first twenty-four prayers in this book for individual Japanese disciples on 18 December 1987 during a Christmas trip to Japan.
25-55. Sri Chinmoy offered these special prayers during the years 1989 to 1997.
25. 26 July 1989, New York.
26. 23 November 1989, New York.
27. 7 January 1992, Tenerife, Canary Islands.
28. 5 December 1992, New York.
29. 18 December 1992, Ho Chi Minh City, Viet Nam.
30. 7 June 1993, en route to Boston.
31. 2 January 1994, Fiji.
32. 8 September 1994, New York.
33. 8 September 1994, New York.
34. 8 September 1994, New York.
35. 8 September 1994, New York.
36. 14 December 1994, Kathmandu, Nepal.
37. 15 December 1994, Kathmandu, Nepal.
38. 16 December 1994, Kathmandu, Nepal.
39. 17 December 1994, Kathmandu, Nepal.
40. 19 December 1994, Kathmandu, Nepal.
41. 20 December 1994, Kathmandu, Nepal.
42. 24 December 1994, Kathmandu, Nepal.
43. 26 December 1994, Kathmandu, Nepal.
44. 2 February 1995, New York.
45. 1 January 1997, Takamatsu, Japan.
46. 2 January 1997, Takamatsu, Japan.
47. 3 January 1997, Takamatsu, Japan.
48. 4 January 1997, Takamatsu, Japan.
49. 7 January 1997, Kumamoto, Japan.

50. 8 January 1997, Kumamoto, Japan.
51. 9 January 1997, Kumamoto, Japan.
52. 12 January 1997, Kumamoto, Japan.
53. 25 October 1997, en route to Kingston, Ontario.
54. 8 December 1997, Nassau, Bahamas.
55. 18 December 1997, Lake Atitlan, Guatemala.

PART XVIII

MY LORD, I PRAY TO YOU

MY LORD, I PRAY TO YOU

1

My Lord Beloved Supreme,
I pray to You to grant me
   Only one Boon
In this incarnation of mine:
Every morning and every evening
   I wish to wash
Your Infinity's Compassion-Feet
With my heart's gratitude-tears.

2

My Absolute Lord Supreme
My outer Success entirely depends
On Your Eye's Compassion-Flower.
My inner progress breathlessly depends
On Your Heart's Satisfaction-Fragrance.

3

My Absolute Lord Supreme,
   I am proud of my
Success-mind-body-thunder-drum,
   And You are fond of my
Progress-heart-life-nectar-flute.

4

My Absolute Lord Supreme,
    From today on
I shall use my heart
    In a new way
To feel spontaneously
Your Compassion and Forgiveness
    Infinitely more
And also to give You
My newly-born love and surrender
Cheerfully and unconditionally.

5

My Absolute Lord Supreme,
Is there any special way
To please You in Your own Way
At every moment of my life?

"My sweet child,
There is a way, there is a way.
Just give Me your obedience —
Cheerful obedience
    And soulful obedience,
Oneness-obedience
    And fulness-obedience.
Lo, you have the capacity
And you are the capacity
To please Me in My own Way
At every moment of your life."

6

My Absolute Lord Supreme,
Alas, why do I feed and nourish
Teeming imaginary sufferings
And thus disappear
    From Your Eye's
Compassion-Illumination-Protection-Nest
To enter into
The desolate desert-Sahara?

7

My Absolute Lord Supreme,
    In my devouring
Animal incarnations
You loved me unconditionally.
    In my doubting
Human incarnations
You loved me unconditionally.
    And now,
In my aspiring divine incarnation
You are loving me unconditionally.
    My Lord,
Do grant me the supreme capacity
To breathe in the sweet fragrance
    Of sacred remembrance.

8

My Absolute Lord Supreme,
My body is hiding my purity.
My vital is hiding my humility.
My mind is hiding my sincerity.
My heart is hiding my divinity.
My soul is hiding my Immortality.
My Lord, my Lord, my Lord,
Do compel them to give me back
My Eternity's treasures
   In infinite measure.

9

My Absolute Lord Supreme,
With my heart's mounting cries
I wish to prove to myself
   That I need You only.
With my eyes' glowing smiles
I wish to prove to myself
   That I love You only.
With my life's self-giving ecstasies
I wish to prove to myself
   That I serve You only.

10

My Absolute Lord Supreme,
When I cheerfully place
   At Your Compassion-Feet
My life's tiny success-leaf,
You immediately, blessingfully
And unconditionally help me
   Climb Your Heart's
Tallest Progress-Tree.

11

My Absolute Lord Supreme,
My desire-mind thinks
   That it can have everything.
My aspiration-heart feels
   That it has everything.
My realisation-life knows
   That it is everything.
My Lord, You are telling me
That I am Your Eternity's
Dream-fulfilling child.

12

My Absolute Lord Supreme
   Who, if not You,
Can and will liberate me
   From the meshes
Of ignorance-night?

My Lord,
   When, if not now
Will You grant me
Your Eternity's Closeness,
Your Infinity's Oneness
And Your Immortality's Fulness?

13

My Absolute Lord Supreme,
My gratitude-heart
   Is the only place
Where I can see
   Your Compassion-Feet.

14

My Lord,
Now is the only time for me
To be a perfect instrument
   Of Your Vision-Eye.

15

My Lord,
I am one of those
Supremely chosen instruments
   Of Yours
Who are going to please You always
   In Your own Way —
      Always!

16

My Lord,
You are telling me
That You are not going to waste
Even a fleeting second with me
   Any more
If spirituality is my mind's luxury.
But if spirituality is my heart's
   Supreme necessity,
Then every day You will teach me
   A new lesson
Absolutely illumining
   And supremely fulfilling.

17

My Absolute Lord Supreme,
My yesterday's dream was
To become another Supreme
　Like You.
My today's dream is
To see Your Infinity's
　Vision-Eye.
My tomorrow's dream shall be
To touch Your Immortality's
　Compassion-Forgiveness-Feet.

18

My Absolute Lord Supreme,
You are the Supervisor
　Of my hesitation-mind,
You are the Inspirer
　Of my dedication-hands,
You are the Lover
　Of my aspiration-heart
And You are the Dreamer
　Of my perfection-life.

19

My Absolute Lord Supreme,
How can I please You
    At every moment
In Your own Way?

"My child, easy!
Just give Me at every moment
Your biting thought-monkeys
    And take from Me
My roaring Will-Power-Lion."

20

My Absolute Lord Supreme,
This morning I was so excited
To see You secretly entering
    Into my heart-room,
And now I am so delighted
To see You smilingly
    Throwing away
My heart-room's exit sign.

21

My Absolute Lord Supreme,
This morning to You I offered
My mind's ten desire-thorns
    To make myself happy,
And now to You I am offering
My heart's seventy aspiration-flowers
    To make You happy.

22

My Absolute Lord Supreme,
This morning You said to me
That You will never revoke
    Your Heart's
Forgiveness-Credit Card.
Please keep Your Promise!

"My child,
This morning you said to Me
That you will never remove
    The gratitude-plant
From your heart-garden.
Please keep your promise!"

23

My Absolute Lord Supreme,
   How can You prove
To the world at large
That I am a supremely chosen
Instrument-child of Yours
To realise You, to reveal You
And to manifest You here on earth
   Unless and until
I forcefully silence
   My doubting mind?

24

My Absolute Lord Supreme,
   This morning
When my heart caught You
In Your Vision-blossoming,
   Playful Mood,
You immediately gave me back
My Eternity's childhood
To smile at You soulfully,
To play with You sleeplessly
And to dance with You
   Breathlessly.

25

My Absolute Lord Supreme,
You are telling me
That You will grant me
Your Eternity's Divinity,
Your Infinity's Quantity
And Your Immortality's Quality
If I just give You
   My sincerity's purity.
My Lord, I am ready.
My heart is ready
And my life is ready.

26

My Absolute Lord Supreme,
   I am offering You
My heart's love-bouquet,
   And You are blessing me
With Your Eternity-Heart's
   Open Door.

27

My Lord Supreme,
My Beloved Supreme,
Your Vision tells me
That my name is Madal,
   The God-dreamer.
Your Compassion tells me
That my name is Chinmoy,
   The God-seeker.
Your Illumination tells me
That my name is Sri Chinmoy,
   The God-lover.
Your Perfection tells me
That my name is Guru,
   The God-server.
And Your Satisfaction tells me
That my name is Gratitude,
   The God-knower.

28

My Lord Supreme,
My Beloved Supreme,
What is a miracle?
A miracle is something
That the finite cannot accomplish
   By itself,
But that the Infinite can easily do
   In and through the finite.
I am the finite.
You are the Infinite.
I am gratitude sleepless.
You are Compassion breathless
   And deathless,
Plus unconditional,
   Unconditional,
      Unconditional.

29

My Lord Supreme,
Do grant me the capacity
To be a sleeplessly
Self-giving child
   Of Yours.

30

My Lord Beloved Supreme,
This morning I am determined
To accomplish something
   Impossible.
At this very moment
I shall start counting one by one
   Seven good qualities
In my most deplorable enemy.
   My Lord,
I desperately need
Your Help.

31

My Lord Beloved Supreme,
This is a day off for me
   From trying to fool You.
Today I shall only
Devotedly and soulfully
   Count and see
How many Compassion-Eyes
And how many
Forgiveness-Hearts
   You have for me.

32

My Lord, my Lord,
I am engulfed in the flames
Of doubt, fear, worry and anxiety.
Prayerfully I invoke You,
Soulfully I implore You
To come to me and save me!

33

My Lord, my only Lord,
It is I who have allowed myself
To be whipped by unwillingness,
And now I am dumbfounded
By the ruthless threats
   Of giant doubts.
My Lord, save me,
Save my existence-life on earth!

34

My Lord Supreme,
Out of Your infinite Bounty
   Do grant me
The blessingful capacity
To choose immediately
My faithful heart
   Over my doubtful mind
Every day, every hour,
Every minute and every second
   Of my life.

35

My Beloved Supreme,
With the purity of my inner eye
And the sincerity of my outer eyes
I wish to cry sleeplessly
   For You, only for You.

36

My sweet Lord Supreme,
Now that I am absolutely certain
That my love for You
Is genuine and unconditional,
I wish to forget once and for all
Even my last stumbling dance
With uncertainty, incapacity
   And unwillingness
When I could not make
My unconditional surrender
   To You.

37

My Eternity's Lord Supreme,
Today You have made me
    A pioneer-citizen
Of the transcendence-delight-world.
May my ever-climbing
    Gratitude-heart-tree
Someday, at Your choice Hour,
Touch Your ever-descending
Golden Feet!

38

My dear Lord, my sweet Lord,
My Absolute Lord Supreme,
As Your unconditional
    Compassion-Ocean
Is far beyond my comprehension,
    Even so, alas,
It seems my conscious love
For the temptation-volcano
Is far beyond Your Comprehension.

39

My Beloved Supreme,
Could You spare a moment?
I shall be eternally grateful to You
If You powerfully put
    Your Purity-Handcuffs
Around my impurity-mind.

40

    My Lord Supreme,
When I tell You
That I have been thinking of You,
I sincerely feel that I am offering You
A piece of good news.
    My Lord Supreme,
When You tell me
That You have been thinking of me,
I immediately feel
That I have made
    Tremendous progress
In my life of aspiration,
And I clearly see
That my life's transformation-goal
Is not a far cry,
But is within my easy reach.

41

    My Lord Supreme,
I have only two friends:
Your Compassion-Eye
And Your Forgiveness-Heart.
    "My child,
I also have only two friends:
Your morning's smiling face
And your evening's singing heart."

42

    My Lord,
I am ashamed
Of my lethargic body.
    "But, My child,
I am proud
Of your strong body."

43

    My Lord,
I am ashamed
Of my aggressive vital.
    "But, My child,
I am proud
Of your sleepless vital."

44

    My Lord,
I am ashamed
Of my suspicious mind.
    "But, My child,
I am proud
Of your searching mind."

45

   My Lord,
I am ashamed
Of my impure heart.
   "But, My child,
I am proud
Of your self-giving heart."

46

   My Lord,
I am ashamed
Of my insecure life.
   "But, My child,
I am proud
Of your perfection-dreaming life."

47

   My Lord Supreme,
I am sure that You are
   Extremely happy today,
For I have finally dethroned
My life's ego-king.
   "My child,
I am more than happy,
More than proud
And more than satisfied.
But now you have to do
Something else for Me.
Soulfully, devotedly
   And cheerfully,
You have to become another God!"

48

My Lord, my sweet Lord,
   My Supreme Lord,
I do know that my life's
Unconditional surrender to You
   Is fast asleep.
But I clearly see that my heart's
Most sincere gratitude to You
Is wide awake.

49

My Lord, my Lord, my Lord,
I may not know
What Your Compassion-Eye
   Looks like,
And I may not know
What Your Forgiveness-Heart
   Feels like,
But I do know
That You have been
Sleeplessly and eagerly waiting
For only one perfection-cry
   From my heart
And for only one satisfaction-smile
   From my life.

PART XIX

SADNESS-HEART-SILENCE.
MADNESS-MIND-ELOQUENCE

SADNESS-HEART-SILENCE. MADNESS-MIND-ELOQUENCE

1

Supreme!
My solemn promise:
I shall never stand
In Your
Unworthy Presence
With my
Sacred palms together
In supplication.

2

Supreme!
You will
Never be able
To break
A single smile
Over my
Beautiful face.

3

Supreme!
I am eagerly waiting
For someone
To replace You,
So that
I can have someone
To swim with me
While I swim
In the sea of tears,
Frustrations
And failures.

4

Supreme!
You want me
To sacrifice
My life to You.
Never!
You do not value
My life,
To say the least.
Therefore,
I am buying a goat
For sacrifice
To satisfy You,
For I feel
The goat-sacrifice
Will be valued
By You.

5

Supreme!
How I wish
It would be
A long-forgotten story
That I have touched Your Feet,
Desired and cried
For anything.

6

Supreme!
I call You
My own:
A mistake
That defies
Correction
And
Redemption.

7

Supreme!
True.
My desires
Were great
In number.
But now
My frustrations
Are a million
Times more.

8

Supreme!
I do not know how
You justify
Your Name:
"Eternity's
Compassion-Eye
And
Immortality's
Forgiveness-Heart."

9

Supreme!
To me
The word "compassion"
Is not applicable
To You.
I have
Luckily ended
My cherished,
Faulty dreams.

10

Supreme!
Destruction I see
Within, without,
All around.
You are untroubled,
Unconcerned
And what not.

11

Supreme!
When necessity demands,
Earthly parents
Warn their children.
I took You
As my only Parents.
You deliberately
Did not warn me.
It seems Your dictionary
Does not house
The word "warning".
Look at my fate:
Abysmal abyss-sorrows
Have befriended me.

12

Supreme!
To worship You
Is to be
Intimately familiar
With the sorrows
And pangs
Of my life-tree
With all its branches,
Flowers, leaves
And fruits.

13

Supreme!
Are You blind?
It seems You see
Only when
I am frustrated
And utterly lost
And I thrust
My anger-finger
In Your
Two uncomely Eyes.

14

Supreme!
My sole desire
Was to become
The golden dust
Of Your Lotus-Feet.
I am so happy
That it is not too late
To withdraw
My desire totally.

15

Supreme!
The less
I think of You,
The more I am free
From the
World-disease
Which You
Undoubtedly
And solely are.

16

Supreme!
In those days,
The moment I touched
Your Feet,
Fears and doubts
Devoured me.
You may not believe —
Fears, doubts, anxieties,
Worries, frustrations,
Unbelief and disbelief
Devoured me
And my life.
Alas, a deplorable,
Despicable experience!
In vain, how hard I try
To delete it
From the tablet
Of my heart.

17

Supreme!
Hard-hearted
You are.
Stony,
In every sense
Of the term,
You are.
From You,
Nothing shall I get,
Nothing do I desire.
I am self-contained,
Self-sufficient.
Believe it or not,
My self-perfection-life
Plus all-satisfaction-life
Is blossoming
Faster than the fastest.

18

Supreme!
I was
A slave
To Your Service.
I am now
The master
Of my will.

19

Supreme!
I shall not give way
To sleep.
My mind-tempest,
My heart-tornado
From now on
I shall
Sleeplessly treasure.
For they are real,
Unlike all Your
Hollow Promises.

20

Supreme!
If anybody asks me
How to pray to You,
I shall tell him
Immediately,
"Do not walk along
That way.
Be not a fool.
Do not invite
The sea of sorrows."
And I mean it!

21

Supreme!
If anybody asks me
How to meditate
On You,
I shall tell him
Immediately
To meditate
On frustration
Instead.
It will definitely give
A satisfying result.

22

Supreme!
I gave up everything
To please You
In Your own Way —
Even the exquisite
Beauty
Of my heart
And the incomparable
Fragrance
Of my soul.

23

Supreme!
I am so glad
That You
Have defeated me
In forgetting me.
Had it been
The reverse,
The whole world
Would have
Looked down
On poor me.

24

Supreme!
You always
Talk about
Progress, progress.
Progress.
How is it
That You have
Not even once
Said one nice word
Of appreciation
To me
About my
Most astonishing
Rainbow-series
Of progress?

25

Supreme!
Knowing fully well
That You would not
Wake deliberately,
I called and called.
Now I do not mind
Even if You enjoy
Your Eternity's
Tranquillity-flooded
Sleep.

26

Supreme!
I had faith in You
For longer than
The longest time.
I am neither
Begging You
Nor forcing You
To change
The game.
But, I assure You,
If You ever change
The game,
You will not be
Disappointed.

27

Supreme!
Positions and possessions
I gave You.
I do not have them.
I do not need them either.
My new life
Is my new possession.

28

Supreme!
I do not want
My case
To be heard any more.
I am now mightily free
From my supreme
Fascination-illusion-delusion-dilemmas.
I am now in a world
Of a newly acquired life.
I alone
Am my Eternity's all.

29

Supreme!
Finally,
I am my
Volcano-anger-eruption.
I like it.
I love it.
I treasure it.
I am, at once,
The dreamer
And owner
Of a billion or trillion
Rainbow-dreams.

30

Supreme!
There was a time
When Your Name
Was my only hope.
Now, my only hope
Is that I can remain
A perfect stranger
To You
Throughout Eternity.

31

Supreme!
I used to cry.
Weep and sob
At Your Feet.
But those
Malignant diseases
Will never be able
To attack me
Any more.

32

Supreme!
You may say
What I am saying
Is absolutely wrong.
You just tell me
If anything is right
In Your creation.

33

Supreme!
I have emptied
The tear-oceans
Of my heart.
I do not mind at all
If You do not
Come out of
Your dear, sweet
And self-amorous
Comatose sleep.

34

Supreme!
You want
Your creation
To please You.
I do not know
How You imagine
Your desire
To be fulfilled
As long as You keep
Your creation
Not only
Unconsciously,
But consciously
Weak, helpless
And hopeless.

35

Supreme!
To repeat
Your Name
Is to welcome
Untold misfortunes.
This is my
Infallible conviction.

36

Supreme!
They say
That there are
Countless
Undivine children,
But no
Undivine parents.
Alas, how I wish
It could be true
In Your case.

37

Supreme!
If You continue
To behave like this,
Then for God's sake,
Do not take
Upon Yourself
The name of the
Compassion-flooded
World-Pilot.

38

Supreme!
To worship You
Is to multiply
One's self-doubts.

39

Supreme!
The whole world
Understands me,
My poor heart.
Either You do not know
How to understand me
Or You purposely
Do not care.

40

Supreme!
My hopes
Never thought that
They would find
Their fulfilment
Elsewhere.

41

Supreme!
I fed You
With my heart's
Nectar-devotion.
I want the world
To continue
To have faith in You.
Therefore,
I am not telling
The world
What You are
Feeding me with.

42

Supreme!
Both of us knew
Something special:
I knew
How to pray.
You knew
How to spurn.

43

Supreme!
I begged You
For protection.
I never thought
That You did not
Even know
The meaning
Of protection.

44

Supreme!
I clasped Your Feet
Most devotedly.
Alas, it was
My delusion-mind
That compelled me
To do so.

45

Supreme!
Happiness I sought
At Your Feet.
But what have I found
And become?
A tear-stained face.

46

Supreme!
Openly,
You tell the doctors
To heal the patient.
Secretly,
You tell death
To kill the patient.
Since the beginning
Of Your creation,
You have been
Playing this game.

47

Supreme!
I desired to become
The dust
Of Your Feet.
I now have become
My greatest victory's
Tallest banner.

48

Supreme!
Do You have
The capacity
To forgive me?
I do not think
You have.

49

Supreme!
Do You want me
To forgive You?
For God's sake,
I do not need
And I do not want
To have
That capacity.

50

Supreme!
It does not matter
Whether You came
To me
Or I came
To You.
We are now
The North Pole
And the South Pole.
This is what
Definitely matters.

PART XX

MY ASPIRATION-HEART CYCLES

MY ASPIRATION-HEART CYCLES

PART 1

MY ASPIRATION-HEART CYCLES

Preface

For the past twelve months, I have been offering prayers in the morning, before I do my weightlifting. Now I have embarked on a new journey. Each time before I do ten minutes cycling, I will offer a prayer. By living here in the West, I have become a man of prayers.

— Sri Chinmoy
12 October 1999

1

My Absolute Lord Supreme!
May the tears of my heart
Feed You
Exactly the way
The Smiles of Your Eye
Feed my heart —
Sumptuously
　And
Unconditionally.

2

My Absolute Lord Supreme!
You love each and every
Human being
Unconditionally.
So must I.

3

My Absolute Lord Supreme!
God-realisation-thirst
I have.
God-manifestation-hunger
I need.

4

My Absolute Lord Supreme!
Sweet, sweeter, sweetest
Are the tears of my heart
    And
The sorrows of my life.

5

My Absolute Lord Supreme!
A mounting aspiration-cry
Is the only requirement
For God-realisation.
A spreading dedication-smile
Is the only requirement
For God-manifestation.

MY ASPIRATION-HEART CYCLES

6

My Absolute Lord Supreme!
May my vital, my body
And all that I have
And all that I am
Be always on Your side.

7

My Absolute Lord Supreme!
May my obedience-heart
Sleeplessly sing for You.
May my surrender-life
Breathlessly dance for You.

8

My Absolute Lord Supreme!
Patience I must practise,
For patience is the pioneer
Of victory.

9

My Absolute Lord Supreme!
You want me to learn
Only devotion-heart-songs
And
Gratitude-life-songs
And sing for You,
For Your Satisfaction.

10

My Absolute Lord Supreme!
I am exceedingly happy
That I am able to cancel
All my desire-trips
Today and forever.

11

My Absolute Lord Supreme!
I shall sleeplessly
Keep my heart's door open
To all God-seekers.

12

My Absolute Lord Supreme!
Today I received a personal call
From my Lord.
He wanted to know
How my gratitude-heart-tears
Are doing.

13

My Absolute Lord Supreme!
The mind may pray
To the unknown God,
But the heart always prays
To the known and familiar God.

14

My Absolute Lord Supreme!
Please, please, please,
Give me back all my old
Blue-gold dreams —
My God-aspiration,
My God-realisation,
My God-manifestation,
My life-transcendence
   And
My God-satisfaction-dreams.

15

My Absolute Lord Supreme!
May my constant surrender
To Your Will
Be my one single
Burning desire.

16

My Absolute Lord Supreme!
Today I must remove
Altogether
My world-possession-desire-hunger.

17

My Absolute Lord Supreme!
My mind departs quickly
Only when I start living
Happily and proudly
Inside my heart.

18

My Absolute Lord Supreme!
I must keep my heart-eye
Open
All the time
To Your Will.

19

My Absolute Lord Supreme!
From now on I shall be
The adamantine determination
Of a God-seeker-hero.

20

My Absolute Lord Supreme!
Today You are asking me
To be a passenger
Of Your Eternity's
Blue-gold Dream-Boat.
My gratitude-heart
I place at Your Feet.

21

My Absolute Lord Supreme!
The mind is pride-pleasure
With no God.
The heart is humility-treasure
Only with God.

22

My Absolute Lord Supreme!
I have been for a long time
A member
Of the God-lovers' society.
Today I have become
A member
Of the God-servers' society
As well.

23

My Absolute Lord Supreme!
My dedication-life,
My aspiration-heart
And
My surrender-breath
Are extremely fond of
One another.

24

My Absolute Lord Supreme!
My peace is
My love-expansion.
My love is
My aspiration-expansion.
My aspiration is
My Lord's Compassion-expansion.

25

My Absolute Lord Supreme!
I am the lover
Of Your Compassion-Eye.
You are the Lover
Of my aspiration-heart.

26

My Absolute Lord Supreme!
Your Forgiveness-Heart
Has made my miserable life
Liveable once more.

27

My Absolute Lord Supreme!
Do give me the strength
To be always ready
For the correction
And perfection
Of my life.

28

My Absolute Lord Supreme!
I must break the age-old,
Tenebrous night of my mind
Into a million pieces.

29

My Absolute Lord Supreme!
God wants my ever-blossoming
Gratitude-heart
To captain the pro-God team.

30

My Absolute Lord Supreme!
In vain I have been trying
For years and years
To tame my monkey-mind —
In vain!

31

My Absolute Lord Supreme!
May I have the heart
That loves and loves
And loves
Each and every human heart.

32

My Absolute Lord Supreme!
The source of
My beatitude-life
   Is
My God-gratitude-heart.

33

My Absolute Lord Supreme!
In the spiritual life,
A heart of devotion-ecstasy
Is a supreme necessity
To realise God.

34

My Absolute Lord Supreme!
My faith-life is not
My mind-frustration.
   It is
My heart-illumination.

35

My Absolute Lord Supreme!
My Lord's Compassion-Eye
Every morning rings
My mind's inspiration-bells,
My heart's aspiration-bells
    And
My life's dedication-bells.
I ring every morning
My Lord's
Victory-Manifestation-Bells.

36

My Absolute Lord Supreme!
Do come and liberate me
From my self-doubt —
The heaviest of all burdens.

37

My Absolute Lord Supreme!
The unaspiring mind
Is a powerful magnet
For nonsense.
The aspiring heart
Is the most powerful magnet
For universal oneness.

38

My Absolute Lord Supreme!
You are commanding my mind
Not to represent the past.

39

My Absolute Lord Supreme!
Your Compassion-Eye
Has employed
My newness-mind,
My eagerness-heart
   And
My selflessness-life
To do public relations for You.

40

My Absolute Lord Supreme!
May my morning start
With my God-gratitude-heart-tears and smiles.

41

My Absolute Lord Supreme!
My prayer is my short-cut
To Your Compassion-Feet.
My meditation is my short-cut
To Your Satisfaction-Heart.

42

My Absolute Lord Supreme!
Every morning
You push my body
Vehemently
And You pull my heart
Gently.

43

My Absolute Lord Supreme!
My heart is throbbing
With the God-Arrival-expectation.

44

My Absolute Lord Supreme!
God smiles and smiles
And smiles
When I ask Him
For instant God-realisation.

45

My Absolute Lord Supreme!
My mind says to me:
"Accept a disciple —
Take a tremendous risk."
My heart says to me:
"Accept a disciple —
Offer a most fragrant flower
To God."

46

My Absolute Lord Supreme!
Your Compassion-Eye
Never closes
Your Heart's
Forgiveness-Door.

47

My Absolute Lord Supreme!
Every day
I must run and run and run
On only one track:
My God-obedience-track.

48

My Absolute Lord Supreme!
My heart most devotedly
Memorises
Your Compassion-flooded
Morning Messages.

49

My Absolute Lord Supreme!
I want to become a heart
Of glowing hopes
And not a mind
Of towering promises.

Notes to *My aspiration-heart cycles, part 1*

1. 12 October 1999, 11:40 pm, New York.
2. 13 October 1999, 4:27 am, New York.
3. 13 October 1999, 5:36 am, New York.
4. 13 October 1999, 6:12 pm, New York.
5. 14 October 1999, 5:21 pm, New York.
6. 14 October 1999, 8:31 pm, New York.
7. 15 October 1999, 12:56 am, New York.
8. 15 October 1999, 8:34 am, New York.
9. 15 October 1999, 5:50 pm, New York.
10. 16 October 1999, 2:01 am, New York.
11. 16 October 1999, 8:25 am, New York.
12. 16 October 1999, 7:41 pm, New York.
13. 17 October 1999, 12:45 am, New York.
14. 17 October 1999, 8:50 am, New York.
15. 18 October 1999, 7:22 am, New York.
16. 18 October 1999, 9:03 pm, New York.
17. 19 October 1999, 5:32 am, New York.
18. 20 October 1999, 1:14 am, New York.
19. 22 October 1999, 7:52 am, New York.
20. 23 October 1999, 8:09 am, New York.
21. 24 October 1999, 9:27 am, New York.
22. 25 October 1999, 8:36 am, New York.
23. 26 October 1999, 8:30 am, New York.
24. 26 October 1999, 12:22 pm, New York.
25. 26 October 1999, 9:23 pm, New York.
26. 28 October 1999, New York.
27. 1 November 1999, 7:46 am, New York.
28. 2 November 1999, 7:39 am, New York.
29. 3 November 1999, 7:49 am, New York.
30. 4 November 1999, 8:04 am, New York.

31. 7 November 1999, 6:26 am, New York.
32. 5 December 1999, 8:06 am, São Paulo, Brazil.
33. 6 December 1999, 7:52 am, São Paulo, Brazil.
34. 8 December 1999, 6:53 am, Nova Friburgo, Brazil.
35. 9 December 1999, 5:25 am, Nova Friburgo, Brazil.
36. 13 December 1999, 6:56 am, Nova Friburgo, Brazil.
37. 14 December 1999, 5:21 am, Nova Friburgo, Brazil.
38. 15 December 1999, 6:14 am, Rio de Janeiro, Brazil.
39. 16 December 1999, 5:01 am, Rio de Janeiro, Brazil.
40. 17 December 1999, 4:37 am, Rio de Janeiro, Brazil.
41. 19 December 1999, 6:38 am, Rio de Janeiro, Brazil.
42. 20 December 1999, 4:56 am, Rio de Janeiro, Brazil.
43. 21 December 1999, 6:25 am, Rio de Janeiro, Brazil.
44. 22 December 1999, 5:00 am, Rio de Janeiro, Brazil.
45. 23 December 1999, 4:38 am, Rio de Janeiro, Brazil.
46. 25 December 1999, 5:19 am, Curitiba, Brazil.
47. 27 December 1999, 5:56 am, Curitiba, Brazil.
48. 28 December 1999, 6:38 am, Curitiba, Brazil.
49. 29 December 1999, 4:57 am, Curitiba, Brazil.

MY ASPIRATION-HEART CYCLES,

PART 2

50

My Absolute Lord Supreme!
I am my doubtful mind.
God is God's tearful Heart.

51

My Absolute Lord Supreme!
I wish to be the golden dust
Of Your Feet,
But You want me to be
The Himalayan pride
Of Your Heart.

52

My Absolute Lord Supreme!
The deeper our heart-roots,
The stronger our love of God.

53

My Absolute Lord Supreme!
Each happy moment
In my inner life
Builds a new castle-glory
In my outer life.

54

My Absolute Lord Supreme!
Every day at sunrise
I shall aim at
A new horizon.

55

My Absolute Lord Supreme!
The desire-days of my mind
Are invariably followed by
The worry-nights of my heart.

56

My Absolute Lord Supreme!
The strength of the mind
Fails to disarm
The hope-power of the heart.

57

My Absolute Lord Supreme!
This morning You came down
To awaken me
To Your Infinity's Silence.

58

My Absolute Lord Supreme!
I have tamed my outer life
To remain still.
I have trained my inner heart
To enjoy the thrill.

59

My Absolute Lord Supreme!
My forgiveness-smile
Is the golden vastness
Of my heart-sky.

60

My Absolute Lord Supreme!
The tears of my heart
   And
The smiles of my soul
Every day play hide-and-seek
To entertain You.

61

My Absolute Lord Supreme!
Whenever angels see
An unconditionally
God-surrendered seeker,
They immediately start trumpeting
God's supreme Victory.

62

My Absolute Lord Supreme!
Man-made friendship
Is a foolish hardship.
God-made friendship
Is a rainbow boat trip.

63

My Absolute Lord Supreme!
My heart is begging God
To use His iron rod
So that my mind can fly
In His boundless Sky.

64

My Absolute Lord Supreme!
I must develop
Intense homesickness
For my Beloved Supreme.

65

My Absolute Lord Supreme!
I have only one desire.
I have only one aspiration.
I have only one aim.
I have only one goal.
I wish to become
My Master's choicest slave.

66

My Absolute Lord Supreme!
Impossible dreams are afraid of
My sleepless and breathless
Faith in God.

67

My Absolute Lord Supreme!
May my heart dance and dance
With new hope-promise-blossoms
Every morning.

68

My Absolute Lord Supreme!
When I secretly and deliberately
Hide inside my mind-jungle,
Only my God the Father
And God the Mother
Searches for me
Full of worries
And full of anxieties.

69

My Absolute Lord Supreme!
God says to my doubting mind
And my strangling vital,
"No more freedom!
No more freedom!"

70

My Absolute Lord Supreme!
May my early morning prayer
Be fragrant with
My God-gratitude-heart-tears.

71

My Absolute Lord Supreme!
A golden hyphen must connect
The beauty of my heart
   And
The fragrance of my soul.

72

My Absolute Lord Supreme!
What are You doing?
What are You doing?
"My child, I am just wiping
The tears from your face.
I am just removing
The thorns from your eyes."

73

My Absolute Lord Supreme!
Every day
God anxiously and eagerly waits
For the arrival
Of my aspiration-heart.

74

My Absolute Lord Supreme!
My God-realisation every day
Lovingly and self-givingly
Ploughs
My life's world-dedication-soil.

75

My Absolute Lord Supreme!
This morning
You secretly entered
Into my desire-mind,
Quickly robbed
All my desires
And ran away.

76

My Absolute Lord Supreme!
My meditation-heart
And God's Ecstasy-Eye
Every day talk and talk and talk
To their fullest satisfaction.

77

My Absolute Lord Supreme!
I came into the world
Only to spread
God-Consciousness-Delight
Here, there and all-where.

78

My Absolute Lord Supreme!
O impersonal God,
You are Your own
Eternity's Love.
O personal God,
You are Your own
Immediacy's Hero.

79

My Absolute Lord Supreme!
When I look at the world,
I am all sadness.
When I look at myself,
I am all madness.
My Supreme,
Save me from my sadness,
Save me from my madness!

"My child, My child,
Throw your sadness into My Heart,
Throw your madness into My Feet.
My Heart and My Feet
Will take care of your sadness
And madness.
My child, do not forget
That I depend on you,
I depend on you."

My Supreme, my Lord, my Beloved,
My Absolute Supreme,
Do accept the sea
Of my gratitude-heart-tears.

80

My Absolute Lord Supreme!
My mind is a member
Of the God-seeker committee.
My heart is a member
Of the God-lover committee.
My life is a member
Of the God-server committee.

81

My Absolute Lord Supreme!
My monkey-mind gives no peace
To my God-loving
And God-roaring heart.

82

My Absolute Lord Supreme!
My meditation does not blame
Anybody or anyone.
My meditation only tames
The undivine in me.

83

My Absolute Lord Supreme!
God says to my heart
That there can be
No frustration-tears
In my heart.

MY ASPIRATION-HEART CYCLES

84

My Absolute Lord Supreme!
May my God-longing, God-crying
And God-surrendering breath
Remain ceaseless and deathless.

85

My Absolute Lord Supreme!
To hear God's Nectar-Voice
My heart needs
An unshakeable poise.

86

My Absolute Lord Supreme!
My heart blooms only
Where my Lord Supreme
Plants my heart.

87

My Absolute Lord Supreme!
Alas, my mind enjoys
Microscope-inspection.
To my greatest joy,
My heart enjoys
Telescope-panorama.

88

My Absolute Lord Supreme!
No more a fault-finding mind.
More a God-loving heart
In every human life, everywhere —
More, ever more.

89

My Absolute Lord Supreme!
God's Eye teaches me
How to love.
God's Life teaches me
How to serve.
God's Heart teaches me
How to surrender.

90

My Absolute Lord Supreme!
When I open my eyes,
I see nothing of the inner world.
When I open my heart,
I see not only the things
Of the inner world
But God Himself.

91

My Absolute Lord Supreme!
Each day I offer
A new surrender-life to You,
I give You a new victory.

92

My Absolute Lord Supreme!
It is a very rare privilege
To feel and say
That my Master is always right,
Not only for me
But also for the entire humanity.

93

My Absolute Lord Supreme!
My prayer-tears
Brighten my eyes.
My meditation-smiles
Sweeten my heart.

94

My Absolute Lord Supreme!
May my unconditional surrender
To God's Will
Be the only joy
In my aspiration-heart
And my dedication-life.

95

My Absolute Lord Supreme!
The mind greedily wants to study
World-destruction-terrorism.
The heart prayerfully likes to study
World-oneness-heroism.

96

My Absolute Lord Supreme!
God's Compassion and Love-Nets
Catch only the true seeker-hearts.

97

My Absolute Lord Supreme!
To please You,
My Lord Beloved Supreme,
I need only the repetition
Of one thought:
Gratitude.

98

My Absolute Lord Supreme!
Desire-indulgence
I was.
Aspiration-effulgence
I now am.

99

My Absolute Lord Supreme!
Finally my soul has succeeded
In taking my life away
From my mind-desert!

100

My Absolute Lord Supreme!
Alas, the human mind
Is always slow to appreciate
And always quick to deprecate.

101

My Absolute Lord Supreme!
If I have true aspiration
For You,
Then only You can give me
True satisfaction.

102

My Absolute Lord Supreme!
Your Compassion treasures
All our self-giving efforts.

SRI CHINMOY

Notes to *My aspiration-heart cycles, part 2*

50. 1 January 2000, 8:00 pm., Curitiba, Brazil.
51. 2 January 2000, 5:44 am, Curitiba, Brazil.
52. 3 January 2000, 7:05 am, Curitiba, Brazil.
53. 5 January 2000, 10:21 am, Curitiba, Brazil.
54. 7 January 2000, 7:59 am, Foz do Iguaçu, Brazil.
55. 8 January 2000, 8:13 am, Foz do Iguaçu, Brazil.
56. 9 January 2000, 8:07 am, Foz do Iguaçu, Brazil.
57. 10 January 2000, 6:26 am, Foz do Iguaçu, Brazil.
58. 11 January 2000, 7:48 am, Foz do Iguaçu, Brazil.
59. 13 January 2000, 6:35 am, Foz do Iguaçu, Brazil.
60. 14 January 2000, 7:43 am, Foz do Iguaçu, Brazil.
61. 15 January 2000, 9:56 am, Foz do Iguaçu, Brazil.
62. 17 January 2000, Asunción, Paraguay.
63. 18 January 2000, 6:21 am, Asunción, Paraguay.
64. 19 January 2000, 8:15 am, Asunción, Paraguay.
65. 20 January 2000, 5:24 am, Asunción, Paraguay.
66. 21 January 2000, 6:18 am, Asunción, Paraguay.
67. 23 January 2000, 6:46 am, Asunción, Paraguay.
68. 26 January 2000, Brasilia, Brazil.
69. 27 January 2000, 8:38 am, Brasilia, Brazil.
70. 28 January 2000, Brasilia, Brazil.
71. 2 February 2000, 10:23 am, New York.
72. 3 February 2000, 9:59 am, New York.
73. 5 February 2000, 8:51 am, New York.
74. 7 February 2000, 8:43 am, New York.
75. 8 February 2000, 8:08 am, New York.
76. 10 February 2000, 11:51 am, New York.
77. 12 February 2000, 9:09 am, New York.
78. 14 February 2000, 9:25 am, New York.
79. 16 February 2000, 8:54 am, New York.

MY ASPIRATION-HEART CYCLES

80. 25 February 2000, New York.
81. 26 February 2000, 7:15 am, New York.
82. 28 February 2000, 9:26 am, New York.
83. 1 March 2000, 8:45 am, New York.
84. 3 March 2000, 9:29 am, New York.
85. 5 March 2000, 6:56 am, New York.
86. 6 March 2000, 12:10 am, New York.
87. 7 March 2000, 8:33 am, New York.
88. 9 March 2000, 7:21 am, New York.
89. 11 March 2000, 4:09 am, New York.
90. 12 March 2000, 7:50 am, New York.
91. 16 March 2000, 9:14 am, New York.
92. 18 March 2000, New York.
93. 21 March 2000, 8:23 am, New York.
94. 25 March 2000, 7:01 am, New York.
95. 29 March 2000, 8:50 am, New York.
96. 31 March 2000, 7:34 am, New York.
97. 4 April 2000, 8:00 am, New York.
98. 6 April 2000, New York.
99. 10 April 2000, 9:23 am, New York.
100. 14 April 2000, New York.
101. 15 May 2000, 7:47 am, New York.
102. 18 May 2000, 7:52 am, New York.

PART XXI

MY RACE-PRAYERS

MY RACE-PRAYERS

PART 1

MY RACE-PRAYERS

1

My Lord,
My God-realisation-aspiration
Has been crying for centuries,
And yet I do not know
Where You are
Or where I am.

2

My Lord,
You are commanding me
    To join You
In Your beginningless
World-transformation-task.
Therefore, my heart is all gratitude
    To You.

3

O Lord,
How beautiful is the morning
When I can see Your Beauty's Eye
And Duty's Hands and Legs
Circling the dreaming hopes
    Of my life,
The streaming tears
    Of my heart
And the blossoming smiles
    Of my soul!

4

My Lord Supreme,
My prayers cannot satisfy You.
My meditations cannot satisfy You.
What else, then, can I do for You
   To satisfy You?

"My child,
How do you know
That your prayers and meditations
Are not satisfying Me?
They *do* satisfy Me.
But I want you to satisfy Me
Sleeplessly and breathlessly,
And infinitely more,
   Infinitely more."

5

When I look into God's Eye,
I see that He is Infinite and I am finite.
When I look into God's Heart,
I clearly see and throbbingly feel
That I am His Eternity's doll
And He is my Eternity's All.

6

My Lord, an unconditionally
God-surrendered seeker
And God-surrendered lover
   Is the beauty
Of the ever-blossoming
Universal Consciousness
   And the fragrance
Of the ever-heightening
Transcendental Consciousness.

7

My Lord, my Lord, my Lord!
My God-discovery has solved
Not only all intricate mysteries,
But also all insoluble problems,
Past, present and future.
My Lord, You have given me
   And I have.

"My child, I have given you
   And you are."

8

My Lord Supreme
Voraciously devours
The beaming smiles
   Of my soul.
My Lord Supreme
Voraciously devours
The streaming tears
   Of my heart.

9

My Lord, my Lord,
The outer runner promises
God-Joy-Manifestation
   On earth.
The inner runner fulfils
   The promise.
The outer runner runs
   For God.
The inner runner runs
   With God.

10

Every morning I gladden
My Lord's Heart immensely
By crying and flying
   In my inner life,
And by smiling and running
   In my outer life.

11

My Lord, my Lord, my Lord,
My running is the rose-beauty
   And jasmine-fragrance
Of my God-blossoming heart.

12

My Lord, my Lord,
You are telling me that
A smiling heart-runner
Is the enjoyer supreme
Of Heaven's infinite Beauty
And immortal Fragrance,
Especially when the runner runs
In inclement weather,
Unpleasant weather,
Uninspiring weather
And undivine weather.

13

My Lord, my Lord,
My implicit faith
In my God-surrender-run
Is speedily and safely
   Taking me
To my God-Destination
Of the ever-blossoming
And ever-heightening Beyond.

14

My Lord, my Lord,
You are reminding me
Again and again
Of the undeniable fact
That a sleeplessly self-giving seeker
Is absolutely the fastest runner
In the worlds of aspiration
   And dedication.

15

I am a morning runner.
   God gives me His Beauty.
I am a midday runner.
   God gives me His Power.
I am an afternoon runner.
   God gives me His Charm.
I am an evening runner.
   God gives me His Peace.
I am a midnight runner.
   God gives me His Pride.

16

O our 3,100-mile-run runners,
My sleepless, prayerful, soulful, powerful
And proud gratitude-heart-throbs
   I have discovered
In your aspiration-mountain-height
And in your dedication-fountain-delight.
O my Saturday two-mile-race runners,
Your running is challenging,
Yet charming and thrilling.

17

My Lord Beloved Supreme,
You have given
My finite gratitude-heart
   The capacity
To bind Your Universal Life
And Transcendental Self
   At the same time.

18

My Lord, my Lord, my Lord!
The Heaven-born fragrance
   Of my inner running-soul
Becomes the earth-transforming beauty
   Of my outer running-life.
My Lord, my Lord, my Lord!

19

My Lord, my Lord,
My morning run unites
My God-readiness-heart
With God's absolute Fulness-Smile.

20

My Lord, my Lord,
When my body, my vital
And my mind walk,
   My name becomes transformation.
When my heart runs,
   My name becomes satisfaction.
When my soul flies,
   My name becomes perfection,
And God tells me who I eternally am.

21

My Lord, my Lord,
My life is my patience.
My patience is God's Satisfaction.
God's Satisfaction is my All
In the inner world
   Of my God-realisation
And in the outer world
   Of my God-manifestation.

22

May every morning
   My life become
The lotus-beauty-fragrance-petals
   Of my God-oneness-heart.

23

This morning God asked my mind
If my mind sleeplessly loves Him.
Then God asked my heart
If my heart breathlessly needs Him.
My mind immediately said to God,
"I definitely love You sleeplessly."
My heart prayerfully said to God,
"My Lord, please give me
   A few years.
Right now I am quite uncertain."
God said to my mind,
"My son, cultivate sincerity!"
God said to my heart,
"My child, develop speed!"

24

Slowly, steadily and unerringly
My earth-life-tree grows,
   Blossoms and glows
Under the Compassion-Vision-Eye
   Of my Absolute Lord Supreme.

25

The mind's greatness-heights
 Are perishable.
The heart's goodness-depths
 Are imperishable.

26

My Lord,
With the beauty
 Of my outer running
And with the fragrance
 Of my inner running,
I shall make my God-manifestation
A must.

27

The outer run inspires me
 To go and see God.
The inner run inspires me
 To come and sit at God's Feet.

28

My Lord,
To love running
In the morning
Is the beginning
Of my God-pleasing life.

29

My Lord,
Not with my earthly skill,
And not with my Heavenly will,
But with my Lord's
Express Arrival-Thrill
I have completely transformed
   My life.

30

In the morning
I am the blossoming beauty of God.
During the day
I am the unending duty of God.
At night
I am the dreaming melody of God.

31

God's golden Touch
   I love.
God's golden Smiles
   I treasure.
God's golden Tears
   I devour.

32

My Lord,
Not the streaming tears
Of the most deplorable defeats,
But the beaming smiles
Of the most laudable victories,
My life and I eternally are.

33

My Lord, I have won
    Your Victory-Face
By running every day
    Your morning Race.

34

My morning run
Shortens my goal.
So says my heart's
Divine blue-gold soul.

35

Because I love God,
    God exists.
Because I need God,
    God smiles.
Because I sing God's Victory-Song,
    God proudly belongs to me.

36

My inner hunger cries;
My life of beauty flies.
My dream-boat-heart sails;
It never, never fails.

37

There is only one victory
In my inner life and outer life,
And that victory is
My self-transcendence
   In God's own Way.

38

My Lord,
Do shower wisdom-light
   Upon me.
In the spiritual run,
Retirement is conscious
Ignorance-bondage-
   Appointment-engagement.

39

Never say that the world is wrong,
But say that the world
   Can be perfected
Slowly, steadily, unerringly
And unmistakably.

40

My Lord,
When I look at Your Feet,
You ask me to look at Your Face.
When I look at Your Face,
You ask me to look at Your Eye.
When I look at Your Eye,
You ask me to enter into Your Heart.
The moment I enter into Your Heart,
You blessingfully and proudly tell me,
    "My child, now you can rest."

41

Light, more light,
Abundant light and infinite light!
    Every day
In our inner life of aspiration
May we observe our festival of lights.

42

Mornings come to me
With the sound-power
   Of the Unknown.
Evenings come to me
With the silence-peace
   Of the Unknowable.
My Lord Beloved Supreme
Comes to me both in the mornings
   And in the evenings
With what He has and what He is:
   Concern.

43

To my greatest joy,
Today I have come to realise
That it is infinitely easier for me
To please my Lord Supreme
   In His own Way
Than to please myself
   In my own way.

44

My Lord,
I have enjoyed the beauty
Of the world.
I have enjoyed the fragrance
Of the world.
What more do I have to do, my Lord?
"My child,
I now want you to become
The streaming tears
And the bleeding hearts
   Of the world
To become My most perfect instrument
   On earth."

45

The pride of the earthly race
And the joy of the Heavenly Race
Have the same goal:
Self-transcendence.

46

Our Lord wants to hear everything
   From our God-union-heart.
Our Lord does not want to hear
Even a single word
   From our God-division-mind.

47

My Lord, my Lord,
Do keep me sleeplessly
Only with the God-necessity-seekers,
And never, never
With those who are self-sufficient.

48

My Lord, You want me to pray.
I pray for Your Compassion-Eye.
My Lord, You want me to meditate.
I meditate on Your Victory-Banner.
My Lord, do tell me
If I am supposed to do anything else.

"Yes, My child,
You have to do something more.
When you are in a bad mood,
Repeat and repeat and repeat,
'My Lord, I am all for You.'
And when you are in a good mood,
Repeat and repeat and repeat,
'My Lord, You are all for me,
　All for me, all for me.' "

49

    Love the world.
Frustration and renunciation
Shall be your two more names.
    Love God.
God's Grace and God's Praise
Shall be your two more names.

50

Surrender, surrender, surrender!
I must surrender my life,
My heart and my very breath
To the Will of my Lord Beloved Supreme
    At every moment.
If I succeed, only then will He claim me
    As His own, very own.

51

My life will be
Of a very, very, very special significance
    Here on earth
If I can be a constantly cheerful
    Self-giver
To the Will of my Lord Beloved Supreme.

52

My Lord, can You not see
That my outer world
Is dark, darker, darkest?

"My child, can you not see
That I have kept your inner world
Bright, brighter, brightest,
Plus pure, purer, purest?"

53

I pray and pray and pray
When my life needs God.
I meditate, I meditate, I meditate
When my heart loves God.

54

No, no, the outer running is not fun.
   It is our heart's joy-invocation.
No, no, the outer running is not fun.
   It is our soul's Godful inspiration.

55

I love my Lord, I love my Lord!
   Therefore I cry and cry.
I need my Lord, I need my Lord!
   Therefore I try and try.

56

My Lord, may I say something to You?
"Yes, My child, yes."
My Lord, I want to be near You.

"No, My child, I want you to say:
'My Lord, I want to touch You.'
No, My child, I want you to say:
'My Lord, I want to catch You.'
No, My child, I want you to say:
'My Lord, I want to embrace You.'
No, My child, I want you to say:
'My Lord, I want to fulfil You.'
No, My child, I want you to say:
'My Lord, I want to surrender
My earth-existence to You.'
My child, then do it!"

My Lord, I am doing it.

"Heaven, look, look! Earth, look, look!
My child has made his unconditional
And complete surrender to Me.
My child, you have now become
The Heart of My Life
And the Breath of My Soul."

57

Victory, Victory,
Our Lord's supreme Victory,
We must proclaim and establish
Here on earth at every moment.

58

Alas, alas,
Our conscious and unconscious pride
    Has completely destroyed
Our long-cherished God-oneness-joy.

59

Devotion, devotion,
Sleepless, breathless God-devotion!
No devotion —
No highest, no higher, no high
God-realisation.

60

I do not want my God-hunger
Only to be a childish hobby.
I want my God-hunger
    To win
God's Satisfaction-Trophy.

61

My Lord, I have seen
The Beauty of Your Eye,
But I have not felt
The Power of Your Heart,
And I have not become
The dust of Your Feet —
Alas, alas, alas!

62

Alas, I cannot remember
The last time when
My heart most sincerely,
Most soulfully and most self-givingly
   Said to God,
"My Lord Beloved Supreme,
I love You only,
And I need You only."

63

In supreme Silence
The Absolute Lord Supreme
Says to the God-Realised souls,
"My supremely chosen children,
I bring you into the world
Not to defend yourselves
Under any circumstances,
But to love Me and serve Me
Unconditionally, sleeplessly
    And breathlessly
In My own Way
In each human being
And also in each earth-planet-creation
    Of Mine.

You must realise that as you claim Me
    To be your All,
Even so, I claim you,
My Oneness-Vision-Reality-children,
    To be My All."

64

    Expectation
Is frustration-poison-drinking.
    A constant self-giving
Is nectar-delight-drinking.

65

My Lord,
I wish to know from You personally
The differences that exist
Between You and me.

"My child,
There are countless differences
But I shall name only three:
Unlike Me, every day
You have a very tight schedule.
You have no time to write to Me.
You have no time to speak to Me.
You do not even have the time
To speak to me over your heart-phone.
I write to you every day.
I try to speak to you every day.
But alas, alas and alas,
I get no response from you.
Now the second difference is this:
I constantly make fun of myself.
Alas, you have not yet learnt
This particular art,
And I have no idea whether
You will ever be able to learn this art.
The third difference is this:
You think and you feel
That you are indispensable
There in Heaven and here on earth.

MY RACE-PRAYERS

In My case, I am absolutely sure
That not only this world,
But also all the worlds
That are in existence,
Can live without Me.
In a sense, you are badly needed
Here, there and all-where.
In My case, nobody wants Me,
Nobody needs Me.
I am left all alone."

66

Each God-seeker
Is the Beauty of God's Heart,
The Divinity of God's Breath
And the Immortality of God's Dream.

67

God loves me
Not because I am a very good
    God-seeker.
God blesses me with His Compassion
Not because I am a very bad
    God-seeker.
God loves me and blesses me
Precisely because I am
His Eternity's child-flower
    And
His Infinity's dream-fragrance.

68

The seeker's spiritual life begins
Only when he sincerely feels
That he is only for God,
Only for God, only for God.

69

I must breathe in every Breath
Of my Lord Beloved Supreme
With a tremendous soulfulness,
Eagerness and intensity.

70

I really love
My ever-blossoming
God-manifestation-tears and smiles,
   I really do.

71

Two kings: the inner and the outer.
The outer king prays to the inner King
   For power, boundless power.
The inner King says to the outer king,
"My child, not power,
But light, light, light!"
The outer king says to the inner King,

"My Father Lord Supreme,
How can I be like You?"
The inner King says to the outer king,
"My child, love Me, pray to Me,
Surrender to Me and claim Me.
You are bound to realise that
Who I am and what I am
You already are in the inner world."

72

My morning running prayer
   Is my heart's
      Silence-bliss.

73

Each new morning
Is a new opportunity for me
To sit in a new way
At my Lord's Feet
And devour the dust
Of my Lord's new Feet
In a new way.

74

My outer running shows me
　The smiling Face of God.
My inner running brings me
　The dancing Heart of God.

75

We must not enjoy
Our comfortable way of thinking
　About God.
We must enjoy only
Our self-giving willingness
　To fulfil God's Will.

76

This morning
My Lord Supreme commanded me
    To use His Mirror.
I immediately obeyed His Command.
To my widest astonishment,
I saw myself as a budding God.
I said to my Beloved Supreme,
"What about Your other children?
You have countless children.
What about them?"
Smilingly and blessingfully
He said to me,
"They are also the same, My child.
All your brothers and sisters
Are also budding Gods and Goddesses."

77

Today my life
Has a new name:
Attachment-extinction.

78

My heart
Is my Master's home,
    Only home.
I must not roam,
I must not roam.

79

God tells me
That if I try to hide
From His Compassion-Eye
And His Forgiveness-Heart,
Then He will deliberately forget
My outer name
And my inner home.

80

Today I am in
The seventh Heaven of delight.
    Why?
My heart's devotion-tears
And my life's surrender-smiles
Are playing hide-and-seek.

81

Smiling,
The breath of the New Year
Has just entered into my heart
And has given me
Three spiritual names:
Excitement, enlightenment
    And fulfilment.

82

This morning
My heart was running
With the God-obedience-currents
   And dancing
With the God-obedience-waves.

83

My Lord,
What is more important,
Your Blessings or Your Love?

"My child,
Both are equally important.
My Blessings you need
To make yourself absolutely divine.
My Love you need
   To become
A supremely choice instrument
Of My Transcendental Vision."

84

If you believe that
To please God in His own Way
   Is essential in your life,
Then why not do it immediately?

85

In spite of being
Shockingly undivine,
Human beings pray to God,
Love God and serve God.
This is, indeed,
The greatest miracle of all.

86

My Lord,
You had to wait
Countless years
For me to come and see You.
How is it that I cannot wait
One single, solitary day
For You to come and see me?

"My child,
Awake, arise —
Arise, awake!"

87

A seeker-runner's life
   Is made of
God's Heart-Songs.

88

When I start counting
My Lord's Blessings
Upon my devoted head
And surrendered life,
In no time I fall asleep.
My Lord blesses me
With the sweetest dream.
In that dream I see and hear
   God telling me,

"My child,
You do not have to count
   My Blessings.
You just be happy and remain happy,
Be happy and remain happy.
Your happiness is all I want
   From your inner life
And your outer life as well."

89

The outer world
Is time-bondage-imprisonment.
The inner world
Is Eternity's
Freedom-enlightenment-achievement.

90

Ignorance-night
Is extremely, extremely proud of
   Disobedience-pride.

91

When we pay any attention
To our doubting mind,
Our aspiring heart starves
   And withdraws.

92

My earthly hope says,
   "I can."
My Heavenly promise says,
   "I already have done:
God-fulfilment-assurance
   On the path."

93

   The human life
Is for the God-hunger.
   The divine life
Is for the universal feast.

94

Run, run, run!
Spirituality needs both
The inner running
And the outer running.
Neither the inner running
Nor the outer running
Is a curiosity-invitation.
In the life of a genuine God-seeker
   And God-lover,
Curiosity-indulgence is an inescapable
And inevitable self-destructive force.
Only when God's unconditional
Forgiveness-Power descends,
Can the seeker make a fresh attempt
At spiritual progress.
Before we accept spirituality,
Curiosity may inspire a certain seeker
To enter into the spiritual life.
But once a seeker is spiritually
   Well-established,
Curiosity-indulgence
Is the most self-destructive force.

95

I am a God-dreamer-life.
I am a God-lover-heart.
I am a God-listener-mind.
I am a God-carrier-vital.
I am a God-server-body.
I am a God-treasurer-soul.
I am a God-whisperer-soul.
I am a God-drummer-soul.
I am a God-messenger-soul.
I am a God-harbinger-soul.

Commentary: How I wish all of you would learn this prayer by heart. It will definitely, definitely help you in your aspiration-life, so all of you kindly learn it by heart. This is a most special prayer. If you can memorise it, I will be so grateful to you.

96

No age will replace
Our Master's tears
And our Master's smiles.

No age will replace
My children's love for me
And their faith in me.

No age will replace
My gratitude to their hearts
And their gratitude to my life.

97

Be brave, be brave, be brave!
Live not in fear-torture-cave.
Be brave, be brave, be brave,
The way to God's Home to pave.

98

My prayerful and soulful service
   To humanity
Is not my sacrifice.
It is the gigantic fulfilment
Of my Heaven-climbing
And God-fulfilling dream.

99

I must transcend my previous
Aspiration-heart-height, I must!
I must surpass my previous
Dedication-life-length, I must!
I must deepen my previous
Ecstasy-soul-depth, I must!

100

The real spiritual life means
Daily, weekly, monthly, yearly
   And eternally
The victory of
Self-transcendence-discovery.

Notes to *My Race Prayers, part 1*

1. 3 December 1999, Curitiba, Brazil.
2. 31 December 1999, Curitiba, Brazil.
3. 8 January 2000, Iguassu Falls, Brazil.
4. 12 January 2000, Iguassu Falls, Brazil.
5. 15 January 2000, Iguassu Falls, Brazil.
6. 19 January 2000, Asunción, Paraguay.
7. 22 January 2000 Asunción, Paraguay.
8. 22 January 2000, Asunción, Paraguay.
8. 27 January 2000, Brasilia, Brazil.
9. 5 February 2000, New York.
10. 26 February 2000, New York.
11. 4 March 2000, New York.
12. 11 March 2000, New York.
13. 18 March 2000, New York.
14. 25 March 2000, New York.
15. 29 April 2000, New York.
16. 29 July 2000, New York.
17. 5 August 2000, New York.
18. 26 August 2000, New York.
19. 16 September 2000, New York.
20. 28 October 2000, New York.
21. 11 November 2000, New York.
22. 2 December 2000, Ayutthaya, Thailand.
23. 20 December 2000, Mandalay, Myanmar.
24. 23 December 2000, Mandalay, Myanmar.
25. 13 January 2001, Bali, Indonesia.
26. 10 February 2001, New York.
27. 17 February 2001, New York.
28. 24 February 2001, New York.
29. 10 March 2001, New York.

30. 17 March 2001, New York.
31. 24 March 2001, New York.
32. 31 March 2001, New York.
33. 7 April 2001, New York.
34. 10 April 2001, New York.
35. 21 April 2001, New York.
36. 28 April 2001, New York.
37. 12 May 2001, New York.
38. 23 June 2001, New York.
39. 30 June 2001, New York.
40. 7 July 2001, New York.
41. 14 July 2001, New York.
42. 21 July 2001, New York.
43. 4 August 2001, New York.
44. 11 August 2001, New York.
45. 25 May 2002, New York.
46. 8 June 2002, New York.
47. 13 July 2002, New York.
48. 20 July 2002, New York.
49. 27 July 2002, New York.
50. 10 August 2002, New York.
51. 1 March 2003, New York.
52. 22 March 2003, New York.
53. 5 April 2003, New York.
54. 17 May 2003, New York.
55. 31 May 2003, New York.
56. 7 June 2003, New York.
57. 14 June 2003, New York.
58. 14 June 2003, New York.
59. 19 July 2003, New York.
60. 26 July 2003, New York.
61. 9 August 2003, New York.

62. 11 October 2003, New York.
63. 25 October 2003, New York.
64. 1 November 2003, New York.
65. 8 November 2003, New York.
66. 15 November 2003, New York.
67. 22 November 2003, New York.
68. 28 November 2003, Singapore.
69. December 2003, Solo, Indonesia.
70. 6 December 2003, Solo, Indonesia.
71. 10 December 2003, Solo, Indonesia.
72. 11 December 2003, Solo, Indonesia.
73. 12 December 2003, Solo, Indonesia.
74. 13 December 2003, Solo, Indonesia.
75. 17 December 2003, Yogyakarta, Indonesia.
76. 18 December 2003, Yogyakarta, Indonesia.
77. 19 December 2003, Yogyakarta, Indonesia.
78. 21 December 2003, Yogyakarta, Indonesia.
79. 24 December 2003, Yogyakarta, Indonesia.
80. 28 December 2003, Yogyakarta, Indonesia.
81. 31 December 2003, Yogyakarta, Indonesia.
83. 7 January 2004, Bali, Indonesia.
84. 14 January 2004, Bali, Indonesia.
85. 17 January 2004, Bali, Indonesia.
86. 21 January 2004, Bali, Indonesia.
87. 22 January 2004, Bali, Indonesia.
88. 23 January 2004, Bali, Indonesia.
89. 25 January 2004, Bali, Indonesia.
90. 27 January 2004, Bali, Indonesia.
91. 28 January 2004, Bali, Indonesia.
92. 29 January 2004, Bali, Indonesia.
93. 31 January 2004, Bali, Indonesia.
94. 21 February 2004, New York.

MY RACE-PRAYERS

95. 28 February 2004, New York.
96. 6 March 2004, New York.
97. 13 March 2004, New York.
98. 20 March 2004, New York.
99. 27 March 2004, New York.
100. 3 April 2004, New York.

MY RACE-PRAYERS

PART 2

101

The outer weather challenges us;
The inner weather frightens us.
But our Lord's infinite Compassion,
Affection, Love and Concern
Enable us to silence and smash
Their pride and torture.

102

A self-conquered
And God-surrendered seeker
Is absolutely the best
   God-lover
And the most perfect
   God-server.

103

Each time an unconditionally
God-surrendered seeker
Meets with God,
God tells him,
"My child, you are the beauty
   Of My Soul's
      Transcendental Dream
And you are the duty
   Of My Heart's
      Universal Reality."

104

Today
My Lord's Compassion-Victory
And my life's surrender-victory
We shall together celebrate.

105

My Lord Supreme,
May Thy Victory be proclaimed
In and through me
At every moment of my life.
My Lord Supreme,
My Lord Supreme,
My Lord Supreme!

106

The human life is
A confusion-dissatisfaction-jungle.
The divine life is
A beauty-fragrance-garden.
A God-seeker's sleepless
   God-surrender-life is
A God-Heartbeat-assimilation-
   Experience-delight.

107

Supreme,
My Supreme,
My Lord Supreme,
My Beloved Supreme,
My heart, my life and I
Wish to learn only two things from You:
Do teach us how to cry for You,
    Only for You,
And how to surrender ourselves
Entirely and completely to You,
    Only to You.

108

Those who love God happily,
Cheerfully, self-givingly, unconditionally,
Sleeplessly and breathlessly
Will never, never, never believe
In God's defeat-failures.
To them, every moment is God's Victory,
God's Supreme Victory,
Even though at times
Our wee human mind
Cannot understand the significance
Of God's constant Victory,
Victory Transcendental
And Victory Universal.

109

My outer running
Is my body's journey —
The destination is known.
My inner running
Is my soul's journey —
The Goal is unknowable.

110

The life that does not believe in
God-loving and God-pleasing prayers
Will end in a most painful failure.
The life that believes in
God-loving and God-fulfilling prayers
Will unmistakably grow into
God's brightest Smile and highest Pride.

111

My body unconsciously loves
Harmful silence-lethargy.
My heart consciously loves
Soulful silence-ecstasy.
I consciously plus self-givingly love
Godful silence-intimacy.

112

For God-realisation,
Needed: no outer skill.
Needed, needed, needed:
Only a God-crying thrill.

113

My Lord, my Lord, my Lord!
I am no more
A "give me" beggar.
From now on I shall be
A "take me" child —
Your child.

114

Learn more truth.
Earn more joy.
Be more perfect.
Be more perfect.
Earn more joy.
Learn more truth.
This message-light
Is for all.

115

I give my money-power to God.
God smiles at me.
I give my name, my fame,
My joy and my pride to God.
God smiles at me twice.
I give my oneness-heart
Unreservedly to God.
God smiles at me a million times
And embraces me a million times.
I give my cheerful, sleepless
And unconditional
Surrender-breath to God.
God smiles at me
And deliberately forgets to stop.
God embraces me
And deliberately forgets to stop.

116

The mind thinks
That God is unapproachable.
The heart knows and feels
That God is not only approachable
But also sleeplessly lovable
And breathlessly adorable.

117

Who is my hero?
No, not a good God-talker.
Who is my hero?
No, not a good God-dreamer.
Who is my hero?
No, not a good God-lover.
Who is my hero?
No, not a good God-server.
Who is my hero?
My hero, indeed:
A God-bleeding heart
And a God-blossoming life.

118

I am proud of myself
Because I think of God every day.
God is proud of Himself
Because He thinks of me
At every moment, at each hush gap.
I am proud of myself
Because I love God only.
God says to me,
"Is it so, My child?
Is it so, My child?
I do not think so, My child.
I do not think so, My child."

119

I fly to please my soul.
I cry to please my heart.
I judge to please my mind.
I challenge to please my vital.
I rest to please my body.
I suffer to please my life.
I love, I serve, I serve, I love
To please my Lord Beloved Supreme.

120

Today's marathon is a unique
God-invocation, God-revelation
And God-manifestation-journey
In the physical body-world.

121

Smiling and smiling,
Whispering and whispering,
Singing and singing,
Dancing and dancing,
Our birthdays descend
From the highest Height
Of Delight-flooded Heaven
And stand before us here on earth
To tell us that God wants us to be
His most powerful soldiers
And His choicest children.

122

Smiling and smiling,
Singing and singing,
God says to each and every
Genuine seeker,
"My child,
Nothing can ever equal
Your heart's climbing cries
And your life's blossoming tears."

123

No minute detail
Can escape God's Attention.
Alas, how can my constant
God-ingratitude-heart
Be an exception?

124

Give me no freedom,
Give me no freedom,
My Lord Supreme.
If You really love me,
Then give me no freedom
Even for a fleeting moment.

125

Love God, serve God,
Sail your life-boat, sail!
If not, my mind,
You fool, wait and fail.

126

My soul is sailing
In God's Pride-Boat.
My heart is sailing
In God's Compassion-Boat.
My life is sailing
In God's Forgiveness-Boat.
I am sailing
In God's Dream-Boat.

127

I place my earthly thoughts
    At God's Feet.
I place my Heavenly will
    Inside God's Heart.
I place myself
    In front of God's Eye.

128

Today I shall break open
My life's ignorance-prison-cell
And ring and ring, sleeplessly ring,
My Lord's Summit-Victory-Bell.

129

When the morning begins,
I sing my Lord's Victory-Song
   Inside my heart.
When the evening sets in,
I strike my Lord's Victory-Gong
Here, there and all-where
   Around the world.

130

My Supreme, my Supreme, my Supreme,
Why do I refuse Your unconditional
Love, Affection, Sweetness and Fondness,
    Why?
My Supreme, my Supreme, my Supreme,
Why do I not sleeplessly and breathlessly
Cry for You,
    Why?
My Supreme, my Supreme, my Supreme,
Why do I not cheerfully give You
What I have and what I am,
    Why?
"Because, because, because, My child,
You have made yourself
The absolute lord of your life."

131

I tried to become great.
God laughed at me.
I tried to become good.
God laughed at me.
I tried to become perfect.
God laughed at me.
Finally I said to God,
"My Lord, I shall become
What You want me to become."
My Lord smiled at me and said,
"My child, now you are truly Mine,
And I am all yours."

132

The outer run
And the inner run
Are two complementary souls.
They help each other
Tremendously.

133

My Lord says to me,
"My child,
Be not a beggar
Of what I have.
Be a chooser
Of who I am."

134

Every morning
God wants my aspiration-heart
And my dedication-life
To run together,
Side by side,
Towards the self-same Goal.

135

My Lord,
How I wish I could tell You
How much I love You!
"My child,
How I wish I could tell you
How much I need you!"

136

My God-running legs
Have made my life
Very precious.
My God-running heart
Has made me
Very gracious.

137

My Supreme has chosen
My heart's streaming tears
To be His Eternity's playmate.

138

My Supreme, my Supreme, my Supreme,
   I love You
Not because You love me infinitely more.
   I love You
Because Your Feet are my only Treasures,
Your Eye is my only Delight
And Your Heart is my only All,
   Only All, only All.
My Supreme, my Supreme, my Supreme!

139

My Lord, my Lord, my Lord,
I am happy, I am happier, I am happiest
Only when I feel that
I am Your bond-slave.

140

I think of You, God.
God says to me, "No good, no good."
   I pray to You, God.
God says to me, "No good, no good."
   I meditate on You, God.
God says to me, "No good, no good."
   I love You, God.
God says to me, "No good, no good."
   I serve You, God.
God says to me, "No good, no good."
   I surrender to You, God.
God says to me, "No good, no good."
   I am all gratitude to You, God.
God says to me, "No good, no good."
   I claim You, God, as my own, very own.
God, You claim me as Your own, very own.
God says to me, "Good, good, very good,
   My child, My child!"

141

My Lord, my Lord, my Lord,
Never, never take a leave of absence.
My heart and I shall die, die, die
   Immediately.

142

Sorrow, sorrow, sorrow, sorrow,
Every day my heart-field
   You harrow.
But before my earth-life is done,
I shall devour God's Nectar-Sun.

143

Hope, hope, my hope,
Do not desert me!
Continue to nurture
My life-tree.

144

Life and death,
Life and death,
Life and death.
Death and life,
Death and life,
Death and life.
Life conquers death
To sing and play and dance
With the ever-blossoming Beyond.
Death conquers life
Not to torture, but to treasure
The beauty of life's heart
And the fragrance of life's soul.

145

When God says yes,
My heart says yes.
When God says no,
My heart says no.
Only then my God-oneness-life
Blooms and blossoms,
And God claims me
As His own, own, own —
Very own.

146

My outer journey cries and smiles.
My inner journey blooms and blossoms.
And I am the hope-promise-journey
   Of Eternity.

147

Every day I feed
My Inner Pilot
With my complete and constant
Surrender to His Will.

148

Before I start my running,
My Lord looks into my eyes
And smiles and smiles.
After I end my running,
I look at my Lord's Feet
And smile and smile.

149

God the Flute-Heart
   I love.
God the Thunder-Eye
   I need.

150

I race, I race, I race, I race
To be my Supreme's boundless Grace.
I race, I race, I race, I race
To see my Supreme's golden Face.

151

God does not want anyone
To fall and roam.
He wants all His children
To live in His Heart-Home.

152

Do not give up hope,
Do not give up hope!
Hope will give you
A Heaven-climbing rope.

153

My life is full of God-Blessings.
My heart is full of God-Songs.
My mind is full of God-Stories.
My vital is full of God-Flames.
My body is full of God-Dreams.
My thoughts are made of God's Will.
    I am in thrill,
    I am in thrill,
    I am in thrill!

154

My Lord,
Your Sun-Fire-Eye
    Frightens me,
Your Moon-Sweetness-Heart
    Enlightens me
And Your Thunder-Kick-Feet
    Liberate me
From the ignorance-world-night.

155

Peace I need to see the Face
Of my Absolute Lord Supreme.
Bliss I need to sail and fly with Him
And breathe and be His Dream.

156

Every morning
My devotion-heart offers
Streaming gratitude-tears
To my Lord Supreme
And devours the golden dust
Of His golden Feet.

157

My heart runs
The world's longest race,
And not my mind.
My Lord runs ahead of me;
My breath runs behind.

158

Every morn and every eve
My heart and I sing
A new Golden Shore-song.
With twinkling eyes
And dancing heads,
The cosmic gods
And goddesses throng.

159

Let me be good.
Let me be self-giving and pure.
My Supreme Lord's express Arrival
    Shall then be sure.

160

My Lord Supreme, I am praying to You
To bless all the marathon runners
With Your sweet and fond Marathon-Love.
My Lord, they desperately need
   Your Compassion.
My Lord, I am also praying to You
To bless our self-giving organisers.
Self-giving is the right word, my Lord.
They always serve You lovingly
   And self-givingly,
And at times sleeplessly.

My Lord, I am also praying to You
To bless profusely the helpers
And also the well-wishers
   Of this marathon.
May all the runners run
   Smilingly and happily
While covering the entire distance.

161

O my rainbow-heart-sky,
   In you I see
The beauty of the Unknowable,
   In you I feel
The silence of the Unknowable.

162

The outer run has a destination.
The inner run knows no destination.
The inner run is a run of the Beyond,
For the ever-transcending Beyond.
The outer run asks me who I was.
My answer: I was a God-dreamer.
The inner run asks me who I am.
My answer: I am a God-lover.
Finally, God asks me who I would like to be.
My answer: My Lord, I would like to be
Your Eternity's server-slave.
My Lord says, "No, not correct!
I would like you to be the co-pilot
Of My Eternity's Golden Boat-Journey."

163

My Lord, please forgive me.
Today I do not have any special prayer
To place at Your Feet.

"My child, tomorrow you must pray to Me
More than usual."

My Lord, today I am unable to think of You.

"My child, tomorrow you must think of Me
Much more than usual."

My Lord, today I am unable to love You.

"My child,
Tomorrow you must and must and must
Love Me infinitely more
Than you usually do.
My child, today I am forgiving you,
But you must not be negligent
   In your prayers.
You must not be negligent
   In thinking of Me.
You must not be negligent
   In loving Me.
If you want to claim Me to be yours
And if I want to claim you to be Mine,
Then you must never, never, never
Forget your morning spiritual
Love-devotion-surrender-disciplines."

164

No more my life will walk along
A God-empty road.
I am now blossoming
With a lifelong
   God-Touch-Smile,
I am now blossoming
With a lifelong
   God-Touch-Song,
And I am now blossoming
With a lifelong
   God-Touch-Embrace.

165

Not true:
God thinks of me only one time
   During my entire life.
God thinks of me
   All the time.

Not true:
God loves me only one time.
God loves me
   All the time.

Not true:
God needs me only one time.
God needs me
   All the time.

Not true:
God highly appreciates me
   Only one time.
God highly appreciates me
   All the time.

Not true:
God wants me to be another God
   Only for a fleeting day.
God wants me to be another God
   For Eternity.

166

My God-gratitude-heart
Blooms and blossoms
In my soul-beauty's
Heaven-plenitude-smiles.

167

My Lord,
You have given me Your own Eye
   To see the world.
You have given me Your own Ears
   To hear the world.
You have given me Your own Heart
   To love the world.
You have given me all that You have
And all that You are
   To give to the world.
My Lord,
Do give me one more thing.
Please, please give me Your own Feet
To worship You
   Sleeplessly and breathlessly,
My Lord, my Lord.

168

Every morning God comes down
From His highest Heaven
To bless my climbing
   Aspiration-heart-flames
With His Infinity's
   Peace-Bliss-Heart.

169

Every day a new morning angel
Wakes me up to celebrate
   God's Birthday
By clasping God's Eye,
   Embracing God's Heart
      And worshipping God's Feet.

170

When I think of God,
God says to me,
"I am not fully satisfied with you."
When I pray to God,
God says to me,
"I am not fully satisfied with you."
When I meditate on God,
God says to me,
"I am not fully satisfied with you."
When I say to God,
"My Lord, I love You only
And I need You only,"
God says to me,
"My child, come to Me
And be with Me
All the time, all the time."

171

My Supreme,
Out of Your infinite Compassion
You have bound Yourself
Tight, very tight, in the finite
So that we can love You,
Catch You, embrace You
And become Your choice instruments
   Here on earth,
My Supreme!

172

God loves me most dearly.
Therefore, He examines me,
He judges me
Constantly and severely.

173

My Lord,
Be pleased to pour more and more
Your Wisdom-Light
Into the mind of the seekers —
To smile at the morning beauty's sun
And continue smiling during the day
To please You in a very special way.

174

The morning hope-beauty blesses
   The morning runners.
The evening peace-fragrance blesses
   The evening runners.
The outer morning runners
And the outer evening runners
Are helping considerably
Their inner runners' aspiration,
Dedication and manifestation.

175

My Lord,
This morning You are asking me
To join Nature
In her prayer to You:
"My Lord,
You have given me
Beauty infinite,
But You have not given me
My duty."
"My child,
Your duty
Is to climb up incessantly
   To clasp My Feet
And devour the golden dust
   Of My Feet."

176

My Lord, my Lord!
In Your Compassion-flooded Eye
I have discovered my All.

177

My Lord,
You want me to run every day.
Do You ever run?
"My child,
I run not only every day,
But also at every moment.
Do you know why?
I run constantly
From one end of My creation
To the other end.
If I do not run ceaselessly,
My creation will become inactive,
Inert and uselessly idle.
At every moment I run
To awaken and energise
My entire creation."

178

My Supreme,
I wish to see You
Either in my heart's happiness
Or in my life's soulfulness.
This is my most sincere prayer
To You, my Supreme!

179

No more self-indulgence,
No more self-indulgence!
I shall run outwardly
To see Nature's God.
I shall run inwardly
To see Heaven's highest Height.
No more self-indulgence,
No more self-indulgence!

180

Every kneeling prayer
Receives God's
Fondness-Blessings.

181

I have given God what I have:
   The tears of my heart.
God has given me what He has:
   The Smiles of His Eye.
But alas,
One thing we have not been able
To give to each other:
Satisfaction, mutual satisfaction.

182

Today's runners:
Brave you are,
Daring you are,
Weather-defying you are,
God-loving you are,
God-fulfilling you are.
Spirituality braves all obstacles
And then it receives
The Victory-Garland from God.

183

Early in the morning
When we offer
Our pure love to God,
   We do the good thing.
And when we offer
Our pure devotion to God,
   We do the better thing.
Finally, when we offer
Our pure surrender to God,
   We do absolutely by far
     The best thing.

184

The early morning running
Is the God-pleasing
And God-fulfilling dedication
Of the body, vital, mind and heart.

MY RACE-PRAYERS

185

Human life is a series
Of inner and outer battles.
Running, jumping, throwing,
Sports and physical fitness
Help us win the outer battles.
Prayers, meditations
And our surrender to God's Will
Help us win the inner battles.

186

I admire God the Dreamer.
I adore God the Smiler.
I love God the Runner.

187

Each time we prayerfully, soulfully
　And self-givingly run,
We make a most serious commitment
　To our God-manifestation-task.

188

The celestial beauty and fragrance
　Of the early morning
Adorn the hearts
Of all God-loving and God-serving
　Children-runners.

189

My outer success gives my Lord
    Immense joy.
My inner progress gives my Lord
    Immeasurable joy.

190

Every morning
God the Hope blesses my life,
God the Promise blesses my heart,
God the Will-Power blesses me.

191

Earth knows only one name:
    Suffering.
Heaven knows only one name:
    Joy.
My soul knows only one name:
    Light.
My heart knows only one Name:
    Lord.
My mind knows only one Name:
    God.
My life knows only one Name:
    Pilot, my Inner Pilot.
And I know only one Name:
    Supreme, my Absolute Supreme.

192

My Lord,
Do give my heart the strength
　To love You most intensely.
My Lord,
Do give my life the strength
　To need You most sincerely.
My Lord,
Do give my legs the strength
　To run most speedily.
My Lord,
Do give me the strength
　To manifest You here on earth
　　Most unconditionally.

193

With the smiles of my soul
And the tears of my heart,
I have made a most beautiful
And fragrant garland,
And I am now placing it
At the Feet of my Lord Supreme.

194

God says to my prayers,
"My children,
I love your sincerity and purity."
God says to my meditations,
"My children,
I love your tranquillity and immensity."
God says to me,
"My child,
I love your outer regularity
And your inner punctuality."

195

Alas,
Because of our teeming self-doubts,
The intense and immense joy
Of our morning hearts
Cannot come to the fore
And bloom and blossom.

196

Morning is the best time
To enter into my rose-garden-heart
   To enjoy deeply
Its exquisite beauty and fragrance.

197

To talk about God
Is infinitely easier
Than to think of God.

To think of God
Is infinitely easier
Than to pray to God.

To pray to God
Is infinitely easier
Than to become one
With God's Will.

198

My sleepless love for God
   Is the beauty
Of my ascending heart
   And the fragrance
Of my descending soul.

199

God's ever-blossoming
   Infinite Beauties
My soul can see.
But God's ever-multiplying
   Infinite Duties
Remain unknowable.

200

The tears of my heart
And the Smiles of my Lord
Play together and sing together
   Sleeplessly.

Notes to *My Race Prayers, part 2*

101. 6 April 2004, New York.
102. 9 April 2004, New York.
103. 10 April 2004, New York.
104. 17 April 2004, New York.
105. 24 April 2004, New York.
106. 8 May 2004, New York.
107. 15 May 2004, New York.
108. 22 May 2004, New York.
109. 5 June 2004, New York.
110. 12 June 2004, New York.
111. 26 June 2004, New York.
112. 3 July 2004, New York.
113. 10 July 2004, New York.
114. 17 July 2004, New York.
115. 24 July 2004, New York.
116. 31 July 2004, New York.
117. 7 August 2004, New York.
118. 14 August 2004, New York.
119. 21 August 2004, New York.
120. 25 August 2004, New York.
121. 28 August 2004, New York.
122. 4 September 2004, New York.
123. 11 September 2004, New York.
124. 18 September 2004, New York.
125. 25 September 2004, New York.
126. 9 October 2004, New York.
127. 16 October 2004, New York.
128. 30 October 2004, New York.
129. 6 November 2004, New York.
130. 13 November 2004, New York.

131. 20 November 2004, New York.
132. 13 December 2004, Xiamen, China.
133. 23 December 2004, Qingdao, China.
134. 26 December 2004, Qingdao, China.
135. 30 December 2004, Qingdao, China.
136. 2 January 2005, Qingdao, China.
137. 9 January 2005, Qingdao, China.
138. 19 February 2005, New York.
139. 26 February 2005, New York.
140. 5 March 2005, New York.
141. 12 March 2005, New York.
142. 19 March 2005, New York.
143. 26 March 2005, New York.
144. 2 April 2005, New York.
145. 9 April 2005, New York.
146. 16 April 2005, New York.
147. 23 April 2005, New York.
148. 30 April 2005, New York.
149. 30 April 2005, New York.
150. 6 May 2005, New York.
151. 11 June 2005, New York.
152. 18 June 2005, New York.
153. 9 July 2005, New York.
154. 16 July 2005, New York.
155. 23 July 2005, New York.
156. 30 July 2005, New York.
157. 6 August 2005, New York.
158. 13 August 2005, New York.
159. 20 August 2005, New York.
160. 25 August 2005, New York.
161. 28 August 2005, New York.
162. 3 September 2005, New York.

163. 24 September 2005, New York.
164. 1 October 2005, New York.
165. 22 October 2005, New York.
166. 29 October 2005, New York.
167. 5 November 2005, New York.
168. 12 November 2005, New York.
169. 19 November 2005, New York.
170. 30 November 2005, Pangkor Island, Malaysia.
171. 3 December 2005, Pangkor Island, Malaysia.
172. 7 December 2005, Pangkor Island, Malaysia.
173. 9 December 2005, Pangkor Island, Malaysia.
174. 14 December 2005, Kuantan, Malaysia.
175. 17 December 2005, Kuantan, Malaysia.
176. 21 December 2005, Kuantan, Malaysia.
177. 24 December 2005, Kuantan, Malaysia.
178. 28 December 2005, Kuantan, Malaysia.
179. 31 December 2005, Kuantan, Malaysia.
180. 2 January 2006, Kuantan, Malaysia.
181. 5 January 2006, Kijal, Malaysia.
182. 7 January 2006, Kijal, Malaysia.
183. 11 January 2006, Kijal, Malaysia.
184. 14 January 2006, Kijal, Malaysia.
185. 18 January 2006, Kijal, Malaysia.
186. 21 January 2006, Kijal, Malaysia.
187. 1 February 2006, Penang, Malaysia.
188. 5 February 2006, Penang, Malaysia.
189. 8 February 2006, Penang, Malaysia.
191. 18 February 2006, Langkawi, Malaysia.
192. 23 February 2006, Langkawi, Malaysia.
193. 4 March 2006, New York.
194. 11 March 2006, New York.
195. 18 March 2006, New York.

196. 25 March 2006, New York.
197. 1 April 2006, New York.
198. 9 April 2006, New York.
199. 15 April 2006, New York.
200. 22 April 2006, New York.

MY RACE-PRAYERS

PART 3

201

O my blue-gold heart-bird,
I love you,
I need you,
I treasure you.
You are my joy,
You are my pride,
You are my All.

202

I love my Lord's
Whisper-Blessings.
My Lord loves my
Hunger-yearnings.

203

Long before God comes to us,
He sends His angels to us.
Before His angels come to us,
God sends us divine thoughts
   And divine feelings.
Before the divine thoughts
   And divine feelings,
He gives us purity-hearts.
With purity we all must begin
   Our spiritual journey.

204

My Lord says to me,
"My child,
Take your outer pain
As your inner gain.
Take your outer failures
As your inner triumphs.
Take your outer life
As an experience.
Take your inner life
As your path-finder."

205

Heaven's Silence-Music
Is only for the hearts
Of God's Victory-singers.

206

In my aspiration-life,
My Master-obedience
Is my heart's
God-blossoming dawn.

207

Only one attachment:
God's Will.
No other attachments,
Old or new!

208

My Lord,
I run and run and run and run
To make You happy.
"My child,
You are the smile of My Eye,
You are the beauty of My Heart
And you are the pride of My Life."

209

Krishna, my Lord,
Your morning flute
Feeds my heart.
Your twilight cows
Feed my eyes.

210

The outer rain
Proudly comes down
From the expansion-sky.
The inner Rain
Blessingfully descends
From God's Compassion-Eye.

211

I have three indispensable Saviours:
My Lord's lavishing Hand,
My Lord's cherishing Heart,
My Lord's protecting Eye.

212

I am the world's longest distance
Daring and shattering runner —
My Supreme Lord's Sun-Power-Smile
And His Moon-Bliss-Love-winner.

213

My tears and smiles
Sleeplessly feed
God's birthless and deathless
Heart-Hunger.

214

I am happy, only happy,
When I place
My naughty mind
And my haughty head
At God's Feet.

215

To all the marathon runners
I am blessingfully offering
My heart's boundless joy,
Boundless gratitude
And boundless pride, pride, pride.

216

Everything is possible.
In a twinkling
I can clasp God's Eye.
In a twinkling
I can touch God's Feet.
In a twinkling
I can breathe God's Heart.

217

The life that has no goal
Is an utter failure-life.
The life that has a goal
Wins the Smile of God.

218

We love our desire-life
Infinitely more than we love God.
God loves only us,
And never, never, never, never
Our desire-life.

219

I speak to God's
Golden Feet.
God speaks to my
Broken heart.

220

True, true, true,
True, true, true —
A pure thought
Can remain unchallenged
In my aspiration-heart.

221

I pray to God's Eye
   For love.
I pray to God's Heart
   For devotion.
I pray to God's Feet
   For surrender.

222

First you must bask
In the sunshine
Of your Master's grace
Before you can see
God's Face.

MY RACE-PRAYERS

223

I pray to God
To see His golden Feet.
I meditate on God
To be His choice instrument.

224

While running,
I feel God's Love,
God's Joy and God's Pride
Inside my heart
At every moment.

225

The outer sun
Sadly tells me
How far I am from God.
The inner sun
Secretly tells me
How close I am to God.

226

A self-giving thought
Is a God-fulfilling
Achievement-joy.

227

The outer running
Is the God-awareness-joy.
The inner running
Is the God-closeness-ecstasy.

228

My Lord, my Lord!
In Heaven I adore
Your dreaming Eye.
My Lord, my Lord!
On earth I worship
Your protecting Feet.

229

Down I bring my Lord
   To earth
To cry with me
And weep with my heart.
Up my Lord carries me
   To Heaven
To dream with Him
For a new creation.

230

My life is a humble
Earth-builder.
My heart is an eager
Heaven-promoter.

231

In secrecy supreme
My Beloved Lord tells me
That I have done extremely well
In all my love-devotion-surrender
    Examinations.

232

My eyes can fool me,
My ears can fool me,
But not my heart
That loves God only.

233

Every morning and every evening
My soul, my heart and I
Salute and salute and salute
Our Lord's Victory-Banner.

234

Not God's Kindness,
Not God's Strictness,
But God's Heart-Tears
Have changed my life completely.

235

My Lord,
Do tell me the secret of secrets:
How I can please You all the time
In Your own Way.
"My child,
Sing, sing and sing
Only surrender-songs."

236

Running early in the morning
With God-devotion-heart-joy
Is absolutely the best way
   To start the day.

237

My Lord Supreme,
May I bask every morning
   In the Sunshine
Of Your Heaven-born Smiles.

238

My Lord, my Lord, my Lord,
You live inside my painful body.
You also live inside my blissful heart.
Which place do You prefer?
"My child,
I have no preference.
I love your body and your heart equally.
I suffer and suffer
With your painful body.
I enjoy and enjoy
Your blissful heart."

239

My Lord,
When I pray, it is all wrong.
When I meditate, it is all wrong.
When I serve, it is all wrong.
My Lord, what can I do?
"My child,
Before you pray,
Ask Me to pray in and through you.
Before you meditate,
Ask Me to meditate in and through you.
Before you serve,
Ask Me to serve in and through you.
Give Me the full responsibility.
You just be the witness.
Watch Me, what I do and how I do it."

240

God's Face I love.
God's Eye I love more.
God's Heart I love much more.
God's Feet I love infinitely more.

241

True, my eyes are empty
    Of God's Face,
But my heart is all
God's blossomed Face.

242

Each running step
Beautifully blossoms
As a divine opportunity
To please God in His own Way
Along His Eternity's Road.

243

My constant upward flight
Solely depends on
My heart's receptivity-depth.

244

In my inner life,
I am a Heaven-climbing cry.
In my outer life,
I am a man-serving tree.

245

My failure-life
    Is painful.
My success-life
    Is delightful.
My progress-life
    Is powerful.

246

I chose God-obedience
    To become
God's Heart-Rose.

247

Fast, faster, fastest
    Go alone.
Every day God will speak to you
    Over the phone.

248

Each God-given responsibility-task
Is a golden opportunity
To please God in His own Way.

249

My sleepless surrender
   To God's Will
Entirely depends on
My unconditional love of God.

250

May my heart
Be the beauty
Of a morning rose-garden.

251

In the morning
I swim in the river
   Of God-aspiration.
In the evening
I swim in the sea
   Of God-surrender.

252

Every morning and every evening
I feed my Lord Supreme
With my soul's beauty,
My heart's sincerity
And my life's simplicity.

253

I love the blossoming Beauty
    Of the morning God.
I love the deepening Peace
    Of the evening God.
I love, I love, I love.

254

This morning my Lord Supreme
Has blessingfully shared with me
His most secret
And most sacred Dream —
The time when this world of ours
Shall be inundated with my Lord's
Peace-Beauty and Peace-Fragrance.

255

My Lord,
Please, please, please
Bless me with a supreme Secret.
"My child,
I do not want you to be great.
I do not want you to be good.
I want you to be Mine, only Mine.
This is My supreme Secret."

256

   I sail
My golden dream-reality-boat
   Between
My God-obedience-life-shore
   And
My God-gratitude-heart-shore.

257

Every morning is the birth
   Of a new hope.
Every day is the birth
   Of a new promise.
Every evening is the birth
   Of a new peace.
Every night is the birth
   Of a new dream.

258

Morning is the sacred time
  To offer the world
My God-happiness-soul.
Morning is the secret time
  To feed
My God-longing heart.

259

My sincere humility-life
  Is God's
Precious utility-joy.

260

I sing for God soulfully.
God sings for me blessingfully.
We'll go on, go on
Through Eternity.

261

When the tears of my heart
Go to my Lord crawling,
My Lord immediately embraces them
With infinite Affection, Love,
Sweetness and Fondness,
And then teaches them
How to sprint
   Faster than the fastest,
How to fly
   Higher than the highest
And how to dive
   Deeper than the deepest.

262

Do not surrender to your fate.
Do not accept your fate.
Love God more and more,
   Unconditionally.
God has two big Ears.
He will transform
Your earth-bound fate
Into the Heaven-free Bliss.

263

God's Eye is my body's
   Protection-Temple.
God's Heart is my life's
   Illumination-Shrine.

264

No lasting defeat,
No lasting failure!
At God's Hour —
Victory, victory!
Now just endure.

265

My Lord does not believe
In my very clever mind-flattery.
He believes only
In my life's world-service-tree.

266

Every morning
And every evening
My soul most devotedly records
The Nectar-flooded Discourses
Of my Lord Beloved Supreme.

267

I must make my heart
A pure God-surrender-song
So that I can strike
God's largest Victory-Gong.

268

Marathon is
An unimaginable joy-experience
Of the heart.
Marathon is
An unbearable suffering-experience
Of the body, the vital and the mind.

Short talk offered before the marathon:

I have invoked special Blessings of my Absolute Lord Beloved Supreme for all the marathon runners. Each marathon is an unimaginable joy for the runner's heart. Again, each marathon is an unspeakable torture for the body, the vital and the mind. Our philosophy is to transcend — transcend the physical pain and transcend our previous achievements. My blessings, my love and my gratitude I am offering to each and every runner.

And my special request to you all is this: when you find you are tired, extremely, extremely tired, exhausted, then do not continue, do not continue.

All my love. Start!

269

May I be a morning
Ascending wave of bliss.
May I be an evening
Descending wave of peace.

270

Every day I ply my life-boat
Between
My dreaming soul-shore
And
My crying heart-shore.

271

My Lord Supreme,
No more will You suffer
For my sake.
My life has stopped swimming
In ignorance-lake.

272

Life is a constant battle
Between the human in us
And the divine in us —
And the divine in us
Will ultimately wear
Victory's garland.

273

The fever of the body
Comes and goes.
May my God-love-heart-fever
Remain forever and forever.
The fever of the body
Is torture unbearable.
My God-love-heart-fever
Is rapture unimaginable.

MY RACE-PRAYERS

Notes to *My Race Prayers, part 3*

201. 29 April 2006, New York.
202. 6 May 2006, New York.
203. 13 May 2006, New York.
204. 20 May 2006, New York.
205. 27 May 2006, New York.
206. 3 June 2006, New York.
207. 10 June 2006, New York.
208. 11 June 2006, New York.
209. 17 June 2006, New York.
210. 24 June 2006, New York.
211. 22 July 2006, New York.
212. 22 July 2006, New York.
213. 5 August 2006, New York.
214. 19 August 2006, New York.
215. 25 August 2006, New York.
216. 9 September 2006, New York.
217. 23 September 2006, New York.
218. 30 September 2006, New York.
219. 7 October 2006, New York.
220. 14 October 2006, New York.
221. 4 November 2006, New York.
222. 11 November 2006, New York.
223. 18 November 2006, New York.
224. 2 December 2006, Belek, Turkey.
225. 7 December 2006, Antalya, Turkey.
226. 10 December 2006, Antalya, Turkey.
227. 13 December 2006, Antalya, Turkey.
228. 16 December 2006, Antalya, Turkey.
229. 20 December 2006, Antalya, Turkey.
230. 23 December 2006, Antalya, Turkey.

231. 26 December 2006, Antalya, Turkey.
232. 30 December 2006, Varna, Bulgaria.
233. 3 January 2007, Varna, Bulgaria.
234. 6 January 2007, Varna, Bulgaria.
235. 10 January 2007, Varna, Bulgaria.
236. 13 January 2007, Varna, Bulgaria.
237. 17 January 2007, Varna, Bulgaria.
238. 27 January 2007, Cha-Am, Thailand.
239. 31 January 2007, Cha-Am, Thailand.
240. 3 February 2007, Cha-Am, Thailand.
241. 9 February 2007, Chiang Mai, Thailand.
242. 13 February 2007, Chiang Mai, Thailand.
243. 16 February 2007, Chiang Mai, Thailand.
244. 20 February 2007, Chiang Mai, Thailand.
245. 23 February 2007, Chiang Mai, Thailand.
246. 3 March 2007, New York.
247. 10 March 2007, New York.
248. 10 March 2007, New York.
249. 31 March 2007, New York.
250. 7 April 2007, New York.
251. 10 April 2007, New York.
252. 14 April 2007, New York.
253. 21 April 2007, New York.
254. 28 April 2007, New York.
255. 5 May 2007, New York.
256. 12 May 2007, New York.
257. 26 May 2007, New York.
258. 2 June 2007, New York.
259. 9 June 2007, New York.
260. 23 June 2007, New York.
261. 7 July 2007, New York.
262. 14 July 2007, New York.

263. 21 July 2007, New York.
264. 28 July 2007, New York.
265. 4 August 2007, New York.
266. 11 August 2007, New York.
267. 19 August 2007, New York.
268. 24 August 2007, Rockland Lake State Park, New York.
269. 26 August 2007, New York.
270. 1 September 2007, New York.
271. 8 September 2007, New York.
272. 15 September 2007, New York.
273. 29 September 2007, New York.

PART XXII

MY BLESSINGFUL AND PRIDE-FLOODED DEDICATION TO THE INDOMITABLE RUNNERS OF THE 3100-MILE SELF-TRANSCENDENCE RACE, 2006

MY BLESSINGFUL AND PRIDE-FLOODED DEDICATION TO THE INDOMITABLE
RUNNERS OF THE 3100-MILE SELF-TRANSCENDENCE RACE, 2006

1

I know
How to run and run
   And run.
My Lord Supreme
   Knows
How to love me
   With His
Blessing-Pride.

2

I run the world's
   Longest Race
To dine with God's
Boundless Grace.

3

   History's
Longest Run-Race
   Is God's
Smile-blossomed Face.

4

   The world's
Longest distance-runners
Are God's
   Heart-treasured
     Children.

5

   Each
Longest distance-runner
Is a very special
Affection-wave of
    God.

6

   The real Name
Of God is Blessing.
   The real Name
Of God's Heart
   Is Love.
The real Name
Of God's Life
   Is Concern.

7

   When
We talk to God,
We show our greatness.
   When
God talks to us,
He gives us His Goodness.

MY BLESSINGFUL AND PRIDE-FLOODED DEDICATION TO THE INDOMITABLE
RUNNERS OF THE 3100-MILE SELF-TRANSCENDENCE RACE, 2006

8

Earth-servers
　Are
God's Heart-Climbers.

9

　Each
Self-giving thought
　Is a
Rainbow-Beauty.

10

God's Eye
　Is God's
Sleepless Compassion
　For
His aspiring children.

God's Heart
　Is God's
Breathless Concern
　For
His serving children.

11

    Each
Longest distance-runner
    Is
God's special
    Prize-winner.

12

Prayer is our
Mountain-climbing
    Pride.
Meditation is our
Fountain-enjoying
    Heart.

13

    A
God-rising life
    Is a
God-shining
    Heart.

MY BLESSINGFUL AND PRIDE-FLOODED DEDICATION TO THE INDOMITABLE
RUNNERS OF THE 3100-MILE SELF-TRANSCENDENCE RACE, 2006

14

My God-dependence
Is the Beauty
Of my life.

My God-dependence
Is the Fragrance
Of my heart.

15

Running dedication
Knows no enjoying
   Vacation.

16

To-day
My mind is
Utterly absent
Of self-doubt.

17

   I
Wish to have
A new name:
God-dedication-heartbeat.

18

My life-boat plies
   Between
My God-invocation-heart
   And
My God-dedication-life.

19

My only Paradise
   Is my
God-aspiration-heart-garden.

20

Every day
I feed on my Lord's
Compassion-Eye-Beauty.

21

My Earth
Tells me:
   "I can."
My Heaven
Tells me:
   "I am."

MY BLESSINGFUL AND PRIDE-FLOODED DEDICATION TO THE INDOMITABLE
RUNNERS OF THE 3100-MILE SELF-TRANSCENDENCE RACE, 2006

22

Earth-mind
Proudly thunders.
Heaven-heart
Sweetly whispers.

23

I need
A new heart
To love God more.
I need
A new life
To need God more.

24

Each
New day
Is flooded
    With
Rainbow-opportunities.

25

The world's
Longest distance runner
Has at once won
God's Compassion-Eye
    And
God's Protection-Heart.

26

My mind wants
God's Power-Tower.
My heart needs
God's Peace-Sea.

27

I do not
Measure God's
Blessingful gifts.
I only treasure
   Them.

28

God prepares
The souls for the earth.
God prepares
The hearts for the Heaven.

29

God's Heart
Is our Progress-thrill.

30

My Lord
Amplifies and amplifies
My heart-cries.

MY BLESSINGFUL AND PRIDE-FLOODED DEDICATION TO THE INDOMITABLE
RUNNERS OF THE 3100-MILE SELF-TRANSCENDENCE RACE, 2006

31

My
Success depends
On my God-loving
Thoughts.

32

My
Progress
Depends upon
My God-surrendering
Will.

33

My
Surrender-heart
Becomes
God the Smile.
My
Surrender-life
Becomes
God the Pride.

34

My
Sleepless God-faith-vigil
Is indispensable.

35

My heart is desperate
For God's Compassion.
I am desperate
For God's instruction.

36

My soul
Is the Earth-discoverer.
My heart
Is the Heaven-discoverer.

37

My heart lives on
God's Compassion-tears.
I live on
God's Forgiveness-Smiles.

38

God
Loves my mind's
Emptiness.
God
Loves my heart's
Sweetness.
God
Loves my life's
Fulness.

MY BLESSINGFUL AND PRIDE-FLOODED DEDICATION TO THE INDOMITABLE
RUNNERS OF THE 3100-MILE SELF-TRANSCENDENCE RACE, 2006

39

God's
Compassion-Eye
Strengthens
My heart.

40

God's
Justice-Eye
Purifies my
Mind.

41

God
Playfully tries
To hide from
Our eyes.
But His Heart
Prevents.

42

A
God-faith-seed
Becomes slowly
But unmistakably
A God-treasure-tree.

43

God's Heaven-Music
Thrills
My heart every
Morning.

44

My
Silence-heart
Is God's microphone.

45

When
My heart cries,
God's Heart-Door
Opens up *immediately*.

46

Each
God-loving thought
Is as fresh as
A breath of dawn.

MY BLESSINGFUL AND PRIDE-FLOODED DEDICATION TO THE INDOMITABLE
RUNNERS OF THE 3100-MILE SELF-TRANSCENDENCE RACE, 2006

47

Come what may,
I shall run and
Run and end my
Pilgrim-Journey
At my Lord's
Feet.

48

God
Feeds my hopes.
God
Feeds my promises.
Alas, when
Will I be able to feed God's
Heart and His Feet,
When?!

49

May my outer
Life succeed.
May my inner
Life proceed.

50

To work
Devotedly
Is to walk very
Fast towards
God.

51

To-day's
Victory
We celebrate
Only to invoke
A new
Goal.

MY BLESSINGFUL AND PRIDE-FLOODED DEDICATION TO THE INDOMITABLE RUNNERS OF THE 3100-MILE SELF-TRANSCENDENCE RACE, 2006

Notes to *My blessingful and pride-flooded dedication to the indomitable runners of the 3100-mile Self-Transcendence Race, 2006*

1. June 21st, 2006.
2. June 22nd, 2006.
3. June 23rd, 2006.
4. June 24th, 2006.
5. June 25th, 2006.
6. June 26th, 2006.
7. June 27th, 2006.
8. June 28th, 2006.
9. June 29th, 2006.
10. June 30th, 2006.
11. July 1st, 2006.
12. July 2nd, 2006.
13. July 3rd, 2006.
14. July 4th, 2006.
15. July 5th, 2006.
16. July 6th, 2006.
17. July 7th, 2006.
18. July 8th, 2006.
19. July 9th, 2006.
20. July 10th, 2006.
21. July 11th, 2006.
22. July 12th, 2006.
23. July 13th, 2006.
24. July 14th, 2006.
25. July 15th, 2006.
26. July 16th, 2006.
27. July 17th, 2006.
28. July 18th, 2006.
29. July 19th, 2006.

30. July 20th, 2006.
31. July 21st, 2006.
32. July 22nd, 2006.
33. July 23rd, 2006.
34. July 24th, 2006.
35. July 25th, 2006.
36. July 26th, 2006.
37. July 27th, 2006.
38. July 28th, 2006.
39. July 29th, 2006.
40. July 30th, 2006.
41. July 31st, 2006.
42. August 1st, 2006.
43. August 2nd, 2006.
44. August 3rd, 2006.
45. August 4th, 2006.
46. August 5th, 2006.
47. August 6th, 2006.
48. August 7th, 2006.
49. August 8th, 2006.
50. August 9th, 2006.
51. August 10th, 2006.

PART XXIII

MY BLESSINGFUL AND PRIDE-FLOODED
DEDICATION TO THE INDOMITABLE
RUNNERS OF THE 3100-MILE
SELF-TRANSCENDENCE RACE, 2007

MY BLESSINGFUL AND PRIDE-FLOODED DEDICATION TO THE INDOMITABLE
RUNNERS OF THE 3100-MILE SELF-TRANSCENDENCE RACE, 2007

52

I offer
My outer run-results
To the Compassion-Eye
Of my Lord Supreme.
I place
My inner run-results
At the Feet of my Lord
Beloved Supreme.

53

My mind
Takes me out to show me
The world-market.
My heart
Brings me in to show me
My Lord's Heart-Garden.

54

Time knows
How to fly.
I know
How to cry.
At least
In one respect
We two
Are perfect.

55

To-day
The flames of my
    aspiration-heart are
Climbing and climbing
    to reach the
Zenith-Height.

56

I
Plan a long
Vacation.
God
Plans my immediate
Illumination.

57

The outer runner
Cries and smiles.
The inner runner
Sees and becomes.

58

I make my Lord
Supreme *extremely*
    happy when I
    claim Him as
    my own, very own.

MY BLESSINGFUL AND PRIDE-FLOODED DEDICATION TO THE INDOMITABLE
RUNNERS OF THE 3100-MILE SELF-TRANSCENDENCE RACE, 2007

59

Everyday
  my heart and I
  can love God a
  little more.

60

My God-gratitude
  is my heart's most
  precious treasure.

61

My Lord's
Silence-praise of
  my great achievements
  is most powerful.

62

My heart has only
  one task:
  love God,
  love God at
  every moment.

63

There are so many
   ways to please God.
The easiest way
   is to SMILE at
   God.

64

A single God-touch gives the seeker
   enormous, ceaseless, unimaginable thrill.

65

Give not what you have.
Give what you are.
Soon, very soon
   your heart will
   become a
   twinkling star.

66

To think of God
   is good.
To pray to God
   is better.
To surrender to God's Will
   is by far the best.

MY BLESSINGFUL AND PRIDE-FLOODED DEDICATION TO THE INDOMITABLE
RUNNERS OF THE 3100-MILE SELF-TRANSCENDENCE RACE, 2007

67

Where is my
Lord Supreme,
   if not in my
   heart's streaming tears
   and my soul's
   beaming smiles?

68

Fear not,
God's Life loves *you*.
Doubt not,
God's Heart is all for *you*.

69

God claims me as
His own, very own.
Alas, when will
I be able to claim
God as my own, very own?
When?

70

My heart was
   born for
God-satisfaction-tears.

71

Each heart-smile
Is an
Enemy-conqueror.

72

Sincerity is the heart's most
    sacred song to please
God in His own Way.

73

To surrender to
God's Will is to become
God's all.

74

You can see God.
You can feel God.
But to describe
God is an impossible task.

75

God loves my streaming tears.
    I love
God's beaming Smiles.

MY BLESSINGFUL AND PRIDE-FLOODED DEDICATION TO THE INDOMITABLE
RUNNERS OF THE 3100-MILE SELF-TRANSCENDENCE RACE, 2007

76

God wants
My meditation-depth
To be the sweetest song
Of His Heart.

77

God
Is equally happy when
He builds and unbuilds
My heart-cottage.

78

To give is to
Become the king of the
Heart-Kingdom.

79

Only one Choice:
My Lord's
Compassion-Eye.

80

The more I love God,
The more I need God.
The more I need God,
The sooner I shall be able to please
God in His own Way.

81

My Lord, do you
    ever think of me?
My child, what
    else do I do?
What else can I do?

82

I am really happy
When I take this world as mine.

83

Happiness-seekers and
Oneness-lovers are
    very special to God.

84

God's affection is boundless for those
    who sing only God-melodies.

MY BLESSINGFUL AND PRIDE-FLOODED DEDICATION TO THE INDOMITABLE
RUNNERS OF THE 3100-MILE SELF-TRANSCENDENCE RACE, 2007

85

A true seeker lives between his mind's
Nothingness and his heart's Fulness.

86

I must never lose contact with my
Lord's Compassion-Eye and
His Forgiveness-Heart.
Never.

87

My Lord has a special fondness
    for two things:
My life of simplicity and
    my heart of sincerity.

88

My Lord's Compassion-Eye
Is my heart-home.

89

My mind takes me out.
My heart brings me in.

90

Aspiration-flames grow into the
Realisation-Sun.

91

God's Heart is the
Beloved Mother of all.
God's Eye is the Beloved Father of all.

92

Ultimately God's
Justice surrenders
    to God's Compassion.

93

The human in me loves to live.
The divine in me lives to love.

94

The happiness of the heart expedites
    the speed of the body.

95

Little by little I must
    change my life only in
God's own Way.

MY BLESSINGFUL AND PRIDE-FLOODED DEDICATION TO THE INDOMITABLE RUNNERS OF THE 3100-MILE SELF-TRANSCENDENCE RACE, 2007

96

A heart of faith is a life of
   tremendous happiness.

97

The body is the patient.
The heart is the sufferer.
The soul is the sympathiser.
God is the Ultimate Curer.

98

Alas, every day
I do so many things deliberately wrong.
It is hard to believe that
   God still *loves* me and *needs* me.

99

The outer runner is a
   Hope of God.
The inner runner is a
   Promise of God.
The God-dreamer-runner is
   God's all.

100

Life is an adventure.
Be brave. Be victorious.
God is waiting for
 you to garland *you* with
His boundless
   Joy and Pride.

101

Be good and remain good:
If you want to be a supremely
   chosen child of God.

102

I love my heart-blossom.
I adore my soul-fragrance.

103

My heart-home is my
Lord's Compassion-Eye.

104

Every day I must strengthen and
   lengthen my love of God.

MY BLESSINGFUL AND PRIDE-FLOODED DEDICATION TO THE INDOMITABLE
RUNNERS OF THE 3100-MILE SELF-TRANSCENDENCE RACE, 2007

105

God remains seated *always* inside
   the heart-body.
Do not seek Him elsewhere.

106

God the Bird has two special wings:
Compassion and Forgiveness.

107

God's Greatness frightens me.
God's Goodness enlightens me.

108

If you do not love humanity,
You are bound to lose contact
   with God.

109

The Journey's start
   is Dreamful.
The Journey's end
   is Godful.

Notes to *My blessingful and pride-flooded dedication to the indomitable runners of the 3100-mile Self-Transcendence Race, 2007*

52. 18 June 2007.
53. 19 June 2007.
54. 20 June 2007.
55. 21 June 2007.
56. 22 June 2007.
57. 23 June 2007.
58. 24 June 2007.
59. 25 June 2007.
60. 26 June 2007.
61. 27 June 2007.
62. 28 June 2007.
63. 29 June 2007.
64. 30 June 2007.
65. 1 July 2007.
66. 2 July 2007.
67. 3 July 2007.
68. 4 July 2007.
69. 5 July 2007.
70. 6 July 2007.
71. 7 July 2007.
72. 8 July 2007.
73. 9 July 2007.
74. 10 July 2007.
75. 11 July 2007.
76. 12 July 2007.
77. 13 July 2007.
78. 14 July 2007.
79. 15 July 2007.
80. 16 July 2007.

MY BLESSINGFUL AND PRIDE-FLOODED DEDICATION TO THE INDOMITABLE
RUNNERS OF THE 3100-MILE SELF-TRANSCENDENCE RACE, 2007

81. 17 July 2007.
82. 18 July 2007.
83. 19 July 2007.
84. 20 July 2007.
85. 21 July 2007.
86. 22 July 2007.
87. 23 July 2007.
88. 24 July 2007.
89. 25 July 2007.
90. 26 July 2007.
91. 27 July 2007.
92. 28 July 2007.
93. 29 July 2007
94. 30 July 2007.
95. 30 July 2007.
96. 1 August 2007.
97. 2 August 2007.
98. 3 August 2007.
99. 4 August 2007.
100. 5 August 2007.
101. 6 August 2007.
102. 7 August 2007.
103. 8 August 2007.
104. 9 August 2007.
105. 10 August 2007.
106. 11 August 2007.
107. 12 August 2007.
108. 13 August 2007.

PART XXIV

MORNING PRAYERS. POEMS ON WAR

MORNING PRAYERS. POEMS ON WAR

I — Morning prayers

1

This morning
During my meditation
My soul blessingfully spoke to me.
My human eyes and human ears
Were the soulful
   And prayerful witnesses.

"My child,
You need love
More, infinitely more,
   To succeed.

"You need devotion
More, infinitely more,
To proceed.

"You need surrender
More, infinitely more,
To make yourself happy
   And
To make Me happy.
There is no other way,
And there can be no other way."

2

My problem is this:
I cannot think
   Of God
Even for seven minutes a day.

God's problem is this:
He cannot stop thinking
   Of me
Even for seven seconds a day.

My problem is this:
I do not want to know
   How great God is,
As long as He is kind to me.

God's problem is this:
He does not want to know
   How undivine I am,
As long as I call Him my Father.

3

My Lord,
Is it possible to have happiness
   In this world?

"Definitely, My child.
I would not have created this world
If I could not create happiness
   In this world.

"My child,
There are two kinds of happiness:
Happiness real
   And happiness unreal.

"When the real in you
Pleases Me in My own Way,
That happiness is real.

"When the unreal in you
Pleases you in your own way,
That happiness is unreal.

"Do you want to know how
You can know the real happiness
   From the unreal happiness?

"When you are really happy,
You are satisfied within,
   Divinely and supremely.

"When you are unreally happy,
You get no sense of satisfaction
Either in your inner life
   Or in your outer life."

4

My Supreme Lord,
When You make me happy
   In my own way,
I feel that I have achieved
   Something great.

My Supreme Lord,
When I make You happy
   In Your own Way
What happens to You?

"My child,
I feel that I have made
   Tremendous progress,
And I also feel that the Hour
   Has struck for Me
To dream of a better, higher
   And deeper creation
In and through you."

5

My Lord Supreme,
Do give me the sweet hope
    To feel that I can
Fulfil You and please You
In Your own Way.

My Lord Supreme,
Do give me the brave courage
    To feel that I will
Fulfil You and please You
In Your own Way.

My Lord Supreme,
Do give me the surrendered life
    To feel that I am
Fulfilling You and pleasing You
In Your own Way.

6

I do not pray
To an unknown God.

I do not meditate
On an unknowable God.

I pray to the God
Whose Transcendental Eye
   Is extremely familiar.

I meditate on the God
Whose universal Heart
   Is extremely popular.

His Transcendental Eye
Tells me to make Him happy
Only in His own Way.

His Universal Heart
Tells me to become perfect
Only in His own Way.

II — Poems on war

7

My Lord,
Please forgive me.
I have not brought anything
For You this time.

"My child,
Next time you come to visit Me
    Here in Heaven,
Will you bring Me
    What I desperately need?"

Definitely, my Lord.
Please tell me what it is
    That You desperately need.

"My child,
Then bring Me
All the nuclear weapons
That the countries of the world,
Especially the superpowers,
    Have produced."

8

My Lord,
What is the difference
Between suicide and war?

"My child,
Suicide you commit
When you are an impossible fool.

"War you declare
When you are absolutely
   The worst sinner."

9

My Lord,
Everybody knows what war is
   And what peace is.
May I learn from You
   The difference?

"My child,
War is the mind's
   World-devouring problem.
Peace is the heart's
   World-illumining solution."

10

My Lord,
How can humanity
   Stop declaring war?

"My child, easily.
Just by not thinking of war,
Exactly the way humanity
   Does not think of Me."

11

My Lord,
After You created the world,
Did You ever think of war?

"My child,
I have infinitely better things
   To think of:
Love, oneness and peace."

12

My Lord,
When the war-mongers die,
Where do they go?

"My child,
I send them to a place
Where I have never been
And I shall never go,
    Never!"

13

My Lord,
Will there be
A Third World War?

"No, My child,
    Because
Every night I make it a point
To threaten and frighten
The war-mongers in their sleep."

My Lord,
Are they conscious of it?

"My child,
I do not care
If they are conscious of it,
As long as I do not allow them
To do what they want to do."

14

My Lord, Rama and Krishna fought
Against their enemies.
I am sure that they did
   The right thing.

"My child,
Rama, Krishna and I
Are inseparably one.
Therefore, how could they
   Do anything wrong?

"At that time,
The divine forces fought
   Against the undivine forces.

"But now,
To manifest the Light of the Divine,
The inner insecurity-forces
   Fight against
The outer security-forces
   To fool the outer world."

15

My Lord,
Will there be a day
   When there will be no war
And this world of ours
   Will be flooded with peace?

"My child,
Do not think of war.
Do not think of peace.
   Just become peace.
Lo and behold, war is nowhere."

16

My Lord,
As You know, thousands of people
Have been killed
   By nuclear weapons.

"My child,
I am sure that you know that
Billions and trillions of people
Have been saved
   By My Compassion-Eye."

17

My Lord,
The superpowers are decreasing
　Their nuclear weapons.
I am sure that You are pleased
　With them.

"My child,
I am indeed pleased with them,
　But not proud of them."

What do You mean,
My Lord?

"My child,
I shall be proud of them only when
They place at My Forgiveness-Feet
　All their nuclear weapons."

18

My Lord,
If I dislike someone vehemently,
What is the best way to deal with
   That person?

"My child,
There is not just one,
But there are many ways
To deal with that person:

"First,
Do not express
Your volcanic anger.

"Second,
Think and feel
That you have the capacity
To mould and shape that person
Into a perfectly lovely human being.

"Third,
Discard all your preconceived ideas
   And judgements about the person,
For if you cherish hostile attitudes
   Towards any person,
Then your own hostility
   Will devour you.

"Next,
Just imagine that right now
Your so-called enemy is having
Nice thoughts about you.
   Not only that,
To your wide surprise, your enemy
   Is speaking highly of you
      To others.

"Finally,
Ask your mind to be a peace-maker.
Ask your heart to be a peace-lover.
Ask yourself to be a peace-observer
   Here and everywhere
   In the Eternal Now."

APPENDIX

FOREWORDS TO FIRST EDITIONS

Preface to the first edition of *Gratitude-Flower-Hearts*

This volume contains monthly messages as well as some other special messages that Sri Chinmoy offered during meetings and meditation sessions from January 1985 through August 1988.

Preface to the first edition of *Three hundred sixty-five Father's Day prayers*

Sri Chinmoy wrote these 365 poems in honour of Father's Day, 16 June 1974. They were written during the 72-hour period from 6:00 pm 10 June (while he was on the plane to Puerto Rico) to 5:45 pm 13 June during the time of his visit to the San Juan Sri Chinmoy Centre.

The Master offered this prayerful gift to his spiritual children of the Puerto Rican Sri Chinmoy Centres, and to his Centres in all other parts of the world. On Father's Day a special dedication of this volume was made to the Guru by the disciples who worked in the printing of the book. On that occasion, each of the 365 poems was recited to the accompaniment of soulful music.

Sri Chinmoy expressed his deepest and most loving gratitude to the disciples who worked for three days and nights on the book, many of them staying up all night for three consecutive nights, and getting only snatches of sleep during the day, typing, varietyping, proofreading, making plates and negatives, masking, printing, collating and binding this book of poems. The temperature hovered near 98° all during this time.

The Guru is extremely proud of his Puerto Rican children.

Preface to the first edition of *My Race-Prayers*

These prayers were mostly offered by Sri Chinmoy at the conclusion of the weekly Saturday morning "Runners are Smilers" two-mile races held in New York. In 2002 Sri Chinmoy renamed them "Self-Transcendence Races". During Christmas trips to other countries, additional races are held on other days of the week over shorter or longer distances. Sri Chinmoy frequently participated in these races.

Preface to first edition of *My blessingful and pride-flooded dedication to the indomitable runners of the 3100-mile Self-Transcendence Race, 2006*

During the summer of 2006, the annual Sri Chinmoy 3,100-mile Self-Transcendence Race took place in Jamaica, Queens. The fifteen runners participating in this event, which is the longest footrace in the world, circled a city block whose circumference is just under one mile. Sri Chinmoy visited the race several times every day to offer the runners his encouragement, support, concern and love. From 21 June until the last runner finished on 10 August, he also offered them a daily prayer. These beautiful and deeply meaningful prayers were distributed to each runner and also posted on the bulletin board at the counting station. The runners and helpers all derived boundless inspiration from Sri Chinmoy's morning prayers. The fifty-one prayers reproduced in this book were originally published as scans of Sri Chinmoy's original handwriting.

Preface to first edition of *My blessingful and pride-flooded dedication to the indomitable runners of the 3100-mile Self-Transcendence Race, 2007*

During the summer of 2007, the annual Sri Chinmoy 3,100-mile Self-Transcendence Race took place in Jamaica, Queens. The twelve runners participating in this event, which is the longest footrace in the world, circled a city block whose circumference is just over a half mile. Sri Chinmoy visited the race several times every day to offer the runners his encouragement, support, concern and love. From 18 June until the last runner finished on 14 August, he also offered them a daily prayer. These beautiful and deeply meaningful prayers were distributed to each runner and also posted on the bulletin board at the counting station. The runners and helpers all derived boundless inspiration from Sri Chinmoy's morning prayers. The fifty-eight prayers were published in the first edition in Sri Chinmoy's original hand-writing.

BIBLIOGRAPHY

SRI CHINMOY:

— Sri Chinmoy, *Twenty-Five Aspiration-Flames*, Agni Press, NY, 1994. [TAF]

— Sri Chinmoy, *Gratitude-Flower-Hearts*, Agni Press, NY, 1993. [GFH]

— Sri Chinmoy, *My Lord's Lotus-Feet versus my devotion-heart, part 1*, Agni Press, NY, 1998. [LLF_1]

— Sri Chinmoy, *My Lord's Lotus-Feet versus my devotion-heart, part 2*, Agni Press, NY, 1998. [LLF_2]

— Sri Chinmoy, *My Lord's Lotus-Feet versus my devotion-heart, part 3*, Agni Press, NY, 1998. [LLF_3]

— Sri Chinmoy, *Three hundred sixty-five Father's Day prayers*, Aum Press, Santurce, Puerto Rico, 1974. [FDP]

— Sri Chinmoy, *O my Pilot Beloved*, Agni Press, NY, 1980. [MPB]

— Sri Chinmoy, *Prayer-Plants*, Agni Press, NY, 1982. [PP]

— Sri Chinmoy, *I pray before I lift, I meditate while I lift, I offer my gratitude-cries and gratitude-smiles*, Agni Press, NY, 1986. [PBL]

— Sri Chinmoy, *My child, you and I are in the same boat*, Agni Press, NY, 1991. [CSB]

— Sri Chinmoy, *My twenty-seven Hungry Prayer-Tears*, Agni Press, NY, 1991. [HPT]

— Sri Chinmoy, *My Lord Supreme, I am falling asleep*, Augsburg,

Germany, 1992. [LSA]

— Sri Chinmoy, *Volcano-agonies of the seekers*, Agni Press, NY, 1995. [VAS]

— Sri Chinmoy, *My Lord, how can You be so heartlessly cruel to me?*, Agni Press, NY, 1999. [LHC]

— Sri Chinmoy, *My Lord, make me Your happiness-child*, Agni Press, NY, 1992. [MLM]

— Sri Chinmoy, *Somebody has to listen*, Agni Press, NY, 1992. [SHL]

— Sri Chinmoy, *O my heart, where are you?*, Agni Press, NY, 1993. [HWA]

— Sri Chinmoy, *O my aspiration-heart, where are you?*, Agni Press, NY, 1999. [MAH]

— Sri Chinmoy, *My sweet Father-Lord, where are you?*, Agni Press, NY, 1999. [SFL]

— Sri Chinmoy, *My Lord, I pray to You*, Agni Press, NY, 1994. [LPY]

— Sri Chinmoy, *Sadness-heart-silence. Madness-mind-eloquence*, Agni Press, NY, 1998. [SHM]

— Sri Chinmoy, *My Aspiration-Heart Cycles, part 1*, Agni Press, NY, 2000. [AHC_1]

— Sri Chinmoy, My Aspiration-Heart Cycles, part 2, Agni Press, NY, 2000. [AHC_2]

— Sri Chinmoy, *My Race Prayers, part 1*, Agni Press, NY, 2004. [RP_1]

— Sri Chinmoy, *My Race Prayers, part 2*, Agni Press, NY, 2006. [RP_2]

— Sri Chinmoy, *My Race-Prayers, part 3*, Agni Press, NY, 2008. [RP_3]

— Sri Chinmoy, *My Blessingful and Pride-Flooded Dedication to the Indomitable Runners of the 3100-mile Self-Transcendence Race, 2006*, Agni Press, NY, 2006. [BDR_1]

— Sri Chinmoy, *My Blessingful and Pride-Flooded Dedication to the Indomitable Runners of the 3100-mile Self-Transcendence Race, 2007*, Agni Press, NY, 2007. [BDR_2]

[Suggested cite-key in brackets]

POSTFACE

Publishing principles

This edition of The works of Sri Chinmoy aims to obey the Author's wish: scrupulous fidelity to his original words, use of typographical style by him selected, specific spelling choices, end placement of any editorial content (i.e. not written by Sri Chinmoy himself), particular treatment of some personal nouns in special cases, etc.

Textual accuracy

The series has been checked to ensure faithful accuracy to the originals. Although much effort has been put in proofreading and comparing different versions of the text, this print may still present lingering errors. The publisher would be grateful to be apprised of any mistypes, possibly with scan of the original page where the text is different. Please use original books only, specifying the year of publication.

Ongoing reprints will include any revised text from these errata.

Acknowledgements

The Publisher is very grateful to the late Professor Lambert and his équipe for his invaluable advice. For many decades Prof. Lambert conducted a small publishing house specialising in hand-made prints of philological edition of the classics. The standard of this edition would not have been the same without his scholarly advice.

The Publisher is also grateful to the international team of collaborators that spent countless hours proofreading and checking the current text against the originals.

Our deepest gratitude to Sri Chinmoy. His living presence can be felt breathing throughout his writings. It is a privilege to be involved with his works, in any form.

Sri Chinmoy Canon

We could not use better words than Professor Lambert's, who kindly offered the name Sri Chinmoy Canon:

> «By defining Sri Chinmoy's first editions as editio princeps we chose to follow classical scholarship criteria, not because we consider Sri Chinmoy's work antique, but because we believe it is among the few post ‹classical antiquity› works to rightly deserve to be considered a classicus, designating by that term superiority, authority and perfection.
>
> «The monumental work Sri Chinmoy is offering to mankind is awe-inspiring and supremely pre-eminent in proportions and quality. It is manifest that Sri Chinmoy's work — which we feel right to call The Sri Chinmoy Canon — will be of profound help and source of enlightenment to anyone seeking a higher wisdom, truth and reality supreme.»

[Translated from French by M.G.S.]

TABLE OF CONTENTS

TWENTY-FIVE ASPIRATION-FLAMES	11
GRATITUDE-FLOWER-HEARTS	25
MY LORD'S LOTUS-FEET VERSUS MY DEVOTION-HEART	57
THREE HUNDRED SIXTY-FIVE FATHER'S DAY PRAYERS	139
MY PILOT BELOVED	301
PRAYER-PLANTS	331
I PRAY BEFORE I LIFT, I MEDITATE WHILE LIFT, I OFFER MY GRATITUDE-CRIES AND GRATITUDE-SMILES	365
MY CHILD, YOU AND I ARE IN THE SAME BOAT	389
MY TWENTY-SEVEN HUNGRY PRAYER-TEARS	405
MY LORD SUPREME, I AM FALLING ASLEEP	413
VOLCANO-AGONIES OF THE SEEKERS	425
MY LORD, HOW CAN YOU BE SO HEARTLESSLY CRUEL TO ME?	442
MY LORD, MAKE ME YOUR HAPPINESS-CHILD	474
SOMEBODY HAS TO LISTEN	489
O MY HEART, WHERE ARE YOU?	503
O MY ASPIRATION-HEART, WHERE ARE YOU?	515
MY SWEET FATHER-LORD, WHERE ARE YOU?	539
MY LORD, I PRAY TO YOU	587
SADNESS-HEART-SILENCE. MADNESS-MIND-ELOQUENCE	613
MY ASPIRATION-HEART CYCLES	638
MY RACE-PRAYERS	681
MY BLESSINGFUL AND PRIDE-FLOODED DEDICATION TO THE INDOMITABLE RUNNERS OF THE 3100-MILE SELF-TRANSCENDENCE RACE	801
MORNING PRAYERS. POEMS ON WAR	833
APPENDIX	855
FORWARDS TO FIRST EDITIONS	858
BIBLIOGRAPHY	863
POSTFACE	869
TABLE OF CONTENTS	873

www.ingramcontent.com/pod-product-compliance
Lightning Source LLC
Chambersburg PA
CBHW030109240426
43661CB00031B/1350/J